Also by Marian Burros

20-Minute Menus
Keep It Simple: 30-Minute Meals from Scratch
The Best of De Gustibus
Pure and Simple
You've Got It Made

With Lois Levine

The Elegant but Easy Cookbook
Second Helpings
Freeze with Ease
Come for Cocktails, Stay for Supper
The Summertime Cookbook

Eating Well Is the Best Revenge

*E*veryday Strategies for Delicious,
Healthful Food in 30 Minutes or Less

❧ ❧ ❧ ❧ ❧ ❧ ❧ ❧

Marian Burros

Simon & Schuster
New York ❧ London ❧ Toronto ❧ Sydney ❧ Tokyo ❧ Singapore

SIMON & SCHUSTER
Rockefeller Center
1230 Avenue of the Americas
New York, NY 10020

Copyright © 1995 by Foxcraft, Ltd.
SIMON & SCHUSTER and colophon are registered trademarks of
Simon & Schuster Inc.

Designed by Levavi & Levavi

Manufactured in the United States of America

10   9   8   7   6   5   4   3   2   1

Library of Congress Cataloging-in-Publication Data
Burros, Marian Fox.
    Eating well is the best revenge / everyday strategies for delicious,
healthful food in 30 minutes or less / Marian Burros.
        p.   cm.
    Includes index.
    1. Quick and easy cookery.   2. Nutrition.   I. Title.
TX833.5.B8677   1995
641.5′55—dc20   95-19
                                                          CIP

ISBN 0-684-80399-2

To the memory of my late husband, Donald,
who was my official taster.
If some of the recipes in this book
aren't up to his standards, I apologize.
D.B.: I hope I haven't let you down.

Contents

Liquid and Dry Measure Equivalencies

CUSTOMARY	METRIC
¼ teaspoon	1.25 milliliters
½ teaspoon	2.5 milliliters
1 teaspoon	5 milliliters
1 tablespoon	15 milliliters
1 fluid ounce	30 milliliters
¼ cup	60 milliliters
⅓ cup	80 milliliters
½ cup	120 milliliters
1 cup	240 milliliters
1 pint (2 cups)	480 milliliters
1 quart (4 cups; 32 ounces)	960 milliliters (.96 liter)
1 gallon (4 quarts)	3.84 liters
1 ounce (by weight)	28 grams
¼ pound (4 ounces)	114 grams
1 pound (16 ounces)	454 grams
2.2 pounds	1 kilogram (1,000 grams)

Oven Temperature Equivalents

DESCRIPTION	FAHRENHEIT	CELSIUS
Cool	200	90
Very slow	250	120
Slow	300–325	150–160
Moderately slow	325–350	160–180
Moderate	350–375	180–190
Moderately hot	375–400	190–200
Hot	400–450	200–230
Very hot	450–500	230–260

Foreword

*I*t seems that sitting down to dinner, once a time of relaxation over a delicious meal with family and friends, has become a guilt-ridden experience when nutrients—not marvelous foods—are consumed. Curiosity about the elusive flavor in the salsa, or the grapes in the wine, has given way to questions such as: Have I gotten enough beta-carotene? Should I have my tuna sandwich at lunch on whole-wheat instead of white bread to get all the fiber I need? Am I over my fat limit? Food has become medicine.

In the words of Jimmy Durante, "What a revoltin' development."

The pleasures of food and healthful eating habits are not mutually exclusive, but learning to make the accommodation does not come naturally in the American kitchen. How could it, when our culinary history since the prosperous post–World War II period has followed one principle: to eat as high on the hog as possible. Rethinking this principle is not quite as basic as learning how to breathe, but more like acquiring a new skill; like good sex—you have to give it some thought and then practice.

Which is the point of this book. If you have never known a gustatory experience while trying to adhere to a healthful eating lifestyle, trust me. After you have tried a few of the menus here, I think you will see the difference between food that is merely good for you and food that is good for you as well as good enough to eat.

It may be useful to know that human beings have not always lived on a diet of french fries, cheeseburgers, and Doritos, though you might not realize that from observing Americans. But the fact is that our diet, which is Anglo-German by background, has never been vegetable-based. That sort of cuisine is more familiar to Europeans from the Mediterranean area, who traditionally have consumed far less meat and saturated fat than their northern cousins. And it is the reason that health professionals today are trying to convince Americans to eat more like the Italians, Greeks, Spanish, and other people from that region. There, vegetables, fruits, and grains dominate the plate, and meat takes up a much smaller part.

Such a diet is not one of deprivation; it's one of plenty, but a different kind of plenty. As it happens, you can eat far larger quantities of vegetables, fruits, and grains than you can of meat and fat and not gain weight because they have far fewer calories. And I'm not talking about bowls of steamed vegetables and brown rice. I'm talking about orange apricot chicken and curried bulgur, corn, and peas; linguine with prosciutto and arugula and warm cauliflower salad; and fresh and smoked salmon with lentils and Brussels sprouts vinaigrette.

Eating well may be the best revenge, but revenge takes careful plotting. And plotting well means having useful information as well as certain skills. Here you can read all about why you should eat certain foods often and others infrequently, and be brought up to date on the latest, best nutrition recommendations.

We all want to do the right thing, but it's hard to hit a moving target. The nutrition information can be overwhelming, and it seems to change constantly; keeping up is a full-time job. Believe me, I know: I do it for a living and if I leave my food-health reporter's desk for a week, it takes me two to catch up.

Admonitions to substitute margarine for butter have blown up in our faces. We were beseeched to load up on calcium until a voice telling us to scarf down the oat bran outshouted the bran fans. If you can remember back to the seventies, you know that sugar was the culprit then; now it is fat. The good guys and the bad guys seem to switch roles.

We used to worry about sodium nitrite in our hot dogs: now we worry about salmonella in our chickens, pesticides in our fruits and vegetables, and lead in our drinking water.

It all comes out sounding like the Tower of Babel. Some people have responded by tuning out and shutting down. Others have cherry-picked the advice they are willing to follow, leaving the rest behind. In the 1990s Americans are practicing a sort of niche nutrition.

The truth of the matter, however, is that it's very simple to do what's right and still enjoy eating. You only need to remember three words that haven't changed since the early 1900s:

EAT LESS FAT

Then if you could add another slogan, you'll be all set:

FOOD IS NOT MEDICINE

You can use this book for the menus alone, following them as a way to a more healthful diet. I've done all the work of figuring out the nutritional values and making sure that these meals meet today's requirements—first and foremost, they keep the fat and animal protein within limits and serve up generous portions of carbohydrates, fiber, and nutrients, along with plenty of flavor. To facilitate matters, I've added a pantry of ingredients to have on hand, mail-order sources, and strategies, hints, and the best equipment for getting the job done.

Beyond that you can use this book as a guide to all those recommendations and learn the rationale behind them. Writing the "Eating Well" column for eight years for the *New York Times,* I've sorted through all the studies, reports, tests, expert opinions, and government-agency press releases, and done my best to make sense of them. Here you will find the abbreviated version. You will also find the information you need on food safety, the new labeling laws, and a rundown on the government agencies that, for better or worse, have a say in what you find in the market and put on your table.

Above all, though, I want this to be a cookbook that meets all the demands of today's busy, concerned, and sophisticated home cook, one that you will turn to eagerly and often for its recipes; I hope you will enjoy it for the pleasurable meals it offers, and appreciate the ease with which they can be executed, all the while knowing that they are as good for you as they are good.

How to Use This Book

It isn't enough to tell people how to make healthful meals: they must also be fast and delicious. If you are familiar with my previous book, *20-Minute Menus,* you know that I am passionate about no-nonsense cooking. Like millions of other American homemakers with professional lives, I have demands on my time that are often overwhelming, and no matter how much I may like to cook—and I do—the reality is that there is a limit to the time I can spend preparing daily dinners. So this is not the book for leisurely menus for entertaining, or for those dishes that benefit from long marinating or slow braising or roasting. Speed and simplicity are the operative words here: don't expect tomato roses and sculpted mushrooms. The techniques of choice in this book are broiling, boiling, sautéing, steaming, and poaching, and the tomatoes aren't even peeled, let alone turned into flowers.

What you will find here are the organization and strategy to prepare these healthful meals, from the trip to the market to the pantry essentials to the game plan for making it all work out.

STRATEGIES FOR QUICK, LOW-FAT COOKING

❧ The Game Plan

To make a complete meal in 20 to 30 minutes you need a strategic approach—you don't complete one dish, tidy up, and then go on to the next. In fact, even within the process of completing just one dish, it may not be efficient to do all the slicing and chopping before you actually start to cook. Instead, to get these meals on the table in the shortest possible time, it is necessary to work among the various dishes, going back and forth to complete the next steps as they occur. That's why I've included Game Plans that put all the chores for the menu at hand in their logical order. People who have cooked these menus from the *New York Times* love them. Cuts down on the thinking!

Generally speaking, the Game Plan sets in motion first the dish that takes longest to prepare, and the steps for the rest fall in line. Cooking times are not always specified; if you follow the plan, everything should be ready at the same moment. Each menu takes between 20 and 30 minutes from the moment you start to the moment it's ready for the table. Nevertheless, you should regard the Game Plan as a guide, and adjust it accordingly if you prefer to follow a different order. No time has been allotted for interruptions or for such chores as setting the table. I assume that someone other than the cook will take care of that, and in my experience anyone between the ages of three and ninety is capable of setting a table.

If you are a novice, getting these meals onto the table may take you a bit longer than the 20 or 30 minutes estimated. It isn't that the techniques are difficult or complicated—it's just that to be truly efficient in the kitchen you have to know your way around. On the other hand, following the Game Plan will help you acquire the organizational skills that will help you operate quickly and confidently when executing any recipe; in any case the recipes go more quickly after they've been prepared once.

Ingredients and Equipment

Quick cooking starts with quick shopping, so it is critical that you go to the market with a short list, which lets you use the express checkout line. As backup it is useful to have a pantry full of staple ingredients to expedite those dishes that you like to cook and your family likes to eat.

With healthful eating in mind, smart shopping is equally important—it also is important to know what to buy, and how, and which products will deliver the best taste with the lowest fat, lower sodium, and the fewest chemicals. You will find here a guide to use when shopping and following a list of ingredients that are used frequently in the book. A section devoted to sensible and relatively inexpensive tools and equipment will help you collect the right stuff to execute the recipes deftly.

The products and ingredients fall into three categories: such fresh items as lemons and yogurt, which are staples even though they don't last forever; items like dried herbs and many condiments that have long shelf lives; and less common items that also have long shelf lives but might require a special trip to a specialty-food shop or ethnic market—for instance, your supermarket may not carry hoisin sauce or arborio rice, so you will want to lay in a supply when you can. And then there are some ingredients that I find are important to cooking that do not keep for very long and are not always readily available. Many of these can be put into the freezer, such as certain fresh herbs—thyme, rosemary, and oregano, to name three very useful ones. I always have a piece of fresh ginger in my freezer, which can be coarsely grated without defrosting or peeling.

For those who don't have easy access to some of these ingredients under any circumstances, I have included a list of mail-order companies on page 26. This list has been developed over a decade of writing the annual Christmas mail-order article for the *New York Times*. From those lists, along with what I've gathered in writing some other articles, I've culled the very best products from the most reliable sources.

A NOTE ABOUT QUANTITIES

One of the most important things to keep in mind as you use this book is not to take the measures of ingredients too literally. If an onion is an ounce or two more or less than what the recipe specifies, use it anyway. You certainly don't want to waste time pawing through the onions at the market for one just the right weight. If a package of chicken breasts is 12 ounces rather than the 8 called for, freeze the excess or make a larger meal; you can save the leftovers for lunch.

Similarly, the cup measures may also be regarded as rough, and I emphasize *rough*. They are included for those ingredients that you have at hand at home, or for those who either don't have a kitchen scale or are not always inclined to use one. If you are very experienced and confident, you will be able to "eyeball" ingredients and skip measuring altogether, at least with some items. And beyond the alternatives that are offered—dried pasta for fresh, dried herbs for fresh—you may see other opportunities for flexibility. The dishes may not come out exactly as they did in the original version, but this is home cooking, not haute cuisine. The important thing is that the dish tastes good and that the meal can be made quickly.

A User's Guide to Quick-Cook Ingredients That Taste Good and Are Good for You

No one ever accused the food industry of missing an opportunity to present new products it claims consumers are demanding. And sometimes products come on the market that none of us even knew we needed or wanted (I can't say I've ever noticed someone standing in the street shouting for yet another breakfast cereal). So it comes as no surprise that the food industry has responded to the public's desire for lighter, more healthful food.

Some reduced-fat and nonfat products add pleasure to a healthful diet; they help limit fat intake without compromising taste. Today they can be found in many well-stocked supermarkets and in the natural-food supermarkets that have been established in recent years, such as Whole Foods in Texas and California; Bread and Circus in Massachusetts and Rhode Island; and Fresh Fields in the Washington, D.C., area and in Chicago. And there are similar independent stores in many cities throughout the country that are equally good. Many of the products included here—and many, many more—can be found at these stores, and they are worth exploring for the range they offer, but many others can be found in any typical big chain market. In some categories, we have moved from low- to lower- to even no-fat products. And many of these ingredients are now available organically grown and raised.

❧ Vegetables and Fruits

READY-CUT VEGETABLES

Cut-up raw vegetables first appeared at salad bars in small markets and now can be found in many supermarkets. These vegetables are already trimmed and sliced or chopped or otherwise prepped for cooking and, because of concerns regarding sanitation, are often packaged. The packaged assortments include peeled baby carrots; shredded carrots; broccoli and cauliflower florets; celery stalks; shredded cabbage; salad mixes; and cut-up fruit, including peeled, cored, and sliced pineapples. Needless to say, these can cut down considerably on some of the most time-consuming (not to mention tedious) cooking chores. Throughout the recipes here, you will find the option to use the most commonly found of these ingredients.

MESCLUN

This traditional French mix of baby greens, wild greens, and herbs is becoming more widely available. It is relatively expensive, but should be virtually waste-free—it also is carefully washed before it reaches the market. The quality can vary, so peer carefully through the plastic wrapper to be sure no old or wilted leaves are included.

GARLIC

Peeled and minced garlic packed in oil is widely available, but it does fall short of fresh. Since it takes only about 30 seconds to smash, peel, and chop a garlic clove, I prefer to stick with fresh.

MUSHROOMS

The assortment has grown from the white, cultivated ones known as champignons de Paris to shiitake, portobello, cremini, enoki, and from time to time, some even more exotic or seasonal sorts, such as porcini, morels, chanterelles, and oysters, to name a few.

HERBS

More fresh ones are coming onto the market all the time and, often thanks to hydroponic gardening, can be found the year round. Besides curly and Italian or broad-leaf parsley (which once accounted for the entire herb selection), basil, thyme, oregano, cilantro, and sage are routinely available; and fresh bay leaves, which are beginning to appear, may make you rethink that particular herb.

CHILES

Most markets carry at least one variety of fresh hot pepper, usually jalapéno, but the assortment increases steadily.

DRIED CRANBERRIES, CHERRIES, AND BLUEBERRIES
These make nice alternatives to raisins and currants in many recipes.

❧ Starches—Rice and Beyond

More and more grains, some of them ancient strains that are once again under cultivation, are appearing on the shelves next to the macaroni and rice. Rice itself, the sustenance grain for most of the world, has become a larger category.

RICE
Long-grain white rice and its relatives, all of which cook in 20 minutes or less, including the more interesting basmati, jasmine, and pecan.

Arborio—the imported Italian variety that cooks up creamy and is the critical ingredient in a perfect risotto.

Brown rice—a quick-cooking variety is now available; while its flavor is not as full as that of regular brown rice, it is good, and of course has the advantage of the fiber that is not present in white rice. To use regular brown rice in quick-cooking meals, soak it for from 4 hours to overnight (you can put it to soak in the morning before you go to work). Soaking the kernels softens them with no appreciable effect on their nutrients. To cook, drain off the soaking liquid and proceed with the directions for cooking white rice; the cooking time may slightly exceed the 17 minutes required for white rice.

PASTA
All fresh pastas, including couscous and thin or small dried shapes like orzo or riso, cook in under 20 minutes. Besides spinach pasta, which has been around for years, fresh pasta is increasingly seen in delicious flavors such as basil, tomato, black pepper, lemon, red pepper, garlic-parsley, and squid ink. Many fresh pastas are now made without egg yolks.

Other Quick-Cooking Nutritious Starches
Bulgur
Buckwheat groats (kasha)
Fine-grind cornmeal (instant polenta)
Quinoa (pronounced KEEN-wa)
Red lentils

BREADS
It is no exaggeration to say that a real movement toward better bread is under way in this country. A number of dedicated bread makers who produce traditional loaves have established themselves, and

their breads, rolls, and muffins can be found at farmers' markets, specialty-food stores, health-food stores, and some supermarkets. There are also a number of fairly large, very good commercial bakeries with wide distribution that turn out more healthful, better-tasting loaves than were previously easy to find. The range of well-made breads, including traditional types of numerous whole-wheat and multigrain varieties, made without fat, is impressive, and they are a good source of carbohydrates and fiber.

There are also new choices among the snack and variety breads:

Tortillas—whole-wheat flour tortillas; sprouted-wheat tortillas; and fat-free flour tortillas
Whole-wheat pita bread, now widely available
Afghan bread—this very thin flat bread is becoming more and more available; it can be used as a very good pizza base.

✦ Dairy Products

MILK
Nonfat; one percent; nonfat and low-fat buttermilk; powdered nonfat buttermilk (Sasco).

SOUR CREAM
Light, with less than half the fat of traditional sour cream

YOGURT
Nonfat plain and flavored

CHEESE
Most cheeses suffer from having their fat content reduced, but some do pass the taste test. When you are cooking with cheese, it is usually better to use small amounts of good-quality full-flavored cheese than the reduced-fat versions. For instance, just a bit of good, imported Parmigiano-Reggiano or Roquefort can bring a lot of flavor to a dish. It is worth knowing that even among traditional cheeses, the fat content varies enormously; in general, for instance, hard and fresh cheese are lower in fat than aged double- and triple-crème cheeses. Knowing your cheeses can help you make the best choice in terms of fat, whether among the reduced-fat or traditional types.

Light cream cheese
Reduced-fat ricotta cheese, with 50 percent less fat than the traditional type
Goat cheese—reduced-fat from Coach Farm and Chavrie

❧ Meat and Poultry

CHICKEN
Skinless, boneless chicken breasts; skinless, boneless chicken thigh meat is sometimes available, and can be a good substitute for breasts; chicken sausages; ground chicken breast meat (see Marketing Note, below)

TURKEY
Whole boneless breasts; sliced breast; turkey sausages; smoked turkey, for the flavor of ham hocks and other smoked pork products, with less fat; ground turkey (see Marketing Note, below)

BEEF
Flank steak; top round—among the leanest cuts, cooks quickly

PORK
The tenderloin is a good, tasty, lean, and quick-cooking cut; ground lean pork (see Marketing Note, below)

LAMB
Boneless leg

MARKETING NOTE

Free-range and organically raised chicken and turkey and hormone- and antibiotic-free beef are available at some natural-food supermarkets and specialty-food shops and through mail order.

A note about ground meats:

Ground lamb, beef, pork, and poultry—turkey as well as chicken—are routinely available. However, to be sure you are getting the least amount of fat possible, you should grind it yourself using a meat grinder or food processor. For poultry, the skin and excess fat should be removed before grinding. Flank steak is the best choice for beef; a well-trimmed piece from the leg best for lamb; the tenderloin for pork. Of course, a reliable butcher can grind your meat for you, if you specify the removal of skin and fat and the cut you want.

Food Note ❧ Poultry can be cooked with its skin on with only a negligible amount of fat leaching into the meat. The skin can then be removed before serving.

❧ Fish and Shellfish

Any fish, even small whole ones, fits right into quick cooking.

Some seafood, such as crab and shrimp, comes already cooked; shrimp is also sometimes available raw and shelled. In any case, it cooks quickly.

Oysters are often sold shucked and packed in jars with their own liquid.

Scallops cook in 2 to 5 minutes, depending on their size.

Cultivated mussels—washed, debearded, and packaged—reduce the preparation time considerably.

❧ Canned and Packaged Products

The assortment of packaged foods that are quick and healthful and that fit into cooking from scratch gets better every year.

TOMATOES
No-salt-added canned tomatoes—whole, ground up, crushed, puréed; tomato paste, canned or in a tube, especially good for the times when you need a small amount.

FROZEN VEGETABLES
These three are indispensable: corn kernels, peas, and lima beans.

BEANS
The best canned beans, without added salt and without preservatives, are made by Eden Foods of Clinton, Michigan. They are certified organic. These beans also seem a little firmer than most canned beans; American Prairie, distributed by Mercantile Food Company, in Georgetown, Connecticut, also certified organic, with a little added salt.

BROTHS AND STOCKS
Frozen vegetable, chicken, fish, and beef stocks. Not easy to find, but worth seeking—they are superior to anything in a can; canned low-sodium stocks made without monosodium glutamate are available, though you may have to go to a natural-food store for them. The flavor isn't good enough for soup or a sauce, but they add some flavor when substituted for water for cooking polenta or rice.

TAHINI
Now available toasted, like Asian sesame paste.

VINEGARS

More flavors and varieties than ever before can be found in the supermarket: raspberry, garlic, and tarragon; Chinese or Japanese rice wine vinegar; balsamic.

OILS

More and better olive oils from more sources, including France, Italy, Spain, Greece, and California, are available, and some are flavored with spices, garlic, or herbs; canola oil is now an established item in most supermarkets. (The last time I wrote about canola oil in a cookbook, one reviewer said there was no such thing); Asian dark or light sesame oil; Chinese hot chili oil.

OTHER ASIAN INGREDIENTS

Reduced-sodium soy sauce; hoisin sauce; chili purée with garlic.

THE LOW-FAT, QUICK-COOK PANTRY AT A GLANCE

Herbs and Spices
Basil—fresh, frozen, dried
Bay leaves
Caraway seeds
Cardamom, ground
Chile powder, pure—hot
Cilantro, fresh
Cinnamon, ground
Coriander seed, ground
Cumin, ground
Curry powder
Fennel seeds
Ginger—fresh, frozen, powdered, pickled, sugared, crystallized
Marjoram—fresh, frozen, dried
Mustard, dry
Nutmeg, ground
Oregano—fresh, frozen, dried
Paprika—preferably Hungarian sweet
Pepper—whole black, cayenne, hot red flakes
Poppy seeds
Rosemary—fresh, frozen, dried

Sage—fresh, frozen, dried
Sesame seeds
Tarragon—fresh, frozen, dried
Thyme—fresh, frozen, dried
Turmeric

Condiments

Anchovy paste or whole anchovies
Beans—salted or fermented black (Chinese)
Capers
Catsup
Cheese—Parmigiano-Reggiano, Cheddar, low-fat goat
Cherries, dried
Chili paste, hot with garlic (Chinese)
Chili sauce
Cranberries, dried
Fish sauce (called *nam pla* if Thai; *nuoc nam* if Vietnamese)
Hoisin sauce
Honey
Hot pepper sauce
Maple syrup
Molasses, unsulfured, dark
Mushrooms, dried wild, such as porcini and Chinese
Mustard—Dijon and grainy (also called country), honey
Nuts—almonds (slivered); peanuts (unsalted, roasted); pecans; pine
Oil—olive, canola, Asian sesame, hot chili, walnut
Olives—black or green packed in brine or oil—French, Greek, Italian; olive paste
Oyster sauce
Raisins
Sesame paste—Asian or toasted tahini
Shallots
Sherry, dry
Soy sauce, reduced sodium
Vermouth, dry
Vinegar—balsamic, cider, red, white wine, raspberry, rice
Wine—red, white
Worcestershire sauce

Pastas, Grains, and Beans

Thin dry pastas such as linguine, spaghettini, or angel hair

Small shells

Orecchiette

Orzo

Couscous, whole-wheat

Bulgur, fine ground

Cornmeal, fine ground (instant polenta)

Lentils, red

Rice, white, brown, arborio, basmati

Beans, canned, no-salt-added, black, red, white

Basics

Beef broth—no-salt-added bouillon or stock

Bread crumbs, whole-wheat

Butter, unsalted

Chicken broth—no-salt-added bouillon or stock

Corn kernels, frozen

Cornstarch

Eggs

Flour, unbleached, whole-wheat

Garlic, fresh heads, minced in oil

Lemons

Lima beans, frozen

Milk, skim

Onions

Orange juice, fresh, frozen concentrate

Peas, frozen

Sour cream, low-fat

Sugar, white granulated, brown

Tomatoes—sun-dried not packed in oil, no-salt-added paste, purée, ground, crushed, and whole canned

Yogurt, nonfat plain

Mail Order

Here is a list of mail-order sources for items that are not easy to find in some cities. Everything organic is noted.

MEAT, POULTRY, AND FISH

(Organic) Chicken and veal. Very little fat and lots of flavor to these white chickens.

Deer Valley Farm, R.D. 1, Guilford, NY 13780; 607-764-8556.

(Organic) Game. The place for farm-raised and wild game is D'Artagnan. Its products are superb. It has free-range chickens and all kinds of fresh duck as well as rabbit and excellent venison.

D'Artagnan, Inc., 399–419 St. Paul Avenue, Jersey City, NJ 07306; 800 DARTAGN; 201-792-0748; fax 792–6113.

Lamb, veal, venison, rabbit, chicken. Naturally raised. The rosy, milk-fed veal puts white veal products to shame. (These animals are raised humanely.)

Summerfield Farm, SR4, Box 195A, Brightwood, VA 22715; 703-948-3100; fax 948-6249.

Sausages. Relatively lean, certainly for sausages, a 3.2-ounce serving has 10 grams of fat. Try the Thai, fresh chicken and apple, fresh chicken and turkey, mild Italian turkey, or turkey with scallions and fresh herbs.

Aidells Sausage Company, 1625 Alvarado Street, San Leandro, CA 94577; 510-614-5450, 800-546-5795.

FRUITS AND VEGETABLES

(Organic) Bananas. Not the varieties you'd expect to find in the grocery store, these have names like Manzan, Blue Java, Brazilian, Mysore. Cook with them, eat them out of hand; directions come with the bananas telling you what to do with them.

Seaside Banana Garden, 6823 Santa Barbara Avenue, La Conchita, CA 93001; 805-643-4061.

(Organic) Kiwis and persimmons. The tart-sweet kiwis and Fuyu persimmons are excellent. The company also has Valencia and navel oranges, pomolos, plums, and Asian pears, depending on the time of year.

Ecology Sound Farms, 42126 Road 168, Orosi, CA 93647; 209-528-3816; fax 528-0227.

(Organic) Produce. Most of the produce sampled is exceptional, full of flavor and good enough to be served without seasoning—but the lettuces did not travel well. In season the company has just about any fruit or vegetable you could ask for.

It also sells organic dairy products, beef, veal, lamb, pork, and chicken, but I have not tasted them.

Organic FoodWorks, Box A1, RR3, Howard, PA 16841; 814-355-9850.

(Organic) Greens as good as or better than anything at the local farm market: mesclun, red chard, radicchio, kale, arugula, frisée. Also available—all kinds of vegetables and fruits.

Diamond Organics, P.O. Box 2159, Freedom, CA 95019; 800-922-2396; fax 408-763-2444.

Wild Mushrooms. Spectacular, fabulous-tasting wild mushrooms like hen of the woods, hedgehog, cauliflower, black trumpets—names that conjure up exotic, earthy flavors.

Hans Johnasson Mushrooms and More, P.O. Box 532, Goldens Bridge, NY 10526; 914-232-2107

Herbs. Potted herbs arrive in a basket that can go directly into a sunlit window, where they are available for snipping.

Frieda's By Mail, P.O. Box 58488, Los Angeles, CA 90058; 800-241-1771.

CHEESES

Monterey Jack. This hard, dry cheese doesn't seem to be in the same family as the unassertive supermarket version of jack cheese. Beneath the brown coating, its robust flavor is in the tradition of Parmigiano-Reggiano or Asiago. Keeps for months in the refrigerator.

Vella Cheese Company, P.O. Box 191, Sonoma, CA 95476; 707-938-3232; 800-848-0505.

Parmigiano-Reggiano. Todaro Bros. has top-quality Parmigiano that keeps for months in the freezer. Just grate a little when you need it.

Todaro Bros. Mail Order, 555 2nd Avenue, New York, NY 10016; 212-679-7766; fax 689-1679.

Goat. Low-fat with creamy texture. You don't miss the fat.

Little Rainbow Chèvre, 15 Doe Hill, Hillsdale, NY 12529; 518-325-4628; fax 325-4409.

Mozzarella—Mozzarella Company has the cheese from cow and water buffalo milk that is superbly fresh.

Mozzarella Company, 2944 Elm Street, Dallas, TX 75226; 214-741-4072; 800-798-2954.

GRAINS, BEANS, AND LENTILS

(Organic) Cornmeal. Johnnycake Meal. Makes the best shortcake I've ever eaten and is perfect in polenta recipes. Keep refrigerated and it will last for months.

Gray's Gristmill, P.O. Box 422, Adamsville, RI 02801; 508-636-6075.

Lentils. Red lentils cook in 10 minutes. Uncooked they keep for months on the shelf.

G. B. Ratto, 821 Washington Street, Oakland, CA 94607; 800-228-3515 in CA; elsewhere 800-325-3483; fax 510-836-2250.

Rice. Arborio to make risotto. See Lentils, G. B. Ratto, above.

Rice. Arborio. See Parmigiano, Todaro Bros., page 26.

Rice. Basmati—delicately flavored Indian rice. See Lentils, G. B. Ratto, above.

CONDIMENTS

Capers. In several sizes. See Parmigiano, Todaro Bros., page 26.

Chinese ingredients—Much of what you need to cook the Chinese-style recipes in this book can be found at one source: sesame oil, chili paste with garlic, hot chili oil, rice vinegar, hoisin sauce.

China Bowl Trading Co., 830 Post Road East, Westport, CT 06880; 203-222-0381; fax 226-6445.

Dried mushrooms. Cèpes, porcini, shiitake, morels, Polish. See Lentils, G. B. Ratto, above, and Parmigiano, Todaro Bros., page 26.

(Organic) Olive oil. Top-quality olive oil.

Gaeta Imports, 141 John Street, Babylon, NY 11702; 516-661-2681; fax 516-661-7629; 800-669-2681.

Olive oil. Especially extra-virgin olive oil, which is excellent for salads. Once opened, keeps in the refrigerator. See Parmigiano, Todaro Bros., page 26.

Olives. See Lentils, G. B. Ratto, above; Parmigiano, Todaro Bros., page 26.

Sun-dried Tomatoes. Dry or in oil. Indefinite shelf life. See Parmigiano, Todaro Bros., page 26.

(Organic) Prunes and walnuts. The biggest and sweetest prunes I've ever tasted; walnuts were free of bitterness they sometimes have. Try any of the company's dried fruits. It also sells organic grains.

Country Life Natural Foods, Oakhaven, Pullman, MI 49450; 616-236-5011; 800-456-7694; fax 616-236-8357.

Dried cherries and cranberries. Wonderful alternatives to raisins and currants.

American Spoon Foods, 1668 Clarion Avenue, P.O. Box 566, Petoskey, MI 49770; 616-347-9030; 800-222-5886.

Vinegar. Balsamic is a sweet, rich vinegar called for in many recipes in the book. You don't need as much oil with it for salad dressing. Indefinite shelf-life.

See Parmigiano, Todaro Bros., page 26.

(Organic) Maple syrup. It's called Grade A medium amber and has a subtle maple flavor.

Maverick Sugarbush, Box 99, Sharon, VT 05065; 802-763-8680; fax 763-8684.

PRESERVES, JELLIES, JAMS, AND RELISHES

Cider jelly. It has a tart, deep, winy apple flavor and is wonderful on toast and also as a glaze on poultry. Keeps on the shelf for months.

Woods Cider Jelly, RFD 2, Box 477, Springfield, VT 05156; 802-263-5547.

Jams. Wild thimbleberry preserves—described as part loganberry, part raspberry—are refreshingly tart, but the tartest of all, and the one with the deepest cherry flavor, is sour cherry spoon fruit. Very few calories. Keeps for months on the shelf.

See dried cherries and cranberries, American Spoon Foods, page 27.

Preserves and toppings. All of these fruit preserves or conserves, or whatever you wish to call them, are deeply fruit-flavored and sweetened with concentrated fruit juice. They are looser in consistency than the usual preserves and they make good sauce.

Chocolate toppings are another treat for frozen yogurt, ice cream, and cakes; they have no fat, no sugar, and few calories.

Wax Orchards, 22744 Wax Orchard Road, SW, Vashon, WA 98070; 206-463-9735; 800-634-6132; fax 463-9731.

Relishes. Red spoon peppers and green spoon peppers are two excellent hot-sweet relishes.

See dried cherries and cranberries, American Spoon Foods, page 27.

Chutneys in many flavors, like cranberry walnut, apple-pear jalapeño, and peach clove, add zing and tingle.

Carol's Chutney, 5555 S.W. Childs Road, Lake Oswego, OR 97035; 503-620-0164.

BEVERAGES

(Organic) Coffee. Superb coffee that comes decaffeinated by the Swiss water process.

Thanksgiving Coffee Company. P.O. Box 1918, Fort Bragg, CA 95437; 800-648-6491.

A useful book for those interested in hundreds of additional sources for organic food is *Green Groceries,* by Jeanne Heifitz (HarperCollins, 1992). It lists hundreds of sources for mail-order food with the items each company has, what form of certification they have, and, of course, their addresses and phone numbers.

EQUIPMENT FOR THE LOW-FAT, QUICK-COOK KITCHEN

Expensive, elaborate equipment designed for lower-fat cooking certainly abounds, and some pieces are marketed as absolutely essential. To my mind, however, a food processor is the only sizable investment needed to cook meals quickly on a daily basis. However, I generally don't recommend one for only one operation; then I find it easier to chop by hand, but you can be your own judge. You don't need a microwave oven for the recipes in this book. In fact, you really don't need an up-to-date kitchen—the recipes were developed and tested in mine, which is 30 years old.

You do need some good pots and pans and, for sautéing, pans with a good layer of nonstick surface. Farberware's Millennium Plus pans are excellent.

Get yourself a top-of-the-stove grill—they cost less than $20—to give your food the grilled taste of an open flame or charcoal fire. The original Max Burton brand grill is still the best.

Buy a steamer basket to use in a regular pot: Forget about separate steamers; they take longer to cook the food.

Invest in the best, sharpest knives you can find. They are worth the money because they last a lifetime. The Henckels and Wüsthof brands are among the best.

Here's a list, lifted from *20-Minute Menus,* of useful and relatively inexpensive equipment to facilitate the recipes in this book—and all your fast, healthful meals.

TOOLS FOR QUICK COOKS

Knives, Forks, Spoons
Chef's knife

Paring knife

Bread knife

2 stirring spoons, one slotted

1 large fork

Pots and Pans
14-inch nonstick skillet with lid

Nonstick sauté pan with lid

6-quart pot with lid

2- to 3-quart pot with lid

1-quart pot with lid

Steamer basket

Aluminum baking sheet

Top-of-the-stove grill (comes round or oblong with a nonstick grill surface on a base that holds water to keep the food from smoking up the kitchen)

Utensils and Machines
Graduated set of stainless-steel bowls

Spatula

4-sided grater

Set of measuring spoons

1-quart measuring cup

Set of measuring cups

Large colander or strainer

Can opener

Bottle opener

Whisk

Vegetable peeler

Hand juicer

Pot holders

Food processor

Toaster oven

How to Reduce Fat in Cooking

- For sour cream: Substitute reduced-fat sour cream or equal parts nonfat yogurt and reduced-fat ricotta cheese. For thinner mixtures, use more yogurt and less ricotta. This mixture cannot be cooked; the heat will cause the curds to separate from the whey.
- In sauces substitute nonfat yogurt for sour cream: For every cup of yogurt stir in 1 tablespoon of cornstarch to prevent the yogurt from separating; low-fat sour cream is a good substitute, too, though it has more fat than yogurt. Low-fat sour cream does not separate, so the cornstarch can be eliminated.
- For cream: Replace with 2 parts nonfat yogurt to 1 part low-fat ricotta, beaten in a food processor or blender until smooth. Do not heat; the mixture will separate. Spoon the mixture directly over hot foods immediately after they are cooked.
- Nonfat or low-fat buttermilk makes another good substitute. To prevent it from separating when heated, thicken with 1 tablespoon cornstarch for each cup of buttermilk.
- Whipped cream: Whip ⅓ cup heavy cream until very stiff. Fold in ⅔ cup nonfat yogurt.
- Eggs: For 2 whole eggs substitute 1 whole egg and 2 egg whites.
- Salad dressings: Use balsamic vinegar, fruit-flavored vinegar, or Chinese rice vinegar in equal parts to oil, or 2 parts oil to 1 part vinegar. (Traditional ratios are 3 parts oil to 1 part vinegar.) Or use equal parts oil, vinegar, and water and add mustard and herbs to increase the flavor.
- Cooking oil: Use a nonstick pan and generally 1 to 2 teaspoons of oil for a dish for 2 people. Make sure the pan is very, very hot before you add the oil, so that you will get a browning effect similar to that which comes from a lot of oil. Reduce the heat to medium-high, add the oil, then add the food. This cuts down on the life of the nonstick surface, but it does wonders for the taste of the food.
- Use highly flavorful condiments like horseradish in salad dressings and yogurt-based sauces.
- Make yogurt "cheese" by draining plain yogurt through a double thickness of cheesecloth overnight in the refrigerator. Use it like fresh cheese or as crème fraîche in sauces, spreads, and soups.
- Use arrowroot or cornstarch dissolved in water or broth as a thickener in place of roux, which contains oil or butter.
- Try mustard not only as an emulsifier in salad dressings but also as a thickening agent when reducing a sauce.
- Instead of a ham hock or other smoked pork product to flavor soup, use a roasted pepper or some smoked turkey to get the smoky flavor without the fat.

Nutrition Simplified

The mixed messages we receive about nutrition from the media, the government, and our friends—and even some doctors—lead easily to befuddlement, and worse. Some surveys now suggest that people are giving up on the goal of following a healthful diet, not only because it's all gotten too confusing, but because the food just doesn't taste good.

In fact, the issue is far easier to deal with than many think. For most Americans, health and fitness through diet can be summed up in three little words:

EAT LESS FAT

The footnote to that simple message is equally easy to grasp: Eat more fruits, vegetables, and grains. The details may change, but not the basic message. I hope this section will give you a clear overview of the current state of the science of nutrition.

TOO MUCH FAT

Today, if you ask just about anyone who has the least awareness of what good nutrition should be, he or she will tell you that fat is the greatest concern. Calories, once the focus of our approach to food-health-fitness issues, have given way to fat. As it happens, the advice to eat less fat is not new at all; it goes all the way back to the turn of the century when W. O. Atwater, the first director of research at the United States Department of Agriculture, recommended that men (apparently women didn't count) reduce their consumption of fat to no more than 33 percent of calories from fat. So dietary advice—at least sound advice—that often seems to change from moment to moment, may be more stable than you've guessed.

Nevertheless, the average American still gets 37 percent of his or her calories from fat. According to health experts, fat should constitute no more than 30 percent of calories, and an increasing number say the amount should not exceed 20 percent. People like Michael Jacobson, executive director of the Washington-based consumer advocacy group the Center for Science in the Public Interest, says that 30 percent "is a compromise between what is ideal and what is realistic. Generally we say 20 percent is a reasonable goal and would be advantageous. People should know what the best possible diet is even if they don't follow it."

When I reported on the issue for the *New York Times* in July 1991, I wrote that "proponents of a diet with 20 to 25 percent of calories from fat base their recommendation on evidence that points to a reduction in the risk of certain cancers, heart disease, stroke, and diabetes as fat intake is lowered. Not all of the evidence is conclusive, but all of it is suggestive."

You may decide to follow a diet that does not exceed 30 percent fat from calories or to follow a 20-percent plan. For each, there is an outline to help you plan your meals: For 30 percent, there is the plan recommended by the United States Department of Agriculture and represented by the Food Guide Pyramid; for 20 percent, the guide is from *The New American Diet,* a book by Dr. William E. Connor and his wife, Sonya (Simon & Schuster, 1986). Dr. Connor is chief of the division of endocrinology, metabolism, and clinical nutrition at Oregon Health Sciences. He says the optimal diet is 20 to 25 percent of calories from fat, while a diet with 30 percent fat is transitional.

The pyramid is based on the National Research Council report of March 1, 1989, which reinforced dietary recommendations made in 1977 by the Senate Select Committee on Nutrition and Human Needs. At the time, the 1977 report was severely criticized. Twelve years later the only criticism leveled at the NRC report, "Diet and Health," was that it didn't go far enough, especially in the amount of fat it recommended for a healthful diet.

The recommendations, as I reported in the March 2, 1989, *New York Times,* were:

FAT   Reduce intake to 30 percent or less of total calories. Saturated fat: Less than 10 percent of calories.

CHOLESTEROL   Less than 300 milligrams daily.

VEGETABLES AND FRUITS   Eat 5 or more half-cup servings every day of vegetables and fruits, especially green and yellow vegetables and citrus fruits.

STARCHES AND OTHER COMPLEX CARBOHYDRATES   Eat 6 or more servings daily of bread, cereals, and legumes, for a total of more than 55 percent of calories.

PROTEIN   Eat no more than twice the recommended daily allowance and no more than 1.6 grams per day per kilogram of body weight.

WEIGHT   Maintain proper weight through diet and exercise.

ALCOHOL   Not recommended; do not exceed an ounce of pure alcohol daily, the equivalent to two cans of beer, two small glasses of wine, or two average cocktails, and avoid alcohol entirely during pregnancy.

SALT   Eat less than 6 grams (2,400 milligrams of sodium) a day. Limit use in cooking, avoid adding it at table, and consume salty foods sparingly. One teaspoon of salt contains 2,000 milligrams of sodium. Some health authorities say you should not consume more than 3,000 milligrams of sodium a day, but many more say that 2,400 is the limit.

CALCIUM   Maintain adequate intake.

DIETARY SUPPLEMENTS   Avoid taking more than recommended daily allowances. (Today many respected experts quibble with what constitutes the appropriate recommended daily allowance.)

FLUORIDE   Maintain optimal intake, especially during years of tooth formation and growth.

The report also said that there is evidence that further reductions in total fat, saturated fat, and cholesterol "may confer even greater health benefits in terms of cardiovascular disease and certain kinds of cancer."

And it added that a reduction of salt to 4.5 grams or less rather than 6 grams "would probably confer greater health benefits than its present recommendation."

The report made no recommendations on fiber consumption but at a news conference one of the panel members said: "There is clear evidence that consumption of food high in fiber lowers the risk of cancer and cardiovascular disease. But it is difficult to say if it's the fiber. It may be other elements that are protective."

Experts generally recommend 20 to 30 grams of fiber a day.

While the report says little about meat, other than to recommend "lean meat in smaller and fewer portions," I asked a panel member at the press conference to translate that into practical terms and she said: "Two three-ounce servings at most," per day.

As you can see, information from the National Research Council is translated into more practical information on the Food Guide Pyramid:

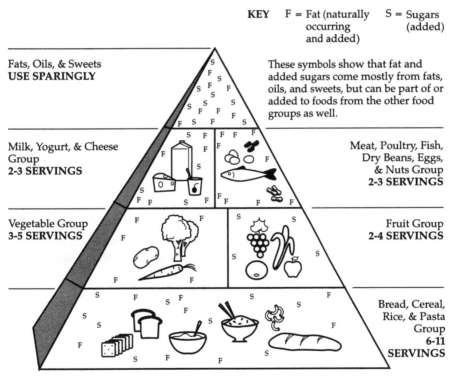

A GUIDE TO DAILY FOOD CHOICES

SOURCE: U.S. Department of Agriculture / U.S. Department of Health and Human Services

Foods have been divided into 5 groups and a range of servings is recommended. The optimal number of servings from each group is a function of how many calories a person should consume each day. For example, a woman who should eat no more than 1,600 calories would need only 6 servings of grains; 11 servings would be appropriate for the teenage boy who should consume 2,800 calories a day. Sedentary women of all ages, older women, and children 4 to 6 need 1,600 calories a day. Active men, very active women, very active teenage girls as well as teenage boys need 2,800, while sedentary men of all ages, older men, active women, teenage girls, and children 7 and older need 2,200 calories.

So what constitutes a serving?

GRAINS   One slice of bread, 1 ounce of ready-to-eat cereal or ½ cup of cooked cereal, rice, or pasta.

VEGETABLES   One cup of raw leafy vegetables, ½ cup of other vegetables, either cooked or chopped raw, or ¾ cup of vegetable juice.

FRUITS   One medium apple, banana, or orange, ½ cup of chopped, cooked, or canned fruit, or ¾ cup of fruit juice.

DAIRY   One cup of milk or yogurt, 1½ ounces of natural cheese, or 2 ounces of processed cheese.

MEATS, DRY BEANS, EGGS, AND NUTS   Two to 3 ounces of cooked lean meat, poultry or fish; ½ cup of cooked dry beans, or 1 egg. Two tablespoons of peanut butter equal 1 ounce of lean meat.

On April 8, 1992, I reported in the *Times:*

"While 6 to 11 servings from the grain group seems like a lot, the amounts most people actually eat at one sitting add up to more than 1 serving, according to the government's standard measure. For example, most people eat 2 servings of cereal in the morning and have 2 slices of bread in a sandwich at lunch. At dinner an average-size portion of pasta as a main course—about 2 cups, which is 4 servings—brings the total in the grain group to 8 servings."

One thing the pyramid does not make clear in the graphic is that all the dairy products should be low-fat and all the meat lean.

THE 20-PERCENT PLAN: "THE NEW AMERICAN DIET"

Here is what you should be eating if you want to reduce your fat intake to 20 percent, according to the Connors in *The New American Diet* and their later book, *The New American Diet System,* published in 1991, which divides food into 6 groups instead of the pyramid's 5. On an 1,800-calorie-a-day diet, 30 percent of calories from fat would allow 60 grams of fat; 20 percent would allow 40 grams.

BEANS, NUTS, AND SEEDS Eat 3 to 5 cups of cooked dried beans a week (kidney, lentil, pinto, chili, and the like). Use nuts and seeds sparingly to spice up grains, beans, and vegetables.

VEGETABLES Eat 2 to 4 cups a day.

WHOLE GRAINS AND POTATOES Eat 2 to 5 servings from this group at each meal (bread, rice, popcorn, cereals, flour, oats, and others). Choose snacks from this group.

FATS Use only 4 to 7 teaspoons added fat a day. Half this amount can be used in cooking, the other half as spreads.

FRUITS Eat 3 to 5 pieces a day. Fresh fruit is preferable to canned fruit or juices.

LOW-FAT ANIMAL PRODUCTS Aim for a daily average of either 6 ounces of fish, clams, oysters, or scallops or 3 to 4 ounces of poultry, shrimp, crab, lobster, or lean meat, or 1 to 2 ounces of low-fat cheese. Use low-fat dairy products as desired (skim milk, nonfat yogurt, and the like).

THE GOOD AND THE BAD IN YOUR DIET

❧ What's Bad: Fat and Its Sidekick Cholesterol

Fat. The trigger word. Watching your cholesterol intake is hardly a problem compared to watching your fat intake. What you want to watch is the cholesterol in your blood, and saturated fat plays as much of a role in your body cholesterol level as the cholesterol in your diet.

The idea that every dish you eat should contain no more than 20 or 30 percent of calories from fat is a misunderstanding and misapplication of the percentage figure, not only by ordinary people who are confused but also by health professionals.

Not everything you eat needs to meet the 30 (or 20) percent fat minimum. If you ate that way you could never have an ice cream cone or a brownie. What you need to do is balance. If you consume a dish that is 80 percent fat you must balance it against a dish with much less fat, making sure the day's, or several days', total does not exceed 30 (or 20) percent.

So far so good. Especially if you were awake when they taught about percentages in school. I wasn't. So try this instead. Count fat grams. That way you don't have to divide and multiply, just add.

The amount of fat you can eat depends on the number of calories to which you are entitled each day to maintain your weight. The charts provide the grams of fat and saturated fat based on 10 to 30 percent of total fat from calories.

For example, if you eat 1,600 calories a day, you are entitled to 53 grams of total fat if you are on a 30-percent-fat-calorie diet.

The figure is calculated as follows: the number of calories consumed each day is multiplied by 30 percent (or less if you choose)—1,600 multiplied by 30 percent, or 480.

Then, because each gram of fat has nine calories, 480 is divided by 9. The result is 53. Never mind. Stick with the right-hand column below. Women, for instance, generally should eat between 1,800 and 2,200 calories a day.

Check the nutrition label on the products you buy for fat grams.

DIET	DESIRED % OF CALORIES FROM FAT	DAILY GRAMS OF FAT
1,600 cal.	30	53
	25	44
	20	36
	15	27
	10	18
2,200	30	73
	25	61
	20	49
	15	37
	10	24
2,800	30	93
	25	78
	20	62
	15	47
	10	31

New York Times, Sept. 8, 1993

TRANS FATTY ACIDS

Until very recently almost everyone believed that it was better to use polyunsaturated fat like margarine than saturated fat like butter. And many dutifully switched to margarine. In most cases all they did was switch. They did not reduce their fat intake, they just changed it.

So it has been something of a minor catastrophe to learn that solid polyunsaturated fats like margarine may be just as bad for you as butter because these polys contain a compound called trans fatty acids.

In a front-page story on October 7, 1992, I wrote: "In response to harsh criticism in the last few years about the amount of saturated fat in the American diet, many food manufacturers have reluctantly switched from palm and coconut oils to partially hydrogenated vegetable oils made from soybean and corn. Now in a stunning example of revisionist nutrition, new data show that these oils —found in margarine, vegetable shortening, and a host of products ranging from doughnuts and pies to cookies and crackers—may also cause heart disease.

"This latest nutritional flipflop may boil the blood of angst-ridden consumers, who in the face of conflicting advice want to throw up their hands and break out the butter. Wrong. The basic message remains the same: Eat less fat."

Trans fatty acids are produced when vegetable oils are converted to margarine or shortenings that are solid or semisolid at room temperature. The trans fatty acids act like saturated fat and raise the harmful elements in cholesterol while lowering the protective elements.

A study published in the British medical journal *Lancet* in March 1993 showed that women who eat 4 or more teaspoons of margarine a day have a 50 percent greater risk of developing heart disease than women who eat margarine only once a month.

It is times like these that people say: I quit. I can't get it right so I'm not going to do any of it.

The trick is to reduce total fat and worry less about the kind.

The implication of trans fatty acids in raising cholesterol levels means that olive oil (or canola oil) is best.

Despite the lack of specific information on package labels, there are certain clues that can help consumers cut down on their consumption of trans fatty acids.

1. Tub margarine is lower in trans fatty acids than the stick kind. Lower still are diet soft margarines and liquid margarine in a squeeze bottle.
2. Margarines and spreads that list liquid oil as the first ingredient are better choices than those listing partially hydrogenated oil first.
3. Olive and canola oils are the best choices: They contain more monounsaturated fat than other oils do.
4. The greater the amount of total fat in a product containing partially hydrogenated vegetable oil, the greater the amount of trans fatty acids. Cutting down on the consumption of high-fat baked goods and processed foods also reduces a person's intake of trans fatty acids.
5. Vegetable oils do not have significant levels of trans fatty acids if they are not hydrogenated, but trans fatty acids are produced as the oils are reused in deep-fat frying.

The chart that follows compares the saturated fat content of polyunsaturated and monounsaturated oils. The oils are listed according to their degree of saturation.

When oils contain less than one-third saturated fat they are considered unsaturates, whether poly or mono. The polyunsaturates include soy, peanut, corn, sesame, sunflower, safflower, walnut, and hazelnut oils.

The monounsaturate oils are olive, almond, avocado, and canola.

Polyunsaturates lower total cholesterol but they also lower beneficial HDL high-density lipoproteins as well as the harmful LDL low-density lipoproteins. Monounsaturates lower LDLs and either leave HDLs untouched or raise them slightly. Saturates raise total cholesterol levels.

Oil	Saturated Fat Content
Peanut	17 percent
Avocado	15 to 20 percent
Soy	14 percent
Roasted sesame	14 percent
Olive	14 percent
Extra-light olive	14 percent
Corn	13 percent
Sunflower	10 percent
Safflower	9 percent
Walnut	9 percent
Hazelnut	7 percent
Canola	6 percent

I'd like to be just one pound thinner for every time I've asked for as little fat as possible in a dish and had the waiter or waitress say, "But it's olive oil and that's good for you."

It's true; olive oil is better for your arteries but it ain't better than margarine, butter, corn oil, or any oil if you also are watching your calories and you want to keep the fat off your hips and thighs. All fats are equal in this—they have 120 calories per tablespoon.

CHOLESTEROL

Health professionals emphasize that while it is a very good idea to cut down on such high-cholesterol foods as eggs and liver in the diet, it's equally important to reduce saturated fat. As Dr. William Castelli, the medical director of the Framingham Heart Study, said in an interview: "For most Americans the reason their cholesterol is too high is more because they eat too much saturated fat than because they eat too much cholesterol."

SODIUM

Just as some people can eat prime steak, baked potatoes with sour cream, and top off the meal with pie à la mode three times a week and live to be ninety, many people can eat salty foods and suffer no ill effects. No high blood pressure, no strokes, no blowing up like a balloon. The problem is you might not know into which category you fit until it is too late. Certainly people with hypertension in the family know they are at greater risk for developing it themselves, but others also develop it. There is a lot of controversy over the importance sodium plays in hypertension, but no one needs as much sodium as the average American eats, something like 4,000 to 5,000 milligrams a day. The maximum recommended by those who believe in the salt-hypertension connection is no more than 2,400 to 3,000 milligrams of sodium a day.

Manufacturers of prepared foods, like canned soups, use a lot of salt for seasoning because it is much less expensive than the seasonings you would use at home to make a similar dish. Salt is cheap; by comparison herbs and spices are not. Salt, like monosodium glutamate, also a significant source of sodium, helps to disguise paltry portions of the costly main ingredients. You don't need chunks of chicken in chicken soup to give it flavor if you add a lot of salt. So one chicken can march through hundreds of cans of soup and increase the manufacturers' profits handsomely.

It's a cinch to control the amount of sodium in your diet if you don't eat processed or prepared foods.

Sodium is a constituent of salt. Six grams of salt equals 2,400 milligrams of sodium. One teaspoon of salt contains 2,000 milligrams of sodium.

When you are cooking a dish for two, $\frac{1}{8}$ teaspoon salt (250 milligrams of sodium) is generally enough to perk up all the flavors; on rare occasions you may need $\frac{1}{4}$ teaspoon (500 milligrams).

❧ What's Good: Carbohydrates and Company

CARBOHYDRATES

Carbohydrates are all anyone talks about these days. But all carbohydrates are not created equal: Some are fabulous while others are tolerable in small doses.

There are complex carbohydrates and simple carbohydrates. The latter provide calories—empty calories, as they are often called, because they give you energy and nothing else. All forms of sugar belong in this group, including honey and molasses and fructose.

As long as you get all the nutrients you need in the rest of the food you eat, and you have some calories to spare, sugar will do no harm if you are a normal healthy person, except maybe rot your teeth.

The problem with sugar is that it generally comes attached to fat, as in ice cream, chocolates, cookies, cakes, and pies. Today, manufacturers have seen a superb marketing opportunity in the low-fat trend and now are producing scads of sweets that are fat-free. Keep in mind that that does not guarantee that they are low in calories. In fact, the calorie levels tend to be about the same as the full-fat versions—high.

It's complex carbohydrates that are receiving all the hosannas. You are supposed to eat more of them than of anything else. They fill you without fattening you; they contain many essential nutrients, including elements that may prevent cancer and heart disease.

Complex carbohydrates are found in fruits, vegetables, grains, dried beans, and peas. Unfortunately Americans aren't devoted to all the foods in this group. We don't eat nearly enough complex carbohydrates, and that's what has been wrong with the traditional American diet since World War II.

A diet based on complex carbohydrates has one enormous plus that is not emphasized enough: For most people it is much easier to lose weight on a diet high in complex carbohydrates than on the traditional American diet.

There are several reasons why fat foods go directly to your hips and thighs and carbohydrates do not. For one thing, a gram of fat has 9 calories whereas a gram of carbohydrate or protein has only 4. So fat has more caloric density.

In addition, fat, protein, and carbohydrates are metabolized differently. Most fat consumed goes into the body's fat stores almost immediately. But it takes very large quantities of carbohydrates to turn to fat.

If you choose a diet with fewer calories than you usually consume, but one that is high in complex carbohydrates, you are likely to feel more satisfied than if you choose a low-carbohydrate diet with the same number of calories. This makes maintaining the diet easier. It is no longer a contest between willpower and hunger: You won't be hungry.

Nancy Goor, who with her husband, Dr. Ron Goor, wrote *The Choose to Lose Diet* (Houghton Mifflin, 1990), said: "Obese people say they don't eat any more than anyone else, and that's true, but what they are eating is filled with fat."

Dr. Goor added: "The amount of food isn't the thing. It's the choice. Plenty of research has shown that if you lower the fat, you do not have to reduce calories. And because you are not hungry, you can do it forever because you feel full and satisfied."

And don't forget to exercise: It makes losing weight even easier.

PROTEIN

Americans eat far more protein than they need, usually in the form of meat or cheese, and both of them come with a lot of fat. (Yes, yes, I know about low-fat cheeses but with rare exceptions I don't consider them cheese and I don't consider them edible.)

You don't need to eat animal protein—the kind from meat and dairy products—to get enough of the nutrient. You can eat beans and peas and corn and pasta and get all the protein you need. Not too many people are ready for the leap to a vegetarian diet, so the best course of action is to do as Dr. Dean Ornish advised First Lady Hillary Rodham Clinton: Eat very small amounts of animal protein, no more than 4 to 6 ounces a day, and fill up with the protein found in vegetables and grains. Dr. Ornish is a cardiologist who has been successfully treating people with heart disease through an extremely low-fat vegetarian diet.

VITAMINS AND MINERALS

This is a minefield. Not long ago I would have written in this space: Healthy individuals who eat a varied diet based on whole foods will get the vitamins and minerals they need.

Now that is not so certain, and some of the most conservative health professionals have been recommending dietary supplements that contain antioxidants because there is a host of intriguing evidence that beta carotene, vitamin C, and vitamin E may reduce the risk of cancer and heart disease. If those words sound familiar it's because these nutrients are found in fruits, vegetables, and whole grains; in other words, in complex carbohydrates.

The April 14, 1993, "Eating Well" column in the *Times* began: "Here's why Americans are confused about nutrition":

Dr. Walter Willett, the chairman of the department of nutrition at the Harvard School of Public Health; Dr. Gladys Block, a professor at the School of Public Health at the University of California at Berkeley, and Dr. Michael Jacobson, the executive director of the Center for Science in the Public Interest, a consumer advocacy group, believe it is prudent to take supplements like vitamins C and E and beta carotene, which is a precursor of Vitamin A. Studies suggest that such antioxidant compounds may help combat heart disease, cancer, and other health problems.

But Dr. Marion Nestle, the chairwoman of the department of nutrition at New York University, Dr. Joan Gussow, professor emeritus of nutrition at Columbia Teachers College; Dr. Catherine Wotecki, at the time the director of the Food and Nutrition Board of the National Academy of Sciences and Dr. Walter Mertz, a retired director of the United States Agriculture Department's Human Nutrition Research Center, disagree.

This group says these nutrients should not be consumed in pills, but rather by eating the foods that contain them: fruits, vegetables, and grains.

Eating only certain elements of food worries Dr. Mertz. In a recent lecture, he said: "There are five hundred carotenoids in food. I am just plain afraid that if I took fifteen milligrams of beta carotene supplement a day, what will happen to the other carotenoids? We just picked one carotenoid out of many."

Those who take supplements consider them insurance: They should be taken in conjunction with healthful diet, not in place of it.

Dr. Block said: "It's very clear we need to be eating fruits and vegetables, because there are hundreds of things in them that are not in a pill and never will be. But at present, only nine percent of the population is eating five fruits and vegetables a day."

And then a bombshell.

The now famous Finnish study, followed by the study of colon cancer and antioxidants, caught a lot of people short. The Finnish study reported in the spring of 1994 set health professionals on their collective ear.

The study set out to determine whether the antioxidants vitamin E and beta carotene, which converts in the body to vitamin A, reduce the risk of heart disease and certain cancers. The subjects were an unhealthy population of 29,000 Finnish men over 50 with many risk factors. They were generally overweight, had used tobacco heavily and for long periods, and had high cholesterol levels and high intakes of fat and alcohol.

Three-quarters of the men were given one or both of the vitamin supplements, and the remaining quarter received neither. The men who took beta carotene were somewhat more likely to die of lung cancer and heart disease. The vitamin E group suffered slightly more strokes.

The final quarter was divided into four groups, depending on how much beta carotene and vitamin E they had at the beginning. Those with the lowest levels of the vitamin and the lowest dietary intake of the nutrients had the most lung cancer, and those with the highest level of nutrients had the least lung cancer.

Dr. Nestle was interviewed for the story and she said: "The findings strongly suggest that diets are more important than supplements, which is what we boring nutritionists have been saying for years."

In July 1994, a study reported in the *New England Journal of Medicine* failed to support the theory that vitamins C and E and beta carotene protected against the development of precancerous growths in the colon.

Foods Rich in Antioxidants

Beta Carotene

Apricots	Papaya
Broccoli	Peaches
Cantaloupe	Spinach
Carrots	Squash, yellow
Kale	Sweet potatoes
Mangos	

Vitamin C

Broccoli	Oranges
Cantaloupe	Peppers
Cauliflower	Potatoes
Grapefruit	Watermelon

Vitamin E

Green, leafy vegetables	Vegetable oils
Liver	Whole-grain products
Nuts	Wheat germ

Note: Liver is not recommended as a regular part of a low-fat diet, and nuts and oils are high in fat.

OTHER DIETARY SUPPLEMENTS

What to do about vitamins and minerals is nothing compared with the land mines surrounding hundreds of other substances that fall in the category of dietary supplements—herbs, amino acids and botanicals, things with names like willow bark, *ma huang,* and evening primrose. None of them has ever been tested scientifically to show whether they actually do what an underground culture of supplement users says they do or what their manufacturers say they do. Which is everything from removing hangnails to curing AIDs.

Some of the more recent examples of dangerous supplements that have been marketed:

Chaparral, an herbal remedy used as an antioxidant and blood purifier; caused toxic hepatitis

Lobelia, marketed to relieve teething symptoms, fussiness, and congestion in babies; has a nicotinelike stimulant

Comfrey, long used as an herbal tea though it has been banned in other countries, now comes in gelatin capsules. It is touted as a tissue healer and bone builder but it can cause permanent liver damage.

Willow bark contains a substance that metabolizes in the body like aspirin. Some products containing willow bark are aimed at children and their labels note that they are aspirin-free. There is a warning on the aspirin label that the product should not be given to children who have the flu or chicken pox because they may develop Reye's syndrome, which can be fatal. No warning is required on the labels of products containing willow bark and may also cause Reye's syndrome.

In the fall of 1994, Congress approved a bill to settle, at least for a while, how to regulate health claims for dietary supplements.

It's a compromise: Only the Food and Drug Administration can decide whether to approve disease-prevention claims. And the agency retains the ability to remove dangerous products, though it may be harder to do so.

However, the bill allows manufacturers to make what are called "structure and function" claims. That means, for example, a label might say, "Vitamin A is necessary for good vision." It's possible such claims could be interpreted to mean that supplements are essential to overcome some bogus deficiency in the diet. Such claims must be accompanied by this disclaimer: "This statement has not been evaluated by the Food and Drug Administration. This product is not intended to diagnose, treat, cure, or prevent a disease."

FIBER

If you remember all the fuss over oat bran, you remember the importance of fiber in the diet. Once again, if you stick to fruits, vegetables, and whole grains, the fiber comes along naturally. You don't have to torture yourself by trying to swallow oat bran. Twenty to 30 grams of fiber should be consumed each day. That translates into 6 to 11 servings of breads, cereals, and starches. A high-fiber cereal, for example, contains 10 to 12 grams in one serving.

ADDING FIBER THE EASY WAY

Instead of 1 cup of cornflakes choose ⅓ cup bran cereal. Fiber gain 8.2 grams.

Instead of 2 slices of white bread choose 2 slices whole-wheat bread. Fiber gain: 5.4 grams.

Instead of 10 cherries choose 1 pear. Fiber gain 3.8 grams.

Instead of 1 cup cooked sliced squash choose cooked asparagus. Fiber gain 2.4 grams.

Instead of 2½ tablespoons all-purpose flour choose 2½ tablespoons whole-wheat flour. Fiber gain 1.1 grams.

Instead of 6 saltines choose 6 whole-wheat crackers. Fiber gain: 1.5 grams.

Instead of ½ cup cooked white rice choose ½ cup cooked brown rice. Fiber gain: 1.3 grams.

(Source: University of California Wellness Letter)

That's the short form of the skinny on dietary guidelines. The real trick is to follow them and still enjoy what you are eating without giving yourself over to hours of shopping and cooking.

A Word About the Nutritional Information Included with the Recipes

The nutritional values given are taken from the database published by the United States Department of Agriculture; it is widely used as a source for this information, but frankly, the nutrition information in this book is approximate and is not meant to be taken as gospel. It can, however, provide a reasonable sense of what's in the meals here. Every figure has been rounded off to the nearest 0 or 5; so, something that has 352 milligrams of sodium will appear with 350, while something with 113 milligrams of cholesterol will be listed with 115.

The nutrition values given for each recipe are per serving of the entire menu, and do not include bread unless it is in the ingredients list. The values are based on the ingredients and quantities given; changes, even small, may have an effect, though minor, on those values. All the menus in this book have less than 30 percent fat from calories; most have 20 percent or less, and some even come in under 10 percent.

A Final Word

Home cooks are always advised to read recipes carefully before proceeding. That advice is particularly well taken here. For one thing, you want to plan your marketing, which is the first step. And then you don't want any missteps that will upset the timetable. So take a few minutes to read the recipe—including the Game Plan—to ensure efficiency and good results. Keep in mind that if you increase the number of servings in a recipe, you also will add to the time for preparation. For instance, if you double a recipe, you probably will add 3 to 5 minutes.

RECIPES

Vegetarian

Eggplant and Tomato Sauce for Fettuccine

Fennel and Mushroom Salad

*E*ggplant has always posed a particular problem for those interested in reducing their fat intake because it is generally sautéed to bring out its flavor before it is added to other ingredients in dishes. But eggplant soaks up oil like a sponge when sautéed or fried, and so requires vast quantities of it. ❧ The alternative is to broil or grill it; it only needs to be lightly sprayed or brushed with oil to keep it from burning while it softens and sweetens. ❧ If you cannot find fresh fettuccine made without eggs, substitute fettuccine made with eggs, which will not add enough fat or cholesterol to worry about.

Eggplant and Tomato Sauce for Fettuccine

16 ounces (1 pound) eggplant

Pan spray

1 large clove garlic

4 ounces (¼ pound) whole onion or 3 ounces chopped ready-cut onion (1 cup)

1 (28-ounce) can no-salt-added chopped or crushed tomatoes

1½ tablespoons no-salt-added tomato paste

1 teaspoon drained capers

8 ounces (1 pound) eggless fresh fettuccine

4 large fresh basil leaves, to yield 1 tablespoon chopped

Freshly ground black pepper

1. Turn on the broiler; cover the broiler pan with aluminum foil.
2. Wash the eggplant and trim off the ends; slice into ¼-inch-thick slices, leaving skin on. Arrange the slices on foil-covered pan and spray lightly with oil spray. Broil 2 or 3 inches from the source of heat about 10 minutes. Watch so they don't burn.
3. Mince the garlic; chop onion.
4. Heat a nonstick frying pan and spray or brush lightly with oil. Sauté garlic and onion until the onion begins to soften.
5. Bring water to boil in a covered pot for fettuccine.
6. Add the tomatoes, tomato paste, and capers to the garlic and onion. Cook over high heat about 10 minutes.
7. Turn the eggplant and spray the second side; continue to broil another 6 or 7 minutes, or until browned.
8. Cook the fettuccine according to package directions.
9. Wash, dry, and chop the basil to make 1 tablespoon. Stir into the tomatoes; season with freshly ground black pepper.
10. Remove the eggplant from the broiler and roughly cut into large chunks; add to the tomato sauce. To serve, drain pasta, and top with the sauce.

Yield: 2 servings

Fennel and Mushroom Salad

1 tablespoon fresh lemon
    juice
2 teaspoons olive oil
5- or 6-ounce fennel bulb
4 ounces (¼ pound) white
    mushrooms
Freshly ground black pepper
½ ounce Parmigiano-
    Reggiano cheese (2 to
    3 tablespoons sliced)

1. Squeeze 1 tablespoon of lemon juice into a serving bowl and whisk
   with the oil.
2. Trim away the top and stem end of the fennel. Wash and thinly slice
   the bulb to yield 1½ cups. Stir into the dressing.
3. Wash, trim, and dry the mushrooms. Slice thinly and add to the
   dressing.
4. Season the salad with the pepper and arrange on 2 salad plates.
5. Thinly slice the Parmigiano and top each salad with the slices.

Yield: 2 servings

G A M E   P L A N

Turn on broiler.

Prepare and broil eggplant.

Prepare garlic and onion and sauté.

Boil water for pasta.

Add tomatoes, tomato paste, capers to garlic and onion.

Turn eggplant.

Make salad dressing.

Prepare basil.

Cook pasta.

Prepare fennel and mushrooms; add to salad dressing.

Add eggplant to tomatoes with basil.

Season salad and sauce.

Prepare Parmigiano.

APPROXIMATE NUTRITION INFORMATION PER SERVING:
610 calories, 10 grams fat, 5 milligrams cholesterol
(105 milligrams with egg fettuccine), 290 milligrams
sodium, 25 grams protein, 120 grams carbohydrate

Linguine with Arugula, Tomatoes, and Potatoes

*T*his one-dish meal is heavy on the carbohydrates, but for anyone who still thinks potatoes, bread, pasta, and the like are fattening, this is a good time to repeat that carbohydrates and protein contain an equal number of calories per gram—4. Fat contains 9 calories per gram. ❧ This is a very filling and easy-to-prepare dish that takes advantage of summer vegetables—tomatoes, tiny new potatoes, and arugula. But most people still feel they need something to round out the meal. For them, a slice of crusty, dense bread fills the bill.

Linguine with Arugula, Tomatoes, and Potatoes

12 ounces (¾ pound) tiny
   new potatoes
16 ounces (1 pound) ripe
   tomatoes
1 clove garlic
1 teaspoon olive oil
¼ teaspoon hot pepper
   flakes
16 ounces (1 pound) arugula
9 ounces fresh no-egg
   linguine
8 small Greek, Italian, or
   French black olives
⅛ teaspoon salt
Freshly ground black pepper
1 ounce Parmigiano-Reggiano
   (about 6 tablespoons
   grated)

1. Scrub but do not peel the potatoes. Cook in water to cover in a covered pot for 15 to 20 minutes, depending on the size of the potatoes.
2. Wash and trim the tomatoes. Chop coarsely.
3. Mince the garlic. Heat oil in a nonstick pan. When hot, sauté the garlic with the hot pepper for about 30 seconds.
4. Bring the water to boil for the pasta.
5. Add the tomatoes to the garlic and cook over high heat to cook off excess moisture.
6. Trim the stems from the arugula; wash thoroughly and shake well. Add to the tomatoes.
7. Cook the linguine according to package directions.
8. Pit the olives and add to the tomatoes. Continue cooking until the arugula is wilted. When the potatoes are cooked, drain, cut into bite-size pieces, and add to the tomatoes. Season with salt, if desired, and pepper to taste.
9. Grate the cheese.
10. Drain the pasta and serve with the sauce. Sprinkle cheese on top.

Yield: 2 servings

GAME PLAN

Follow recipe.

Pasta with Tomatoes and Arugula | Broccoli with Lemon and Garlic

*W*hen summer's best tomatoes come to market, it's time to make one of those pasta sauces that pair hot cooked pasta with cold raw tomatoes. Any tomatoes that fall short of that standard will result in a sauce that has to be doctored and that's not the idea at all. ❧ Traditional cold tomato sauces call for basil, an eternally superb combination. But now that arugula is fairly easy to find, it makes a very good change of pace, the sweetness of the tomatoes providing an interesting contrast to the slightly bitter arugula. ❧ Broccoli cooked with garlic and lemon offers a simple and attractive side dish.

Pasta with Tomatoes and Arugula

1 tablespoon olive oil
6 ounces Vidalia or other sweet onion
3 medium-large ripe tomatoes
2 bunches arugula (1¼ cups)
12 ounces (¾ pound) penne, fusilli, rigatoni, or similar shaped pasta
⅛ teaspoon salt (optional)
Freshly ground black pepper

1. Bring the water for pasta to boil in a covered pot.
2. Chop the onion finely.
3. Heat nonstick pan until it is very hot. Reduce heat to medium-high and add oil. Add the onion and sauté until very soft; do not let the onion brown.
4. Wash, trim, and coarsely cut the tomatoes; coarsely chop in the food processor and place in a large serving bowl.
5. Wash, trim, and dry arugula and chop coarsely.
6. Cook the pasta.
7. Stir the onion and arugula into the tomatoes, and when the pasta is cooked, drain it and mix well with tomato mixture. Season with salt and pepper.

Yield: 3 servings

Broccoli with Lemon and Garlic

24 ounces whole broccoli or
  12 ounces ready-cut
  broccoli florets (4 to
  5 cups)
1 large clove garlic
1½ tablespoons olive oil
1½ tablespoons lemon juice

1. Trim the tough stems from whole broccoli and cut florets into bite-size pieces; discard the stems or use them in another dish. Steam the broccoli till tender but not soft, 5 to 7 minutes.
2. Mince the garlic. Heat the oil in a nonstick skillet, add the garlic, and sauté.
3. Add the cooked broccoli and the lemon juice to the garlic, cooking briefly to combine well.

Yield: 3 servings

G A M E   P L A N

Boil water for pasta.

Prepare and steam broccoli.

Sauté onion; set aside.

Dice tomatoes.

Wash and chop arugula.

Cook pasta.

Mix sauce for pasta.

Use nonstick pan in which onion sautéed to sauté garlic; add broccoli and lemon juice.

Finish pasta dish.

APPROXIMATE NUTRITION INFORMATION PER SERVING, WITHOUT SALT: 620 calories, 15 grams fat, 0 milligrams cholesterol, 155 milligrams sodium, 20 grams protein, 105 grams carbohydrate

GoodFellas Linguine with Tomato Sauce | Green Salad

We came home at 10:30 one night after seeing the movie *GoodFellas*. I didn't feel like cooking but we did feel like eating something, so I made do with what was easy and handy: garlic, olive oil, canned tomato purée, some leftover red wine, and Parmigiano-Reggiano. There was fresh linguine in the freezer. ❧ The result is worth recording: The red wine added several interesting notes as well as body to the tomato purée and it cut the acidity. The garlic spiked it up. ❧ The sauce cooked in the same time needed for the pasta. If only all quick fixes were this good. If you have some salad greens resting in the refrigerator, beat some olive oil with some balsamic vinegar, pour it over them, and you've made your meal. ❧ Without the optional cheese, the calorie count and the fat go down considerably.

GoodFellas Linguine with Tomato Sauce

12 ounces (¾ pound) fresh linguine or other fresh pasta

1 clove garlic

1½ teaspoons olive oil

½ a 28- or 29-ounce can no-salt-added tomato purée

6 tablespoons dry red wine

1 ounce Parmigiano-Reggiano or ⅓ cup coarsely grated (optional)

1. Bring water to boil for the linguine.
2. Mince the garlic and cook in hot oil in a deep saucepan for about 30 seconds. Stir in the tomato purée and wine; cover and simmer.
3. Cook the pasta.
4. Grate the cheese, if using.
5. Drain the pasta.
6. Serve sauce over the linguine and pass the cheese.

Yield: 2 servings

Green Salad

4 ounces (¼ pound) assorted
   salad greens (about
   4 cups packed)
2 teaspoons olive oil
2 teaspoons balsamic vinegar
½ teaspoon reduced-sodium
   soy sauce

1. Wash and dry the greens and break into bite-size pieces.
2. Whisk the oil, vinegar, and soy sauce in a serving bowl. Add the greens and toss to coat well.

Yield: 2 servings

GAME PLAN

Prepare linguine and sauce through step 2.

Start salad.

When water boils, cook pasta.

Grate cheese.

Finish salad.

Finish linguine.

APPROXIMATE NUTRITION INFORMATION PER SERVING:
885 calories, 15 grams fat, 10 milligrams cholesterol,
590 milligrams sodium, 30 grams protein, 150 grams
carbohydrate

Fettuccine with Creamy Basil–Pine Nut Sauce | Tomato Salsa

There is no way to include pesto in a low-fat cookbook—any authentic version simply calls for too much oil. But it is possible to obtain that rich creamy texture and distinctive basil and pine nut flavor by using plenty of fresh basil, low-fat ricotta and yogurt, and a bit of blue cheese. The pale green of the sauce provides a stunning contrast when served over fettuccine and alongside a fresh tomato salsa.

Fettuccine with Creamy Basil–Pine Nut Sauce

9 ounces fresh fettuccine
1 large clove garlic
1 cup lightly packed fresh
    basil leaves
½ cup reduced-fat ricotta
    cheese
½ cup nonfat plain yogurt
2 ounces blue cheese
2 teaspoons sherry wine
    vinegar
Freshly ground black pepper
2 tablespoons pine nuts

1. Bring 3 quarts water to boil for the fettuccine.
2. Turn the food processor on and put the garlic through the feed tube to process.
3. Add the basil, ricotta, yogurt, blue cheese, and vinegar to the processor workbowl. Process to blend thoroughly. Season to taste with pepper and mix in pine nuts by hand.
4. Cook the fettuccine, drain, and serve with the sauce.

Yield: 3 servings

Tomato Salsa

16 ounces (1 pound) ripe
   tomatoes
1 jalapeño pepper
1 small clove garlic
1 small red onion, to yield
   ¼ cup finely chopped
1 bunch cilantro, to yield
   ½ cup chopped
6 to 8 sprigs parsley, to yield
   2 tablespoons finely
   chopped
Juice of 1 small lime

1. Chop tomatoes. Seed and mince the jalapeño; mince the garlic.
2. Finely chop onion; chop cilantro and parsley. Squeeze lime.
3. Combine all the ingredients and mix well.

Yield: 3 servings

G A M E   P L A N

Boil water for fettuccine.

Prepare sauce for fettuccine.

Start salsa.

Cook fettuccine.

Finish salsa.

APPROXIMATE NUTRITION INFORMATION PER SERVING:
680 calories, 20 grams fat, 175 milligrams cholesterol,
555 milligrams sodium, 40 grams protein, 100 grams
carbohydrate

Orzo with Spicy Broccoli, Cauliflower, and Raisins

Arugula and Oranges

*T*his very simple vegetable dish takes advantage of the best the late fall has to offer, particularly at farmers' markets. ❧ You might use the same vegetable combination with polenta or bow ties, but there is something particularly comforting about the texture of orzo. The mixture of sweet—the raisins—with heat—the hot pepper flakes-—adds a Sicilian accent to the dish.

Orzo with Spicy Broccoli, Cauliflower, and Raisins

16 ounces (1 pound) whole onion or
14 ounces chopped ready-cut onion
(3⅓ to 3½ cups)
1 large clove garlic
1 teaspoon olive oil
12 ounces (¾ pound) whole broccoli or
6 ounces ready-cut broccoli florets
(3½ to 4 cups)
10 ounces whole cauliflower or
5 ounces ready-cut cauliflorets
(3 to 3¾ cups)
¼ teaspoon hot pepper flakes, or to
taste
½ cup dry white wine
¼ cup raisins
¼ teaspoon salt
Freshly ground black pepper
¾ cup orzo
2 ounces sharp Cheddar cheese (¾ cup
minus 1 tablespoon coarsely grated)

1. Bring 2 quarts of water to boil in a covered pot for the orzo.
2. Chop the whole onion and mince the garlic.
3. Heat the oil in a nonstick skillet and sauté the onions and garlic until the onions begin to soften and take on color.
4. Cut the tough stems off whole broccoli and cut the florets into bite-size pieces. Remove cauliflorets from head and cut into bite-size pieces.
5. Add the broccoli, cauliflower, hot pepper flakes, wine, raisins, salt, and freshly ground pepper to the onions. Cover pan; reduce heat, and simmer until the vegetables are tender, about 10 minutes.
6. Meanwhile cook the orzo in boiling water until tender, about 10 minutes.
7. Coarsely grate the cheese.
8. Drain and mix the orzo with the vegetables and cheese.

Yield: 2 servings

Arugula and Oranges

1 large navel orange
1 teaspoon olive oil
2 ounces arugula (about
   2 cups), washed, drained, and
   trimmed

1. Peel and cut the orange into chunks. In a small bowl mix the orange sections with the oil.
2. Wash the arugula, dry, and trim away the tough stems. Arrange arugula on two salad plates and top with the orange pieces.

Yield: 2 servings

G A M E   P L A N

Prepare orzo and vegetables through Step 6.

Make salad.

Grate cheese and finish dish.

APPROXIMATE NUTRITION INFORMATION PER SERVING:
675 calories, 15 grams fat, 30 milligrams cholesterol,
510 milligrams sodium, 25 grams protein, 100 grams
carbohydrate

Gorgonzola Cream Sauce with Angel Hair Pasta

Mixed Greens and Dressing

*I*s it possible to make a cheese-flavored cream sauce that comes within a country mile of judicious eating? Some pasta sauces call for heavy cream, butter, and Parmigiano-Reggiano. Is it better to have just a little of the real thing or to try to produce a reasonable facsimile for a full-size portion? ❧ That was the test. This is the result. Low-fat buttermilk was substituted for the cream, the amount of Gorgonzola reduced, nutmeg added to take the sharp edge off the cheese, and some cornstarch added to thicken the sauce. This is the kind of sauce that coats every strand of the pasta, imparting a slightly sharp but creamy flavor. For the final punch sprinkle the pasta with Parmesan cheese. ❧ Add some crusty country bread to complete the menu, if you like.

Gorgonzola Cream Sauce with Angel Hair Pasta

½ cup frozen peas
1 cup low-fat buttermilk
1 tablespoon cornstarch
2 tablespoons sweet
   Gorgonzola
Large dash ground nutmeg
2 tablespoons chopped
   walnuts
1 ounce Parmigiano-Reggiano
   (⅓ cup coarsely grated)
8 ounces (½ pound) fresh
   angel hair pasta

1. Bring 4 quarts of water to boil in a covered pot for the pasta. Turn the oven to 350 degrees.
2. Measure out the peas and leave at room temperature.
3. Mix a tablespoon of the buttermilk with the cornstarch to make a smooth paste. In a heavy-bottomed saucepan stir buttermilk-cornstarch mixture, remaining buttermilk, Gorgonzola, and nutmeg.
4. Cook over medium heat, stirring almost constantly, to melt the cheese and thicken the mixture.
5. Spread the walnuts on a baking sheet and toast them in the oven for 10 minutes, taking care not to burn them.
6. Grate the Parmigiano.
7. When the water boils stir in the pasta and cook according to package directions, about 45 seconds; drain.
8. Just as the cheese mixture begins to thicken, stir in the peas and cook long enough to heat the peas through.
9. Stir in the toasted walnuts and serve the sauce over the pasta with Parmigiano on the side.

Yield: 2 servings

Mixed Greens and Dressing

2 teaspoons olive oil
2 teaspoons balsamic vinegar
¼ teaspoon Dijon mustard
4 ounces mixed leaf lettuce
  and fresh herbs such as
  Boston lettuce, Bibb
  lettuce, basil, and parsley
  (about 3 cups, packed)

1. Whisk the oil, vinegar, and mustard together in a serving bowl.
2. Wash and dry the greens and toss them in the serving bowl to coat with dressing.

Yield: 2 servings

G A M E   P L A N

Boil water for pasta.

Turn on oven.

Make sauce and cook.

Toast walnuts; grate cheese.

Start salad.

Cook pasta.

Finish salad.

Finish sauce for pasta.

Drain pasta and top with sauce.

APPROXIMATE NUTRITION INFORMATION PER SERVING:
700 calories, 20 grams fat, 22 milligrams cholesterol,
615 milligrams sodium, 30 grams protein, 105 grams
carbohydrate

Linguine with Wild Mushrooms in Buttermilk Sauce

Yellow Tomatoes, Black Olives, and Red Onion

The variety of mushrooms in specialty stores, even supermarkets, now is dazzling, and while they may cost as much or more than a rack of lamb or lobster, to my mind they are equally sumptuous. ❧ When you want to serve something special, but do it quickly, linguine with wild mushrooms will please everyone. ❧ If you want to make a less costly version of this dish, use ordinary champignons de Paris (the white mushrooms in the supermarket), then add a few reconstituted dried porcini. The dried porcini will give the dish a deep mushroom flavor. ❧ The salad needs no dressing if the tomatoes are local, ripe, and sweet and the basil sparkling fresh.

Linguine with Wild Mushrooms in Buttermilk Sauce

16 ounces (1 pound) assorted wild
  mushrooms—cremini, shiitake,
  oyster, morels—and champignons
  de Paris (white mushrooms)
9 ounces whole onion or 8 ounces diced
  ready-cut onion (1¾ cups)
1 tablespoon olive oil
1 clove garlic
1 or 2 sprigs fresh oregano, to yield
  1½ tablespoons chopped
6 tablespoons Marsala
1 tablespoon fresh lemon juice
8 ounces (½ pound) fresh linguine
1 cup nonfat buttermilk
1 tablespoon cornstarch
Freshly ground black pepper
¼ teaspoon salt

1. Clean, trim, and slice the mushrooms ¼ inch thick. Dice the whole onion.
2. Boil water for the pasta.
3. Heat the oil in a nonstick pan over high heat. Reduce heat to medium-high: sauté the onion and mushrooms until they are soft.
4. Mince the garlic; wash, dry, and mince the oregano. Stir the garlic and oregano into the mushrooms with the Marsala and lemon juice; raise the heat slightly and cook to reduce excess liquid, stirring occasionally.
5. Cook linguine.
6. Blend a bit of buttermilk with the cornstarch to make a smooth paste, then stir the paste into the rest of the buttermilk. Add the buttermilk to the mushrooms and cook until the mixture thickens. Season with pepper and salt, and serve over hot linguine.

Yield: 2 servings

Yellow Tomatoes, Black Olives, and Red Onion

12 to 16 yellow cherry tomatoes
10 oil-cured black olives
2 thin slices red onion
10 to 12 fresh basil leaves

1. Stem and wash the tomatoes. Arrange on two salad plates.
2. Pit olives. Mince onion. Wash basil leaves.
3. Arrange olives, onion, and basil leaves on tomatoes.

Yield: 2 servings

G A M E   P L A N

Follow directions for linguine and mushrooms through Step 3.

Prepare tomatoes for salad.

Pit olives.

Prepare garlic and oregano and add with other ingredients to mushrooms.

Cook pasta.

Prepare onion and basil for salad.

Blend buttermilk with cornstarch and stir into mushrooms.

Finish salad.

Finish linguine and mushrooms.

APPROXIMATE NUTRITION INFORMATION PER SERVING:
645 calories, 15 grams fat, 140 milligrams cholesterol,
650 milligrams sodium, 25 grams protein, 100 grams
carbohydrate

Rotini with Fresh Tomato Sauce

Corn on the Cob

*N*othing says summer like a cold fresh herbaceous tomato sauce on top of steaming hot pasta. Add some corn fresh from the farmer and you have made a quick supper with little effort, the kind of meal you can enjoy for just a few months of the year. ❧ Serve with crusty French or Italian bread.

Rotini with Fresh Tomato Sauce

1 clove garlic

8 ounces (½ pound) ripe
    flavorful tomatoes

1 sprig oregano, to yield
    1½ teaspoons chopped

1 sprig fresh parsley, to yield
    1 tablespoon chopped

1 or 2 sprigs fresh basil
    leaves, to yield 3 heaping
    tablespoons chopped

1 teaspoon olive oil

Freshly ground black pepper

8 ounces (½) rotini

1 ounce Parmigiano-Reggiano
    (⅓ cup coarsely grated)

1. Bring water to boil in a covered pot for the pasta.
2. Cut the garlic in half, and with the food processor running, put through the feed tube to mince.
3. Wash, trim, and cut the tomatoes in half, squeeze out seeds, and cut into large chunks.
4. Wash and dry the oregano, parsley, and basil.
5. Add the tomatoes, oregano, parsley, basil, olive oil, and pepper to the processor and process until the mixture is coarsely puréed. Spoon into a serving bowl.
6. When the water boils, cook the pasta according to package directions.
7. Grate the cheese.
8. Drain the pasta and mix immediately with the sauce. Serve with cheese.

Yield: 2 servings

Corn on the Cob

2 ears corn

Shuck the corn and steam over a little water for about 3 minutes. Drain and serve.

Yield: 2 servings

G A M E   P L A N

Follow pasta recipe through Step 6.
Prepare and steam corn.
Finish pasta.

APPROXIMATE NUTRITION INFORMATION PER SERVING, INCLUDING SLICE OF BREAD: 675 calories, 10 grams fat, 10 milligrams cholesterol, 275 milligrams sodium, 25 grams protein, 120 grams carbohydrate

Couscous and Fragrant Vegetables

*S*ometimes the best strategy for the quickest and easiest menus is a willingness to use whatever precut vegetables the local market has to offer, cooked with couscous in a single pan. The results are good meals on busy days. ❧ The assortment available the day this loosely translated North African dish was created included carrot sticks, cauliflower florets, and broccoli florets. A can of Italian plum tomatoes, a few onions, and spices—cumin, garlic, and hot pepper flakes—add zest, and cinnamon and ginger give the dish a seductive fragrance. This is so good it is worth the time and trouble to cut up the vegetables yourself if that's necessary. ❧ In any case, be patient with the onions and let them become very soft and golden so that all their sweetness comes through.

Couscous and Fragrant Vegetables

12 ounces (¾ pound) whole onion or
   11 ounces sliced ready-cut onion
   (2¼ to 2½ cups)
1 tablespoon olive oil
1 clove garlic
1 teaspoon ground cumin
½ teaspoon ground cinnamon
⅛ to ¼ teaspoon hot red pepper flakes
4 ounces whole peeled carrots or
   younger ready-cut carrot sticks
   (about 1 cup)
8 ounces cauliflower or 4 ounces
   cauliflorets (1½ to 2 cups)
16 ounces (1 pound) whole broccoli or
   8 ounces (½ pound) broccoli florets
½ a 28-ounce can no-salt-added plum
   tomatoes, drained
Freshly ground black pepper
⅛ teaspoon salt (optional)
1 bunch fresh cilantro, to yield ½ cup
   chopped (optional)

1. Thinly slice whole onion.
2. Heat a nonstick skillet over high heat. Reduce heat to medium-high. Heat oil, add the onion, and sauté gently until it is golden and very soft.
3. Mince garlic and add to the skillet with the cumin, cinnamon, and hot pepper flakes; cook, stirring, about 1 minute.
4. Add the carrots and cook 5 minutes.
5. Cut the whole cauliflower into small florets; trim the tough stems from the broccoli and cut florets into small pieces.
6. Drain liquid from tomatoes. Stir cauliflower, broccoli, and tomatoes into the skillet, crushing the tomatoes with fingers. Season with pepper and salt. Cover and simmer 10 minutes so that flavors can meld.
7. Wash, dry, and chop the cilantro.
8. Serve the sauce over couscous, sprinkled with cilantro.

Yield: 2 servings

Couscous

Water

1 cup quick-cooking whole-wheat
couscous

1. Following the package directions, bring water to boil in a covered pot.
2. Stir in couscous; cover, remove from heat, and allow liquid to be absorbed, about 5 minutes.

Yield: 2 servings

G A M E   P L A N

Prepare vegetables through Step 5.

Prepare couscous.

Chop optional cilantro.

APPROXIMATE NUTRITION INFORMATION PER SERVING, WITHOUT SALT: 580 calories, 10 grams fat, 0 milligrams cholesterol, 95 milligrams sodium, 20 grams protein, 105 grams carbohydrate

Risotto with Arugula

*R*isotto is a pretty speedy dish when you are using flavorings that do not require additional cooking. It can be made in a total of 25 minutes. ❧ If you would like to add some chicken to the risotto, grill thin strips while the rice is cooking, then cut the strips into small pieces and stir into the finished dish. ❧ Have some good crusty bread with it.

Risotto with Arugula

4 to 5 cups no-salt-added
   vegetable or chicken stock
   or broth
2 ounces onion (½ cup
   chopped onion)
1 tablespoon olive oil
12 ounces (¾ pound)
   arugula (3 or 4 bunches)
1 cup arborio rice
½ cup dry white wine
2 ounces Parmigiano-
   Reggiano (½ cup plus
   2 tablespoons coarsely
   grated)
Freshly ground black pepper

1. Heat the broth to a simmer in a saucepan.
2. Chop the onion. Heat the oil in a deep, heavy-bottomed pot; add the onion and sauté until it takes on a little color.
3. Meanwhile, trim the tough stems off arugula and wash the leaves thoroughly. Drain and dry.
4. Add the rice to the onion and stir until well coated.
5. Add the wine and stir until the wine cooks away, about 2 minutes.
6. Chop the arugula coarsely.
7. Add about a cup of simmering broth to the rice and cook over medium-high heat, stirring often, until the broth is absorbed. Continue adding broth as it is absorbed into the rice, while stirring almost continuously. Just before adding the last of the liquid (you may not need all the broth) stir in the arugula.
8. Grate the cheese. When the rice is tender, and there is still enough broth left to make it slightly runny, add the cheese, stirring well; season with pepper to taste and serve.

Yield: 2 servings

G A M E   P L A N

Follow recipe.

APPROXIMATE NUTRITION INFORMATION PER SERVING:
665 calories, 20 grams fat, 25 milligrams cholesterol,
645 milligrams sodium, 25 grams protein, 90 grams
carbohydrate

Spinach Risotto | Tomatoes

*T*he colors of this risotto recipe are so appealing—the bright green of the lightly cooked spinach and the creamy white of the rice. ❧ Why anyone ever said risotto is too time-consuming to bother with remains a mystery when really it is one of the easiest dishes to prepare. Here, slices of local tomatoes are all that is needed for dinner for three hungry people.

Spinach Risotto

8 ounces (½ pound) whole onion or 7 ounces chopped ready-cut onion (1⅔ cups)

1 tablespoon olive oil

5 cups no-salt-added chicken or vegetable stock or broth

2 cups arborio or other Italian rice for risotto

½ cup marsala wine

10-ounce package fresh spinach or 1 pound loose fresh spinach

1 clove garlic

3 tablespoons Dijon mustard

¼ teaspoon salt

Freshly ground black pepper

1 ounce Parmigiano-Reggiano (⅓ cup coarsely grated)

1. Chop the whole onion. Heat the oil in a large, heavy-bottomed pot, add the onion, and sauté until softened.
2. Meanwhile heat the chicken stock in a separate pot.
3. Add the rice to the onion and stir to coat; add the marsala and cook until liquid has been absorbed.
4. Add 1 cup of simmering stock to the rice. Stirring often, cook over medium-low heat until the liquid is absorbed.
5. Wash the spinach thoroughly and trim off the tough stems; chop coarsely.
6. Add a second cup of stock to the rice and continue cooking and stirring. Repeat.
7. Mince the garlic. Stir spinach, garlic, and mustard into the rice; immediately add the last cup of stock and continue cooking until the liquid has been absorbed and the rice is soft but firm and the mixture is creamy.
8. Grate the cheese.
9. Season the risotto with salt and pepper, sprinkle with the cheese, and serve.

Yield: 3 large servings

Tomatoes

3 large ripe tomatoes

Wash, trim, and thickly slice tomatoes and arrange on salad plates.

Yield: 3 servings

G A M E   P L A N

Prepare risotto through Step 8.
Prepare tomatoes.
Finish risotto.

APPROXIMATE NUTRITION INFORMATION PER SERVING:
780 calories, 15 grams fat, 20 milligrams cholesterol,
865 milligrams sodium, 25 grams protein, 125 grams
carbohydrate

Risotto with Asparagus and Porcini

Mesclun and Tart-Sweet Dressing

I am partial to risotto, not just because it is a comfort food for me, but because it is so easy and quick to prepare. ❧ Rice, like pasta, is a tabula rasa, taking on flavors that are added—and nearly anything can be, like asparagus and the intense flavor of dried mushrooms. Dried porcini would be the perfect choice with asparagus but just about any other dried mushroom will give a similar nice woodsy flavor. ❧ To contrast with the richness of the risotto, a simple mesclun salad with a dressing with some honey mustard provides the right sweet-acidic bite.

Risotto with Asparagus and Porcini

4 to 5 cups no-salt-added
  vegetable or chicken stock
  or broth
½ ounce dried porcini or
  other dried mushrooms
2 ounces onion (½ cup
  chopped)
1 tablespoon olive oil
16 ounces (1 pound)
  asparagus
1 cup arborio rice
½ cup dry white wine
2 ounces Parmigiano-
  Reggiano (½ cup plus
  2 tablespoons coarsely
  grated)
⅛ teaspoon salt
Freshly ground black pepper

1. In a saucepan, heat the stock to a simmer.
2. Add the dried mushrooms to the stock to reconstitute.
3. Chop the onion. Heat the oil in a deep, heavy-bottomed pot; add the onion and sauté until it takes on a little color.
4. Wash the asparagus.
5. Add the rice to the onion; stir well to coat.
6. Add the wine to the rice, stir, and let the wine cook away, about 2 minutes.
7. Snap the tough stem ends of the asparagus, breaking them at the point where the woody part meets the tender part. Cut spears just below the tips and cut the rest of the stems into ½-inch pieces.
8. Add about a cup of simmering stock (avoiding the mushrooms) to the rice and cook over medium-high heat, stirring about every 2 minutes until the liquid has been absorbed. (Leave the mushrooms in the remaining stock to continue soaking.) Repeat this procedure, adding more stock as it is absorbed into the rice, while stirring often.
9. Grate the cheese.

CONTINUED

10. Five minutes before the rice is ready, stir in the asparagus and the soaked mushrooms.
11. When the rice is tender but before all the stock has been absorbed —the mixture should be slightly runny—add the cheese; stir well, season with salt and pepper to taste, and serve.

Yield: 2 servings

Mesclun and Tart-Sweet Dressing

1 teaspoon olive oil
2 teaspoons balsamic vinegar
1 teaspoon honey mustard
3 ounces mesclun or other
   baby salad greens (about
   3 cups packed)

1. Whisk together the oil, vinegar, and mustard in a serving bowl.
2. Wash and dry the mesclun, add it to the dressing, and toss well.

Yield: 2 servings

GAME PLAN

Prepare risotto through Step 7.
Begin salad preparation and go back and forth between risotto and salad,
adding more stock to risotto, until both are completed.

APPROXIMATE NUTRITION ANALYSIS PER SERVING:
685 calories, 20 grams fat, 20 milligrams cholesterol,
530 milligrams sodium, 30 grams protein, 100 grams
carbohydrate

Mexican-Italian Polenta | Mesclun Salad

*C*orn, black beans, and jalapeño mean Mexican. So what do you make of those ingredients when they are plopped on top of polenta and sprinkled with fresh mozzarella? ❧ Call it another one of those culinary cross-cultural meetings taking place in more and more American kitchens. ❧ For the salad, if you cannot find mesclun, make your own mixture of greens and herbs, possibly including frisée.

Mexican-Italian Polenta

2 large cloves garlic
8 ounces whole red onion or
    7 ounces finely chopped
    ready-cut onion (1⅔ cups)
2 teaspoons canola oil
3½ cups no-salt-added
    vegetable or chicken stock
    or broth
½ to 1 jalapeño pepper
12 ounces (¾ pound) fresh
    plum tomatoes
¾ cup instant or fine-ground
    polenta
¼ teaspoon salt (optional)
1 (15-ounce) can no-salt-
    added black beans
2 large sprigs fresh basil, to
    yield 3 tablespoons
    chopped
1 cup frozen corn niblets
4 ounces fresh unsalted
    mozzarella cheese

1. Preheat the broiler. Cover the broiler pan with aluminum foil. Set oven rack at lowest possible level.
2. With the food processor running, put the garlic through the feed tube to mince. Finely chop whole onion in the food processor by pulsing. Squeeze any excess liquid from the onion.
3. Heat the oil in a nonstick pan, add the onion and garlic, and sauté until the onion begins to brown.
4. Bring the chicken stock to a boil in a covered pot.
5. Wash, trim, and seed the jalapeño. With the food processor running, put the jalapeño through the feed tube to mince.
6. Wash and trim the tomatoes. Slice them about ⅛ inch thick in the food processor. Add the tomatoes and jalapeño to the onion mixture; reduce the heat and cook until the tomatoes begin to soften.
7. Slowly add the polenta to the boiling stock, constantly stirring. Add the salt if you wish. When the polenta begins to thicken, but before it gets too firm to spread, remove it from the heat and spread it evenly in a 9- by 13-inch glass or metal baking pan. Set the pan aside.
8. Rinse and drain the beans. Wash and chop the basil. Add the beans, basil, and corn to the onion mixture and heat through. Spoon the mixture evenly over the polenta.
9. Coarsely grate the cheese and sprinkle it over the bean mixture.

CONTINUED

10. Place the pan under the broiler. Broil just long enough for the cheese to melt, about 1 minute.

Yield: 3 servings

Food Note ❥ There are those who will tell you that instant polenta is not as good as regular polenta, but in fact, instant polenta is simply more finely ground cornmeal, just as readily available in Italy as the more coarsely ground cornmeal. What may be lost in the resulting texture is made up by reduced cooking time.

Mesclun Salad

4 ounces (¼ pound) mesclun or other mixed baby greens (about 4 cups packed)
1 tablespoon olive oil
1 tablespoon balsamic vinegar
½ teaspoon Dijon mustard

1. Wash and dry the greens.
2. Whisk the oil, vinegar, and mustard together in a serving bowl; toss with the greens to coat thoroughly.

Yield: 3 servings

Food Note ❥ Frisée is not a new salad green, but one that is newly fashionable in recipes and on restaurant menus. Frisée is the French name—in the grocery store this pretty pale green vegetable is often called curly endive.

G A M E   P L A N

Prepare sauce and polenta through Step 8.

Start salad.

Grate cheese.

Finish polenta.

Finish salad.

APPROXIMATE NUTRITION INFORMATION PER SERVING, WITHOUT SALT: 595 calories, 15 grams fat, 20 milligrams cholesterol, 405 milligrams sodium, 30 grams protein, 80 grams carbohydrate

Polenta and Grilled Vegetables | Lemony Tomatoes and Cucumber

*G*rilling the vegetables brings out their sweetness. To speed up the cooking time, cover them while they are on the grill. If you don't have a stove-top grill yet, splurge on one—at about $20, it's a great investment. ❧ In season use ripe fresh tomatoes: When they are gone you can still make a reasonably good version of the salad with yellow or red cherry tomatoes.

Polenta and Grilled Vegetables

12 ounces (¾ pound) zucchini

12 ounces (¾ pound) Japanese eggplant or other small eggplant

6 scallions

2 teaspoons olive oil

2 teaspoons balsamic vinegar

½ teaspoon dried thyme

½ teaspoon dried oregano

Approximately 2½ cups no-salt-added vegetable or chicken stock or broth

2 ounces Parmigiano-Reggiano (½ cup plus 2 tablespoons coarsely grated)

½ cup instant or fine-ground polenta

¼ teaspoon salt

Freshly ground black pepper

Fresh basil leaves for garnish (optional)

1. Preheat the broiler, if using. Cover the broiler pan with aluminum foil.
2. Wash, trim, and quarter the zucchini.
3. Wash, trim, and halve the eggplant.
4. Wash and trim the scallions.
5. Whisk the oil, vinegar, thyme, and oregano together in a large bowl.
6. Place the vegetables in the oil-and-vinegar mixture and coat well.
7. Prepare top-of-the-stove grill, if using. Broil or grill the vegetables. If grilling, cover the vegetables with a tent of aluminum foil so that they cook quickly. When they begin to soften and brown on one side, turn and continue cooking until they are softened through. The scallions will be ready before the other vegetables.
8. Bring the chicken stock to a boil in a covered pot. For a softer polenta use 2½ cups of liquid to ½ cup of polenta; for firm polenta use 2 cups liquid.
9. Coarsely grate the cheese.
10. When the liquid is boiling, slowly stir in the polenta; stir often until the mixture thickens, 3 or 4 minutes. Stir in the cheese and season with salt and pepper.
11. Spoon the polenta onto two dinner plates and arrange vegetables on top; garnish, if desired, with basil leaves.

Yield: 2 servings

Lemony Tomatoes and Cucumber

1 lemon, to yield ¼ teaspoon
    grated rind and
    2 teaspoons juice
1 teaspoon olive oil
1 sprig fresh oregano, to
    yield
    1 teaspoon chopped
2 small, ripe tomatoes
1 medium Kirby cucumber,
    about 3 ounces

1. Grate the lemon rind; squeeze the juice; reserve remaining lemon for another use. In a medium bowl, whisk the rind and juice with the olive oil.
2. Wash, dry, and chop the oregano and stir into the lemon mixture.
3. Wash, trim, and cut the tomatoes into small chunks; add to the dressing.
4. Wash and trim but do not peel the cucumber. Cut into small chunks; add to the dressing and mix well.

Yield: 2 servings

G A M E   P L A N

Preheat broiler, if using.

Make vegetable marinade, prepare vegetables.

Prepare stove-top grill, if using.

Grill vegetables.

Make salad.

Boil water for polenta.

Grate cheese.

Cook polenta and finish dish.

APPROXIMATE NUTRITION INFORMATION PER SERVING:
415 calories, 15 grams fat, 20 milligrams cholesterol,
550 milligrams sodium, 20 grams protein, 50 grams
carbohydrate

Polenta with Zucchini, Peppers, and Cheese

Mizuna with Sweet Vinaigrette

*T*t will take no more than 20 minutes to put this very savory meal together. ❧ The polenta dish is adapted from one of Michel Rostang's bistros in Paris. Leave it to the French to provide a different take even on polenta, which they appear to have adopted along with pasta and other things Italian. ❧ You can substitute any slightly bitter green, like arugula or baby spinach, for the mizuna. The sweetness of the honey mustard in the dressing contrasts nicely with the bitterness of the greens.

Food Note ❧ Mizuna is a bitter green that looks like a thicker version of carrot tops.

Polenta with Zucchini, Peppers, and Cheese

16 ounces (1 pound) whole red peppers or 14 ounces ready-cut chopped pepper (4 cups)

1 tablespoon olive oil

16 ounces (1 pound) whole zucchini

3 cups no-salt-added chicken broth or stock

3 ounces Parmigiano-Reggiano (1 scant cup coarsely grated)

¾ cup instant or fine-ground polenta

¼ teaspoon salt

Freshly ground black pepper

1. Wash, trim, and seed whole red peppers and dice them finely.
2. Heat the oil in a large nonstick skillet; add the peppers and sauté over medium heat.
3. Wash, trim, and finely dice the zucchini; add to the peppers and continue to sauté until the vegetables have softened.
4. Bring the chicken stock to a boil in a covered pot.
5. Grate the cheese.
6. Slowly stir the polenta into the boiling chicken stock and cook until the mixture thickens, just a couple of minutes.
7. When the polenta is cooked, stir it into the vegetables along with the cheese; season with salt and with pepper.

Yield: 2 servings

Mizuna with Sweet Vinaigrette

4 ounces (¼ pound) mizuna
   (about 4 cups packed)
1 teaspoon olive oil
1 teaspoon balsamic vinegar
1 teaspoon honey mustard

1. Trim, wash, and dry the mizuna and cut it into small pieces.
2. Whisk together the oil, vinegar, and mustard in a serving bowl and toss with the mizuna, mixing well.

Yield: 2 servings

G A M E   P L A N

Prepare polenta through Step 4.

Start salad.

Grate cheese.

Finish salad.

Cook polenta and finish dish.

APPROXIMATE NUTRITION INFORMATION PER SERVING:
555 calories, 20 grams fat, 35 milligrams cholesterol,
690 milligrams sodium, 25 grams protein, 60 grams
carbohydrate

Curried Potatoes, Tomatoes, and Peas

*B*y the time the potatoes are cooked, the rest of this one-dish meal will be ready. You will have time to wash the dishes while you wait. Many combinations work equally well in dishes of curried vegetables, and cauliflower, green beans, or carrots could comfortably replace the peas in this one. ❥ If possible, use the tiniest new potatoes, which cook in no time. Large thin-skinned potatoes, unpeeled and cut into cubes, can be substituted.

Curried Potatoes, Tomatoes, and Peas

16 ounces (1 pound) tiny new potatoes

11 ounces whole onion or 10 ounces chopped ready-cut onion (2 to 2¼ cups)

¼ to ½ jalapeño pepper

1 tablespoon canola oil

¼ teaspoon ground turmeric

1 teaspoon ground cumin

½ teaspoon ground ginger

1 teaspoon ground coriander

16 ounces (1 pound) ripe tomatoes

1 (10-ounce) package frozen peas

⅛ teaspoon salt (optional)

Freshly ground black pepper

1½ cups nonfat plain yogurt

1. Scrub but do not peel the potatoes and place them in a pot with water to cover. Cover and boil about 17 minutes, or until tender.
2. Chop the whole onion and mince the jalapeño. Heat the oil in a large nonstick skillet; add the onion and jalapeño along with the turmeric, cumin, ginger, and coriander, and sauté until the onion begins to brown.
3. Coarsely cube the tomatoes and add to the skillet along with the peas; cook just until the peas are heated through and the tomatoes have given up their juices.
4. When the potatoes are cooked, drain them and cut into halves or quarters; add them to the vegetables. Season with salt and pepper. Stir to coat, and serve with yogurt on the side.

Yield: 2 servings

Food Note ❥ Potatoes offer much more nutrition than noodles: vitamins, minerals, and fiber. If you cannot find tiny new potatoes, you can use larger ones and cut them up to cook them quickly. Unfortunately, cut potatoes lose their vitamin C while cooking in water.

Food Note ❧ Most curry powders are a blend of many spices, among them cumin, turmeric, coriander, and cayenne. So anything containing those ingredients, or some combination of them with others, is rightly called a curry. Indian cooks combine their spices according to the dish they are preparing, and don't use premixed curry powders.

G A M E   P L A N

Follow recipe directions.

APPROXIMATE NUTRITION INFORMATION PER SERVING, WITHOUT SALT: 555 calories, 10 grams fat, 5 milligrams cholesterol, 180 milligrams sodium, 25 grams protein, 95 grams carbohydrate

Yellow Potatoes and Green Peppers

Puréed Spinach and Spiced Yogurt

*F*or those who have always loved fried potatoes and green peppers, here is the updated and trimmed-down version. ❧ The dish is prettiest if made with yellow potatoes, such as Finns or Yukon Golds. But any thin-skinned potato will do. ❧ For an Indian touch, spinach is cooked and puréed with yogurt, cumin, and coriander and makes a delightful foil of saucelike consistency for the potatoes and green peppers.

Yellow Potatoes and Green Peppers

20 ounces (1¼ pounds)
   yellow or other
   thin-skinned potatoes
16 ounces (1 pound) whole
   green bell peppers or
   14 ounces chopped
   ready-cut peppers
   (4 cups)
1 tablespoon olive oil
½ jalapeño pepper
½ teaspoon turmeric
¼ teaspoon salt
Freshly ground black pepper
¼ cup water

1. Scrub but do not peel the potatoes; cut into 1-inch cubes. Cook in water to cover in a covered pot until tender, about 10 minutes.
2. Wash, trim, chop, and seed the whole peppers. Heat the oil over medium-high heat in a nonstick skillet large enough to hold all the ingredients. Sauté the chopped peppers in the oil.
3. Wash, seed, and chop the jalapeño and add to the green pepper along with the turmeric, cooking until the peppers are tender, about 4 minutes.
4. Drain and add the cooked potatoes to the peppers with the salt, pepper, and water. Stir well. Cover and cook 1 or 2 minutes to soften vegetables.

Yield: 2 servings

Puréed Spinach and Spiced Yogurt

1 (10-ounce) package
   trimmed fresh spinach or
   1 pound fresh loose
   spinach
¾ cup nonfat plain yogurt
¼ teaspoon ground cumin
¼ teaspoon ground coriander
Freshly ground black pepper

1. Wash and trim the tough leaves and stems from the spinach. In a covered pot, steam the spinach in the water clinging to its leaves until it wilts, about 3 or 4 minutes.
2. In a serving bowl combine the remaining ingredients and mix well.
3. When the spinach is cooked, drain thoroughly and purée or finely chop in a food processor or by hand. Combine thoroughly with the yogurt mixture and serve at room temperature.

Yield: 2 servings

G A M E   P L A N

Prepare potatoes and peppers through Step 3.
Prepare and cook spinach.
Add potatoes, seasoning, and water to peppers.
Finish spinach dish.

APPROXIMATE NUTRITION INFORMATION PER SERVING:
435 calories, 10 grams fat, almost no cholesterol,
625 milligrams sodium, 15 grams protein, 80 grams
carbohydrate

Persian Spinach, Potatoes, and Peas | Oranges, Olives, and Onion

*T*he spinach and yogurt combination that is a traditional Persian or Iranian side dish can, with the addition of potatoes, be turned into a meatless main dish. ❧ The dish includes plenty of cooked onion and a little nutmeg, which add sweetness and mellowness to food that would otherwise be tart. ❧ All it needs to balance its richness is the sharp, salty sweetness of an orange salad with a little raw onion, some imported black olives, and the tiniest bit of oil and vinegar.

Persian Spinach, Potatoes, and Peas

16 ounces (1 pound) tiny new potatoes
12 ounces (¾ pound) whole onion or 11 ounces chopped ready-cut onion (2¼ to 2½ cups)
2 teaspoons olive oil
2 cloves garlic
1 (10-ounce) package fresh spinach or 1 pound loose spinach
1 cup frozen peas
⅛ teaspoon nutmeg
1 cup nonfat plain yogurt
⅛ teaspoon salt
Freshly ground black pepper

1. Scrub but do not peel the potatoes, and place them in a pot with water to cover. Cover the pot and cook potatoes until fork-tender, about 20 minutes, depending on size.
2. Chop whole onion and sauté in a nonstick pan in very hot oil over medium-high heat until it begins to soften and brown.
3. Mince the garlic, and add to the onion as it cooks.
4. Wash the spinach; remove tough stems, and cook in another covered pot in the water clinging to it until it wilts, 3 or 4 minutes, stirring once or twice.
5. Stir the peas into the onion mixture and cook 2 or 3 minutes.
6. When the spinach is cooked, drain it, thoroughly pressing the water out. Cut up and add to the cooked onion, along with nutmeg and yogurt.
7. When the potatoes are cooked, drain and cut into bite-size pieces; stir into the spinach mixture. Season with salt and pepper and serve.

Yield: 2 servings

Oranges, Olives, and Onion

1 teaspoon olive oil

1 teaspoon white wine vinegar

2 large navel oranges

4 medium or large black Italian, French, or Greek olives

2 tablespoons finely chopped red onion

1. In a serving bowl, mix the oil and vinegar.
2. Peel the oranges with a sharp knife to remove pith along with skin; slice. Add to the bowl.
3. Pit the olives. Cut up and add to the bowl.
4. Chop onion and stir into bowl, mixing all the ingredients well.

Yield: 2 servings

G A M E   P L A N

Prepare spinach and potatoes through Step 4.

Make salad dressing; prepare oranges and olives.

Add peas and spinach to onion mixture.

Finish salad.

Finish spinach and potatoes.

APPROXIMATE NUTRITION INFORMATION PER SERVING: 625 calories, 10 grams fat, almost no cholesterol, 435 milligrams sodium, 25 grams protein, 120 grams carbohydrate

Curried Greens and Potatoes

*G*reens—turnip greens, mustard greens, kale, collards, beet greens—have not been among America's favorite vegetables because of their strong flavor, bitter edge, and bite. But little by little those of us not brought up on them are being encouraged to try them. The best first encounters with such vegetables are in dishes where their sharpness is mellowed by other ingredients. This one-dish meal is an effort to convince more people that greens make wonderful eating. ❧ Choose any combination of greens for this and serve with crusty bread.

Curried Greens and Potatoes

16 ounces (1 pound) tiny
   new potatoes
16 ounces (1 pound) mixed
   greens such as mustard,
   collard, kale, turnip, beet,
   or dandelion
1 large clove garlic
1 teaspoon olive oil
1 teaspoon ground cumin
1 teaspoon ground coriander
½ teaspoon turmeric
⅛ to ¼ teaspoon hot red
   pepper flakes
2 cups canned crushed
   no-salt-added tomatoes
2 slices crusty bread

1. Scrub but do not peel the potatoes. In a covered pot, boil the potatoes in water to cover 17 to 20 minutes, until they are just cooked.
2. Trim all tough stems from the greens; wash well and break into small pieces.
3. Mince the garlic. Heat the oil in a nonstick pan large enough to hold all the ingredients; add the greens and garlic.
4. When the greens begin to soften add the cumin, coriander, turmeric, red pepper flakes, and tomatoes; reduce the heat and continue cooking.
5. Drain the potatoes and cut them into bite-size pieces. Add them to the greens and continue cooking over low heat to blend the flavors well. Serve with crusty bread.

Yield: 2 servings

Follow recipe.

APPROXIMATE NUTRITION INFORMATION PER SERVING:
455 calories, 5 grams fat, 0 milligrams cholesterol,
265 milligrams sodium, 15 grams protein, 95 grams
carbohydrate

Hot Escarole with Potatoes and Garlic | Fennel and Parmigiano-Reggiano

*A*s greens have become more popular in this country, Americans have begun to use them for more than salads. The flavor of escarole is brought out by cooking, and like most greens, it is delicious with garlic and hot pepper. If you are a real garlic lover you may want to add a third clove. ❧ Another natural combination is fennel and Parmigiano-Reggiano. No real dressing is needed for such a salad: A squeeze of lemon juice is enough.

Hot Escarole with Potatoes and Garlic

24 ounces (1½ pounds) tiny new potatoes
2 cloves garlic
½ jalapeño pepper
1 tablespoon olive oil
1 large head escarole
2 tablespoons balsamic vinegar
⅛ teaspoon salt
Freshly ground black pepper

1. Scrub but do not peel the potatoes. Cover with water and bring to a boil; cook potatoes about 20 minutes, until tender.
2. Slice the garlic and mince the jalapeño. Heat the oil in a nonstick skillet and sauté the garlic and jalapeño for about 30 seconds.
3. Remove the tough stems and any spoiled leaves from the escarole. Wash and dry. Trim off the bottom; cut the leaves in half crosswise and add to the garlic. Cook over medium heat just a few minutes, stirring occasionally to wilt leaves completely.
4. When the potatoes are cooked, cut into bite-size pieces and stir into the escarole along with the vinegar. Season with salt and pepper.

Yield: 2 servings

Fennel and Parmigiano-Reggiano

6-ounce fennel bulb (about
   1½ cups diced)
2 ounces Parmigiano-
   Reggiano (½ cup plus
   2 tablespoons coarsely
   grated)
½ lemon

1. Wash and trim the leaves and stems from the fennel bulb. Slice off the bottom. Slice the bulb thinly and then cut into small dice.
2. Shave very thin slices of cheese and arrange over fennel on two salad plates.
3. Sprinkle with fresh lemon juice.

Yield: 2 servings

G A M E   P L A N

Prepare escarole and potatoes through Step 3.

Make salad.

Finish escarole dish.

APPROXIMATE NUTRITION INFORMATION PER SERVING:
595 calories, 15 grams fat, 25 milligrams cholesterol,
525 milligrams sodium, 20 grams protein, 100 grams
carbohydrate

Roasted Tomato and Sweet Onion Pizza

To make a pizza in 20 or 30 minutes, you will need to use something other than pizza dough. Here, flour tortillas make a good substitute, cooked separately from the topping to keep them crisp. Maybe these don't qualify it as genuine pizza, but by whatever name, the flavors of the topping are rich and satisfying, the sweet and the tart play off one another. About a dozen pitted, chopped olives can be substituted for the olive paste. (See Mail Order, page 27) ❧ The tortillas are cut into quarters before toasting because it is impossible to cut them after they become crisp. ❧ Olive paste or spread has been around for a few years, but I never used it until recently. Made with black or green olives, olive oil, vinegar, and other seasonings, it is a speedy and zesty alternative to Italian or French olives. Very little is required to produce a lot of distinctive olive flavor, and a small jar will last a long time in the refrigerator.

Roasted Tomato and Sweet Onion Pizza

1 to 2 sprigs fresh oregano, to yield 1 tablespoon chopped

32 ounces (2 pounds) ripe plum tomatoes

24 ounces (1½ pounds) whole onions or 22 ounces thinly sliced ready-cut onions (5 to 6 cups)

1 tablespoon olive oil

3 (9- or 10-inch) flour tortillas

1 sprig fresh rosemary, to

1. Turn the oven to 350 degrees.
2. Chop the oregano. Wash the tomatoes and trim the stem ends. Using the thick slicing blade of the food processor, place the tomatoes on their sides in the feed tube and slice. Cook with the oregano on the top of the stove in an enameled oven-roasting pan (but without oil) set over medium-high heat, stirring often to prevent sticking.
3. Cut whole onions into quarters and slice, using the thin slicing blade of a food processor. Heat the oil in a large nonstick skillet, add the onions, and sauté over medium-high heat 5 to 7 minutes, until softened.
4. Cut the tortillas into quarters, arrange directly on oven rack, and bake until they are brown and crisp, just a couple of minutes; watch carefully, as this happens quickly.

CONTINUED

yield 1 tablespoon chopped leaves

½ cup dry white wine

⅛ teaspoon hot pepper flakes

2 teaspoons olive paste or spread

1½ ounces Parmigiano-Reggiano (7 heaping tablespoons coarsely grated)

5. Chop the rosemary and add with the wine and pepper flakes to the onions. Reduce the heat to medium, cover, and simmer for 10 to 15 minutes, until the onions are very soft and the liquid has been absorbed. Thoroughly stir in the olive paste.

6. Spread the tomatoes over the tortilla wedges and top with the onion mixture. Place the wedges on a cookie sheet and heat through in the oven, just a couple of minutes.

7. Grate the cheese, and sprinkle about 1 teaspoon of cheese on each triangle.

Yield: 2 servings

G A M E   P L A N

Follow recipe.

APPROXIMATE NUTRITION INFORMATION PER SERVING:
600 calories, 20 grams fat, 15 milligrams cholesterol, 590 milligrams sodium, 20 grams protein, 75 grams carbohydrate

Goat Cheese and Red Pepper Pizza

I've tried everything I could think of as a base for quick pizza: bialys, Armenian bread, pitas, ready-to-bake pizza dough, and flour tortillas. The quickest are the flour tortillas. If you have more time, use ready-to-bake pizza rounds. ❧ Try this with whole-wheat tortillas—they taste wonderful and have fiber.

Goat Cheese and Red Pepper Pizza

4 (10-inch) whole-wheat or white flour tortillas

8 ounces (½ pound) whole onion or 7 ounces chopped ready-cut onion (1⅔ cups)

1 tablespoon olive oil

1 clove garlic

2 tablespoons olive paste

1 (15-ounce) can no-salt-added tomato purée (about 1⅓ cups)

¼ cup red wine

18 ounces (1½ pounds) red, yellow, and green peppers and carrots or 16 ounces (1 pound) sliced (ready-cut) red, yellow, and green peppers and carrots (4½ cups)

¼ cup reduced-fat goat cheese

6 tablespoons skim milk

1 pound Japanese or other small eggplant

1 cup canned no-salt-added black beans

1. Turn the oven on to broil. Arrange a double layer of aluminum foil on the broiler pan and place the tortillas on the foil 3 or 4 inches from the source of heat—do not preheat the broiler. Heat the tortillas until a few brown spots appear and the tortillas begin to crisp—2 to 3 minutes. (This will depend on the broiler.) Turn and brown on the second side. Watch carefully; as the broiler heats up, the tortillas brown faster. Do this in two batches if 4 tortillas do not fit flat on broiler pan.

2. Chop whole onion. Heat the oil in nonstick skillet, add the onion, and cook until it begins to brown.

3. Remove the tortillas and set aside.

4. Mince the garlic and put in a small pot with the olive paste, tomato purée, and wine; simmer about 10 minutes.

5. Slice whole peppers and carrots, add to the onion mixture, and sauté over medium heat.

6. Whisk the goat cheese with the milk to make a smooth blend.

7. Peel the eggplant, quarter, and cut into thick slices; add with ¼ cup tomato mixture to the vegetables. Cover, reduce the heat, and simmer until the eggplant is soft, just a few minutes.

8. Drain and rinse the beans and add to the vegetables, cooking just long enough to heat through.

9. Brush the tortillas generously with the tomato sauce. Add any remaining tomato sauce to the vegetables. Divide the vegetables among the tortillas. Top with the goat cheese mixture. Place under the broiler for about 20 seconds, but take care that they don't burn! (Again, broil in two batches if necessary.)

Yield: 2 servings

GAME PLAN

Follow recipe.

APPROXIMATE NUTRITION INFORMATION PER SERVING:
750 calories, 15 grams fat, 5 milligrams cholesterol,
665 milligrams sodium, 30 grams protein, 125 grams
carbohydrate

Lemon Grass Spicy Vegetables

*T*his Thai-inspired one-dish meal is adapted from one served at the Golden Door, the spa in Escondido, Calif. It calls for things like lemon grass, coconut milk, galangal, and chili paste with garlic—ingredients that might be difficult to find in some places. ❧ Lemon grass, which looks like a piece of dried bamboo with a knob on the end, has an exotic citrus fragrance and flavor for which there is no true substitution. You can use lime, but the dish will not taste the same. The same is true of coconut milk. Soy milk could be used, but the taste will be different. ❧ Ginger, on the other hand, is a very close relative of galangal and can be substituted with impunity. In shopping for chili paste with garlic, you can buy either the Thai version or the Chinese version. ❧ Once you have assembled the unusual ingredients, the making of the meal is a cinch. It will be ready in less than 30 minutes, especially if you take advantage of your market's salad bar or produce department for ingredients like already prepared carrots, celery, and broccoli.

Lemon Grass Spicy Vegetables

¾ cup long-grain rice
1 tablespoon Thai galangal, or coarsely grated fresh or frozen ginger
3 shallots
1 clove garlic
1 bunch scallions, to yield 1 cup chopped
2 stalks lemongrass
2 teaspoons chili paste with garlic
2 tablespoons fresh lime juice

1. Combine the rice and 1½ cups water in a heavy-bottomed pot; bring to a boil. Reduce heat to low, cover, and simmer for 17 minutes, until the water has been absorbed and the rice is cooked.
2. Coarsely grate the galangal or ginger; mince the shallots and garlic; chop the scallions.
3. Trim the tough outer leaves from the lemon grass; trim off roots. Thinly slice the lemongrass at the root end into rounds, and then cut each in half.
4. Combine the galangal or ginger, shallots, garlic, lemon grass, chili paste, lime juice, and sugar and set aside.
5. Chop the whole celery and coarsely grate the carrots.
6. Wash, trim, and slice shiitake caps thinly.
7. Remove stems from whole broccoli; cut florets into small pieces.

CONTINUED

4 teaspoons sugar

14 ounces whole celery and peeled carrots or a 12-ounce (¾-pound) mixture of finely chopped celery and shredded ready-cut carrots, about ⅔ carrots and ⅓ celery

4 ounces (¼ pound) shiitake mushrooms

4 ounces (¼ pound) whole broccoli or 2 ounces ready-cut broccoli florets

2 teaspoons toasted sesame oil

¼ cup no-salt-added vegetable stock or broth

¼ cup canned coconut milk

2 teaspoons reduced-sodium soy sauce

8. Heat the oil in a large nonstick skillet until it is very hot. Reduce heat to medium-high, add the lemongrass mixture, and stir for about 1 minute.
9. Add all of the remaining vegetables, and stir-fry another minute.
10. Add the stock, coconut milk, and soy sauce, and continue cooking over medium-low heat until the vegetables are crisp but tender.
11. Serve over rice.

Yield: 2 servings

G A M E   P L A N

Follow recipe.

APPROXIMATE NUTRITIONAL ANALYSIS PER SERVING:
520 calories, 15 grams fat, almost no cholesterol, 320 milligrams sodium, 10 grams protein, 90 grams carbohydrate

Warm Broccoli and Potatoes Vinaigrette

Corn and Red Pepper Salad

ere's a summertime meal to make when vegetables are at their best and don't require a lot of fussing. Add some crusty Italian country bread for a complete meal.

Warm Broccoli and Potatoes Vinaigrette

8 ounces (½ pound) tiny new potatoes

8 ounces (½ pound) whole broccoli or 4 ounces ready-cut broccoli florets (1½ to 2 cups)

1 clove garlic

1 scallion

2 tablespoons olive oil

2 tablespoons cider vinegar

¼ teaspoon dry mustard

¼ teaspoon paprika

Freshly ground black pepper

1. Scrub but do not peel the potatoes. Cook in a covered pot in water to cover until tender, about 20 minutes; drain and cut into quarters.
2. Trim the tough stems from whole broccoli; cut heads into bite-size florets. Steam the broccoli over simmering water until just tender, about 7 minutes.
3. Mince the garlic; wash, trim, and finely slice the scallion. Combine the garlic and scallion with the olive oil, vinegar, mustard, and paprika in a bowl large enough to hold all the vegetables.
4. When the potatoes and broccoli are cooked, drain and add them to the bowl, stirring carefully to coat.

Yield: 2 servings

Corn and Red Pepper Salad

2 ears corn
8 ounces (½ pound) whole
    red pepper or 7 ounces
    chopped ready-cut red
    pepper (2 cups)
¼ teaspoon jalapeño or
    serrano pepper (or more)
1 slice red onion about
    ½ inch thick
10 sprigs fresh cilantro, to
    yield 2 tablespoons
    chopped
1½ teaspoons fresh lime
    juice

1. Shuck the corn and steam in the same pot with the broccoli from the last recipe, about 3 minutes.
2. Chop whole red pepper medium-fine. Mince the chile. Finely chop the onion. Wash, dry, and chop the cilantro. Stir everything together in a serving bowl with the lime juice.
3. When the corn is cooked, scrape the kernels directly into the serving bowl and stir to combine.

Yield: 2 servings

GAME PLAN

Cook potatoes.
Cook broccoli.
Husk corn.
Prepare remaining ingredients for corn salad.
Cook corn.
Prepare dressing for broccoli and potatoes.
Add corn to salad.
Finish broccoli and potatoes dish.

APPROXIMATE NUTRITION INFORMATION PER SERVING,
INCLUDING A SLICE OF BREAD: 455 calories, 15 grams fat,
almost no cholesterol, 260 milligrams sodium,
10 grams protein, 70 grams carbohydrate

Corn Risotto | Green Salad

*T*he current fad of giving dishes names they should never have has infected me. This corn risotto has no rice in it, even though in Italian *risotto* means a rice dish. Risotto is also a slow method of cooking rice that produces a creamy texture. In this dish the corn becomes creamy by putting it in a food processor for a few twirls. ✦ For a fat-free salad dressing, the balsamic vinegar is mixed with a little stock. You can use more of the stock used for the corn risotto.

Corn Risotto

4 large shallots, peeled

3 ounces whole peeled carrots or 3 ounces shredded carrots (¾ cup)

2 teaspoons butter

6 ears fresh corn

1 cup skim milk

4 or 5 sprigs fresh thyme, to yield 1 tablespoon chopped leaves

6 large shiitake or other mushrooms

2 ounces sharp white Cheddar cheese

½ cup vegetable or chicken broth or stock

1. With the food processor on, put the shallots through the feed tube to mince.
2. Add the whole carrots and chop.
3. Heat the butter in a nonstick skillet. Add the shallots and carrots and sauté over medium heat about 5 minutes.
4. Shuck the corn and strip the kernels from the cobs. Add to the skillet along with the milk, and cook over high heat.
5. Wash, dry, and chop the thyme; add to the skillet and continue cooking until most of milk has evaporated.
6. Meanwhile, remove the stems from the shiitake mushrooms and discard. Wash, dry, and slice the mushrooms into thin strips.
7. Grate the cheese in the food processor; set aside.
8. Spoon the corn mixture into the food processor and pulse two or three times to break up the corn. Return the mixture to the skillet with the mushrooms and vegetable or chicken stock. Cook a few minutes, just to cook the mushrooms through. Stir in cheese and serve.

Yield: 2 servings

Green Salad

4 ounces (¼ pound) salad
greens (any combination)
(4 cups packed)
1 tablespoon balsamic
vinegar
1 tablespoon chicken or
vegetable stock

1. Wash, dry, and break salad greens into bite-size pieces.
2. Mix vinegar and stock in a serving bowl, add greens, and toss to coat.

Yield: 2 servings

GAME   PLAN

Prepare risotto through Step 5.
Start salad.
Finish risotto.
Finish salad.

APPROXIMATE NUTRITION INFORMATION PER SERVING:
540 calories, 15 grams fat, 45 milligrams cholesterol,
370 milligrams sodium, 25 grams protein, 85 grams
carbohydrate

Lentil Baba Ghanouj

Red and Green Salad

*I*f this version of baba ghanouj seems a bit strange, that's because it is: Here, lentils replace the traditional chick-peas and cut the cooking time to a fraction of what it would be otherwise. ❧ The richness of the eggplant-lentil-tahini mixture contrasts dramatically with the crispness and sharpness of the arugula and radicchio salad.

Lentil Baba Ghanouj

1 large eggplant
    (1½ pounds)
Oil pan spray
¾ cup red lentils
1¾ cups water
1 large clove garlic
2 ounces onion, to yield
    ½ cup minced onion
2 or 3 sprigs oregano, to
    yield 1½ tablespoons
    chopped
2½ tablespoons tahini
2 tablespoons fresh lemon
    juice
¼ teaspoon salt
Freshly ground black pepper

1. Turn on broiler.
2. Slice the eggplant in 1-inch-thick slices and coat lightly with oil spray on both sides. Cover the broiler pan with aluminum foil and arrange the eggplant slices on the foil. Broil the eggplant close to the heat source about 5 minutes on one side; turn and broil on the second side until tender, about 5 to 7 minutes longer.
3. Meanwhile, bring the lentils and water to a boil in a covered pot; reduce the heat and simmer for about 10 minutes, until the lentils are tender but not mushy.
4. Mince the garlic. Mince the onion. Chop the oregano. In a serving bowl combine the garlic, onion, oregano, tahini, lemon juice, salt, and pepper.
5. When the lentils are cooked, drain and add them to the mixture in the bowl.
6. When the eggplant is cooked, remove skin and add the flesh to the bowl. Mash with a fork and mix thoroughly with the remaining ingredients.

Yield: 2 servings

Red and Green Salad

2 ounces arugula
  (about 2 cups)
4 ounces (¼ pound)
  radicchio (small head)
  (about 3 cups)
1 teaspoon olive oil
1 tablespoon Dijon mustard
¼ teaspoon Worcestershire
½ teaspoon white wine
  vinegar
1 teaspoon water

1. Trim, wash, and dry the arugula and radicchio; break the radicchio into small pieces.
2. Combine the remaining ingredients in a salad bowl. Stir in the arugula and radicchio and toss to coat well.

Yield: 2 servings

G A M E   P L A N

Follow lentil recipe through Step 4.

Begin salad.

Drain lentils and add to bowl.

Finish salad.

Finish baba ghanouj.

APPROXIMATE NUTRITION INFORMATION PER SERVING:
510 calories, 15 grams fat, 0 millligrams cholesterol, 505 milligrams sodium, 30 grams protein, 75 grams carbohydrate

Lentils, Potatoes, and Peas in Indian-Style Tomato Sauce | Green Beans

For those who wonder what New Age cooking is all about, a dinner in which two starches—lentils and potatoes—star is a good place to begin. ❧ Such dishes are common in India, but Americans have been slow to take to them, in part because the myth still exists that carbohydrates are fattening. ❧ Like anything else, carbohydrates will turn to fat if eaten in excess, but they can't go directly to your hips and thighs the way fat does. In addition, vegetables and grains and pulses (lentils) are thought to contain some ingredients that may reduce the risk of cancer. ❧ All this health information aside, the reason you will want to eat this dish is that it tastes so good. When green beans are crisp and slender, they make a perfect side dish.

Lentils, Potatoes, and Peas in Indian-Style Tomato Sauce

12 ounces (¾ pound) new potatoes
½ cup red lentils
8 ounces whole onion or 7 ounces
    chopped ready-cut onion (1⅔ cups)
2 teaspoons olive oil
1 clove garlic
1 teaspoon ground cumin
½ teaspoon ground coriander
⅛ to ¼ teaspoon hot pepper flakes
1 (15- or 16-ounce) can no-salt-added
    tomato purée
1 teaspoon sun-dried tomato paste
½ cup dry red wine
1 cup frozen peas
1 tablespoon balsamic vinegar
3 tablespoons raisins
Freshly ground black pepper

1. Scrub but do not peel the potatoes; cut them into 1-inch pieces. Place in a pot with the lentils and 3 cups of water. Cover and bring to a boil; watch carefully because lentils have a tendency to boil over. Cook over medium-high heat for about 10 minutes, until lentils and potatoes are tender.
2. Chop whole onion and sauté in hot oil in a nonstick skillet.
3. Mince the garlic and add to the onion; stir in the cumin, coriander, and hot pepper flakes; cook until the onion is soft.
4. Stir in the tomato purée, tomato paste, and wine and simmer over low heat.
5. When the lentils and potatoes are cooked, drain well and stir into the tomato mixture along with peas, vinegar, and raisins. Continue cooking just long enough to meld flavors. Season with black pepper.

Yield: 2 servings

Green Beans

8 ounces (½ pound) fresh green beans

1. Wash and trim green beans.
2. Steam over boiling water 5 to 7 minutes, until beans are tender but crisp. Drain and serve.

Yield: 2 servings

GAME PLAN

Prepare lentil dish through Step 3.

Bring water to boil for green beans.

Wash and trim green beans.

Add tomato purée, tomato paste, and wine to lentils and simmer.

Cook green beans.

Finish lentils.

APPROXIMATE NUTRITION INFORMATION PER SERVING:
600 calories, 5 grams fat, 0 milligrams cholesterol,
160 milligrams sodium, 25 grams protein, 130 grams
carbohydrate

Red Lentils and Chili Sauce with Quinoa

Warm Asparagus Vinaigrette

*E*ven though this menu requires four pots—one more than my self-imposed limit—it is so speedy to make that you will have time to do some cleaning up while the lentils and sauce finish cooking. ❧ Instead of rice, quinoa (pronounced *keen*-wa) is used as the base for the lentils and chili-flavored sauce. Quinoa is an ancient grain that once proliferated in pre-Columbian South America. Now on the comeback trail, it cooks as quickly as rice but has a slightly crunchy, nutlike taste and texture. You will find it in natural-food stores and some supermarkets.

Red Lentils and Chile Sauce with Quinoa

¾ cup quinoa

8 ounces (½ pound) whole onion or 7 ounces chopped ready-cut onion (1⅔ cups)

2 teaspoons olive oil

1 cup red lentils

1 large clove garlic

8 ounces (½ pound) peeled baby carrots or 8 ounces chopped ready-cut carrots (1⅓ cups)

1 teaspoon ground cumin

½ teaspoon ground coriander

½ teaspoon, or more, hot plain chile powder

3 ounces no-salt-added

1. Combine the quinoa with 1½ cups water and bring to a boil, uncovered. Cover, reduce the heat to a simmer, and cook for a total of about 15 minutes.
2. Meanwhile, chop whole onion. Heat the oil in a nonstick skillet, add the onion, and sauté on medium-high heat while preparing the rest of the dish.
3. Cover the lentils with water and bring to a boil; simmer about 10 minutes, partly covered, until they are tender but not mushy.
4. With the food processor on, put the garlic through the feed tube to chop. Add to the onion and continue cooking until the onion is soft and beginning to brown.
5. Chop whole carrots in the food processor.
6. Reduce the heat under the onion; stir in the cumin, coriander, and chili powder and cook over low heat for about 20 seconds.
7. Add the tomato paste and stock to the onion mixture and stir to blend. Stir in the carrots; cook until the carrots are soft, about 10 minutes.

CONTINUED

tomato paste (½ a
6-ounce can)
1½ cups no-salt-added
vegetable or chicken stock
or broth
About 15 sprigs fresh
cilantro, to yield
3 tablespoons chopped
¼ teaspoon salt (optional)

8. Wash, dry, and chop the cilantro.
9. When the lentils are cooked, drain them well and stir into the sauce mixture. Season with salt, if desired.
10. Drain the quinoa, arrange the lentil mixture over it, and sprinkle with cilantro.

Yield: 3 servings

Warm Asparagus Vinaigrette

24 asparagus spears
2 teaspoons olive oil
1½ tablespoons balsamic
vinegar

1. Wash and trim the asparagus by breaking the stems at the point where they yield easily. Steam over hot water about 3 to 7 minutes, depending on the thickness of the stems.
2. Stir the oil and vinegar together in a serving dish.
3. Drain the asparagus and turn in the serving dish to cover with dressing.

Yield: 3 servings

G A M E   P L A N

Prepare lentils through Step 7.
Prepare asparagus and cook.
Make dressing for asparagus.
Finish lentil dish.
Drain asparagus and dress.

APPROXIMATE NUTRITION ANALYSIS PER SERVING, WITHOUT
SALT: 560 calories, 10 grams fat, 0 milligrams cholesterol,
105 milligrams sodium, 30 grams protein, 95 grams
carbohydrate

Red Lentil and
Goat Cheese Salad

*R*ed lentils cook fast. So fast, in fact, that a few seconds too long and nice red lentils turn to mush. ❧ This salad is vegetarian, but an easy variation can be made with bits of ham (in the same amount) in place of the goat cheese. ❧ Pick some nice crunchy salad greens for coolness and contrasting texture. And be sure you have bread that has enough character to stand on its own.

Red Lentil and Goat Cheese Salad

¾ cup red lentils

2 cups water

1 large clove garlic

1 bay leaf

¼ teaspoon ground cloves

1 teaspoon dried thyme or 4 sprigs
　fresh thyme leaves, to yield
　　1 tablespoon chopped leaves

3 ounces whole peeled carrots or
　3 ounces chopped ready-cut carrots
　(about ¾ cup)

6 ounces whole red onion or 5 ounces
　chopped ready-cut onion (1⅓ cups)

3 ounces whole red, yellow, or orange
　pepper or 2 ounces chopped
　ready-cut peppers (¾ cup)

2 tablespoons balsamic vinegar

Freshly ground black pepper

5 cherry tomatoes

1 ounce fresh goat cheese, crumbled
　(about 2 tablespoons)

Approximately 6 leaves curly endive,
　red leaf lettuce, or other firm lettuce

1. Bring the lentils, water, garlic, bay leaf, and cloves to a boil in a covered pot; chop the fresh thyme, if using, and add; reduce the heat and simmer.
2. Finely chop whole carrots in a food processor; set aside.
3. Finely chop whole onion in a food processor; squeeze any excess liquid from the onion. Set aside 2 tablespoons chopped onion.
4. Add the chopped onion and carrots to the lentils. Continue to simmer until the lentils are done, about 10 minutes total cooking time. The lentils should be firm but tender.
5. Wash and seed whole pepper and finely chop it in the food processor; squeeze out any excess liquid.
6. Drain the lentils and remove and discard bay leaf.
7. Spoon the lentil mixture into a serving bowl with the peppers, the reserved 2 tablespoons onion, the vinegar, and black pepper to taste.
8. Wash and dry the tomatoes and cut them into small dice; add the tomatoes to the lentils along with the goat cheese and stir gently.
9. Wash and dry the lettuce and arrange it on a serving plate. Mound the lentils on the lettuce.

Yield: 2 servings

Follow recipe directions.

APPROXIMATE NUTRITION INFORMATION PER SERVING, WITHOUT BREAD: 355 calories, 5 grams fat, 0 milligrams cholesterol, 170 milligrams sodium, 25 grams protein, 55 grams carbohydrate

Red Lentil Soup

Radicchio Salad

*T*he quintessential cold-weather supper is soup, salad, and bread. But a hearty soup brings to mind a day-long project, which does not fit in with the present penchant for quick and easy solutions. Red lentil soup, however, can be prepared in less than half an hour, because red lentils cook in about 10 minutes. And it doesn't take a day to coax the full flavor out of the vegetables that play such an important role in this soup. To tell the truth, this soup is so thick it is more like a lentil stew. ❧ After the taste, the greatest satisfaction in the preparation of this meal is to see the results so quickly. And for those without huge appetites, there should be enough left over for lunch the next day.

Red Lentil Soup

1 cup red lentils
1 bay leaf
1 clove garlic
8 ounces (½ pound) whole onion or 7 ounces chopped ready-cut onion (1⅔ cups)
2 teaspoons olive oil
4 ounces (¼ pound) peeled carrots or 4 ounces chopped ready-cut carrots (1⅓ cups)
2 ribs celery or 4 ounces ready-cut celery (¾ cup)
1 teaspoon dried rosemary
¼ teaspoon hot pepper flakes
1 cup no-salt-added canned chopped tomatoes

1. Combine the lentils and bay leaf with 5 cups water in a large saucepan and bring to a boil, partly covered. Cook lentils at a simmer until soft, 10 to 12 minutes; watch carefully so that they do not boil over.
2. With the food processor running, put the garlic through the feed tube to mince.
3. Chop whole onion by pulsing in the food processor.
4. In a large, deep, nonstick skillet, heat the oil until it is very hot. Add the onion and garlic and reduce heat to medium-high. Sauté until the onion begins to brown and soften.
5. Slice whole carrots in the food processor; slice celery ribs in the food processor. Add carrots and celery to onions and continue cooking until the vegetables begin to soften.
6. Add the rosemary, hot pepper flakes, tomatoes, and vinegar, and continue cooking at a simmer.
7. Grate the cheese and sprinkle it on the bread slices. Toast or broil in a toaster oven until the cheese melts.
8. When the lentils are cooked, drain, reserving the cooking liquid. Discard bay leaf. Purée half of the lentils in the food processor. (You may need to add a little of the cooking liquid to purée.) Add

CONTINUED

1 tablespoon distilled white
    vinegar
1 ounce Parmigiano-Reggiano
    (about 6 tablespoons
    coarsely grated)
2 slices crusty Italian or
    French bread
¼ teaspoon salt
Freshly ground black pepper

the puréed lentils and the whole lentils to the tomato mixture, along with enough of the cooking liquid to make a thick soup. Heat through, and season with salt and pepper.

9. Grate cheese; sprinkle on bread and broil bread a minute or two. Serve soup with the cheese bread.

Yield: 2 servings

Radicchio Salad

1 small head (4 ounces)
    radicchio (about 3 cups)
1 teaspoon olive oil
1 teaspoon balsamic vinegar
½ teaspoon Dijon mustard

1. Trim, wash, and separate the leaves of the radicchio.
2. Whisk together the oil, vinegar, and mustard in a serving bowl; add radicchio and stir to coat well.

Yield: 2 servings

G A M E   P L A N

Prepare soup through Step 6.

Start salad.

Grate cheese and broil cheese-topped bread.

Finish salad.

APPROXIMATE NUTRITION INFORMATION PER SERVING:
645 calories, 15 grams fat, 10 milligrams cholesterol, 690 milligrams sodium, 35 grams protein, 95 grams carbohydrate

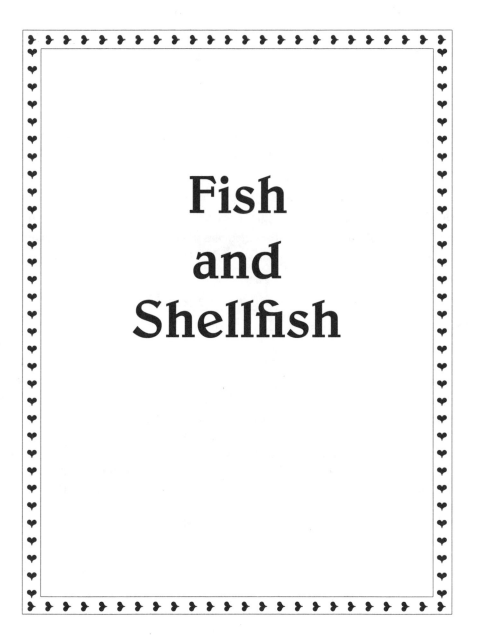

Fish
and
Shellfish

Grilled Salmon on Spinach Bed

Orzo with Vegetables Vinaigrette

*T*he idea of putting salmon on a bed of spinach comes from one of James Beard's many cookbooks. If you take care not to overcook the spinach, it makes a pretty picture. ❧ For the side dish any green vegetable would be equally attractive in combination with the carrots, but when asparagus is in season, it is the vegetable of choice. ❧ The orange juice adds a citrusy, slightly sweet taste to the vinaigrette and complements not only the vegetables in the orzo salad but the spinach and the salmon. This is a meal I would not be ashamed to serve if company were coming for dinner.

Grilled Salmon on Spinach Bed

10 ounces packaged fresh spinach or 1 pound loose fresh spinach

1 small clove garlic

1 to 2 sprigs fresh tarragon, to yield 2 teaspoons chopped

1 pound, 2 ounces skinless salmon fillet

1. Preheat the broiler, if using. Cover the broiler pan with aluminum foil.
2. Wash the spinach and remove the tough stems.
3. Mince the garlic and chop the tarragon.
4. Place the spinach, garlic, and tarragon in a pot and cover, using only the water clinging to the spinach leaves. Cook over medium heat until the spinach is wilted, just a couple of minutes. Drain and arrange in a serving dish large enough to hold the salmon and keep warm.
5. Prepare stove-top grill, if using.
6. Grill the salmon on both sides, following the Canadian rule: Measure the fish at its thickest part and cook 8 to 10 minutes per inch. Place on spinach.

Yield: 3 servings

Food Note ❧ The Canadian rule—measure the fish at its thickest part and cook 8 to 10 minutes per inch—is so-called because it comes from the Canadian government's department of fisheries.

Orzo with Vegetables Vinaigrette

1 cup orzo

8 ounces (½ pound) whole peeled carrots or 7 ounces thinly sliced ready-cut carrots (1⅓ cups)

8 stalks asparagus

3 tablespoons frozen orange juice concentrate

4 teaspoons Dijon mustard

2 tablespoons balsamic vinegar

1½ tablespoons olive oil

2 scallions

⅛ teaspoon salt

Freshly ground black pepper

1. Bring 2 quarts of water to boil in a covered pot.
2. Add orzo and cook for 5 minutes.
3. Meanwhile thinly slice whole carrots.
4. Wash and trim the asparagus, breaking off the woody stems. Cut the asparagus just below the tips, then cut the remaining stalks into ½-inch pieces.
5. Add the carrots and asparagus to the orzo and cook 3 to 5 minutes longer, only until everything is just tender.
6. Beat together the orange juice concentrate, mustard, vinegar, and oil in a serving dish.
7. Wash and trim the scallions; thinly slice.
8. When the orzo and vegetables are cooked, drain, rinse under cold water, and drain again; stir into the dressing with the scallions and season with salt and pepper.

Yield: 3 servings

GAME PLAN

Preheat broiler, if using.

Cook orzo.

Prepare spinach, garlic, and tarragon for salmon and cook.

Prepare carrots and asparagus and add to orzo.

Prepare stove-top grill, if using.

Broil or grill salmon.

Make dressing for orzo.

Cut scallions and mix with orzo, vegetables, and dressing.

APPROXIMATE NUTRITION INFORMATION PER SERVING:
550 calories, 15 grams fat, 30 milligrams cholesterol, 515 milligrams sodium, 40 grams protein, 65 grams carbohydrate

Fresh and Smoked Salmon with Lentils

Brussels Sprouts Vinaigrette

*T*his combination of plain and fancy—lentils and salmon—is increasingly common because the results are so pleasing. Combining smoked salmon with fresh salmon provides a burst of flavor and interesting textures that neither offers alone. ❧ Red lentils, available in Indian markets and specialty food stores—and sometimes supermarkets—are the quick-cooking variety. This dish can be made with green lentils, but it will take longer.

Fresh and Smoked Salmon with Lentils

3 ounces whole peeled carrots or
   3 ounces chopped ready-cut carrots
   (¾ cup)
6 ounces whole onion or 5 ounces
   chopped ready-cut onion (1⅓ cups)
1 cup red lentils
1 bay leaf
4 ounces (¼ pound) fresh salmon
   fillets
½ cup dry white wine or dry vermouth
1 sprig fresh oregano, to yield
   2 teaspoons chopped
5 shallots
4 ounces (¼ pound) smoked salmon,
   preferably unsliced
8 ounces (½ pound) ripe plum
   tomatoes
Freshly ground black pepper
⅛ teaspoon salt (optional)

1. Chop the whole carrots and onions and combine with the lentils, bay leaf, and 4 cups water in a heavy-bottomed pot; cover and bring to a boil. Reduce heat to medium-high and cook the lentils until they are soft but still hold their shape, about 10 minutes.
2. Place the fresh salmon in a skillet along with the wine; cover and bring to a simmer; cook according to the Canadian rule: Measure the fish at its thickest part and cook 8 to 10 minutes per inch.
3. Wash, dry, and chop the oregano; finely chop the shallots, and cut the smoked salmon into small pieces; wash, dry, trim, and finely dice the tomatoes.
4. When the lentils are cooked, drain them and stir in the tomatoes, oregano, shallots, and smoked salmon. Season with black pepper, and salt if you wish.
5. When the fresh salmon is cooked, drain it and cut into 1-inch chunks; carefully mix in with the lentil mixture and serve.

Yield: 2 servings

Brussels Sprouts Vinaigrette

10 ounces brussels sprouts
1 teaspoon olive oil
1 teaspoon balsamic vinegar

1. Wash and trim the sprouts and steam for 7 to 10 minutes; drain.
2. Whisk the oil and vinegar together in a serving bowl and stir in the drained sprouts.

Yield: 2 servings

G A M E   P L A N

Cook lentils.

Cook fresh salmon.

Prepare and cook brussels sprouts.

Chop oregano and shallots, dice smoked salmon, dice tomatoes.

Make dressing for brussels sprouts.

Finish lentil and salmon dish.

Drain brussels sprouts and mix with dressing.

APPROXIMATE NUTRITION INFORMATION PER SERVING,
WITHOUT ADDED SALT: **645 calories, 10 grams fat,
25 milligrams cholesterol, 240 milligrams sodium,
50 grams protein, 90 grams carbohydrate**

Salmon with Grainy Mustard and Lime Topping

Broccoli, Sautéed Onion, and Potato Purée

*T*his entire menu has only 2 teaspoons of added fat. The salmon contributes enough natural fat—the good kind. Not to suggest this is a menu for Puritans: this one tastes good. ❧ The sharpness of the mustard and the tartness of the lime, both juice and rind, provide a superb contrast to the richness of the salmon. ❧ The potato and broccoli purée gets its depth of flavor and texture from the sautéed onions. Nonfat yogurt makes the mixture creamy and the onions add sweetness, making the dish as good as it would be if it were laced with butter.

Salmon with Grainy Mustard and Lime Topping

10 ounces fresh salmon
   fillets
1 small lime
2 tablespoons grainy mustard

1. Turn on the broiler; cover the broiler pan with aluminum foil.
2. Remove the skin from the salmon, if necessary.
3. Grate the rind of lime to yield ¼ teaspoon; squeeze the lime to make 2 teaspoons juice. Mix the rind and juice with the mustard and spread on top of the salmon.
4. Broil the fish 2 inches from heat, following the Canadian rule: Measure the fish at its thickest point and broil 8 to 10 minutes per inch.

Yield: 2 servings

Broccoli, Sautéed Onion, and Potato Purée

12 ounces (¾ pound) tiny new potatoes

12 ounces (¾ pound) whole onion or 11 ounces sliced ready-cut onion (2½ to 2⅔ cups)

2 teaspoons olive oil

16 ounces (1 pound) whole broccoli or 8 ounces ready-cut broccoli florets (3½ to 4 cups)

¼ cup nonfat plain yogurt

¼ teaspoon salt

Freshly ground black pepper

1. Scrub the potatoes (do not peel) and cook in water to cover in a covered pot for 10 to 20 minutes, depending on the size of potatoes, until they are just tender.
2. Slice the onion and break into rings.
3. Heat the oil in a nonstick skillet, add the onion, and sauté to brown lightly.
4. Remove the tough stems from whole broccoli. Cut broccoli into bite-size florets. Five minutes before the potatoes are cooked, add the broccoli to the cooking water.
5. When the broccoli and potatoes are cooked, drain and put half of each into a food processor along with half the onions and half the yogurt. Process to purée and spoon into a serving bowl. Repeat with the remaining ingredients. Add to the bowl and season with salt and pepper.

Yield: 2 servings

G A M E   P L A N

Turn on broiler.

Cook potatoes.

Prepare and cook onion.

Prepare salmon and salmon topping.

Cook broccoli.

Broil salmon.

Drain potatoes and broccoli and purée with onion and yogurt; season.

APPROXIMATE NUTRITION INFORMATION PER SERVING:
575 calories, 20 grams fat, 90 milligrams cholesterol, 605 milligrams sodium, 40 grams protein, 60 grams carbohydrate

Grilled Salmon with Gazpacho Salsa

Jalapeño-Cilantro Rice

*G*azpacho may be a summer soup, but in a less liquid form it also can be used as a year-round salsa. Here, it brings a superb contrast in texture and flavor to the richness of the salmon. ❧ This meal is so quick to make that you will have time to do some of the cleaning up while you wait for the rice to finish cooking.

Grilled Salmon with Gazpacho Salsa

4 ounces (¼ pound) Kirby cucumber

6 ounces whole red peppers or 5 ounces chopped ready-cut peppers (1¼ cups)

2 ounces red onion (⅓ cup quartered)

6 ounces ripe cherry tomatoes

1 large clove garlic

1½ teaspoons Worcestershire sauce

2 tablespoons red wine vinegar

⅛ teaspoon salt (optional)

10 ounces skinless salmon fillet

1. Turn on the broiler, if using. Cover the broiler pan with aluminum foil.
2. Scrub, trim, and cut the cucumber in quarters.
3. Wash, trim, and cut the whole peppers into chunks.
4. Quarter the onion.
5. Stem and wash the tomatoes; cut the garlic in half.
6. Combine the cucumber, peppers, onion, tomatoes, and garlic in the food processor and pulse until the vegetables are finely chopped.
7. Stir in the Worcestershire sauce, vinegar, and optional salt.
8. Prepare a stove-top grill, if using. Grill or broil the salmon according to the Canadian rule: Measure the fish at its thickest part and cook 8 to 10 minutes to the inch.
9. When the fish is cooked, arrange on dinner plates and spoon salsa over the top of each piece.

Yield: 2 servings

Jalapeño-Cilantro Rice

8 ounces (½ pound) whole onion or 7 ounces chopped ready-cut onion (1⅔ cups)

1 teaspoon olive oil

1 large clove garlic

1½ cups no-salt-added chicken stock or broth

¾ cup long-grain rice

½ to 1 jalapeño pepper

1 small bunch cilantro, to yield ¼ cup chopped

1. Chop the whole onion and sauté in hot oil in a heavy-bottomed pot large enough to hold the rice.
2. Mince the garlic and add to the onion; continue to sauté until the onion begins to soften.
3. Stir in the chicken stock or broth and the rice. Reduce heat, cover, and cook rice until all the liquid has evaporated and the rice is tender, 17 minutes total.
4. Wash, trim, seed, and mince the jalapeño. Wash, dry, and chop the cilantro. Remove the rice from the heat and stir in the jalapeño and cilantro.

Yield: 2 servings

G A M E   P L A N

Turn on broiler, if using.

Prepare onion for rice; sauté.

Prepare garlic for rice and add.

Start to prepare vegetables for salmon.

Add stock and rice to onion and garlic for rice and cook.

Finish chopping vegetables for salmon; add Worcestershire, vinegar, and salt.

Prepare stove-top grill, if using. Grill or broil salmon.

Prepare jalapeño and cilantro for rice.

Finish salmon and salsa.

Finish rice.

APPROXIMATE NUTRITION INFORMATION PER SERVING:
530 calories, 10 grams fat, 25 milligrams cholesterol, 480 milligrams sodium, 30 grams protein, 80 grams carbohydrate

Potato Salad with Smoked Salmon

Eggplant Tahini

*B*ored with chicken salad, not eager to have meat, I remembered all the dishes in which smoked salmon is used in place of fresh. It seemed just the right touch for the potato salad that I had been wanting to make. It doesn't take much smoked salmon to permeate a potato salad, so you have all the flavor with little of the fat or salt. ❧ Add eggplant tahini salad to the menu and serve with some crusty country bread.

Food Note ❧ Tahini is ground-up sesame seeds. It adds richness to a dish and is popular in the Middle East, Greece, and Turkey.

Potato Salad with Smoked Salmon

16 ounces (1 pound) tiny new potatoes

1 tablespoon rice wine vinegar or other mild vinegar

1 tablespoon dry white wine

2 teaspoons Dijon mustard

3 tablespoons nonfat plain yogurt

2 ounces lightly smoked salmon

3 tablespoons chopped red onion

1 sprig fresh dill, to yield 1 tablespoon finely chopped

2 ounces arugula (about 2 cups)

2 slices crusty bread

1. Scrub but do not peel the potatoes. Cook in water to cover in a covered pot until they are tender, 10 to 20 minutes.
2. In a serving bowl whisk together the vinegar, white wine, and Dijon mustard; stir in the yogurt.
3. Cut the salmon into bite-size chunks.
4. Finely chop the onion.
5. Wash, dry, and finely chop dill. Stir the dill and onion into the dressing.
6. Trim the roots and tough stems from the arugula and wash thoroughly; dry.
7. When potatoes are cooked, drain them well and cut them into quarters or halves. Gently combine the salmon and potatoes with the dressing.
8. Arrange half the arugula leaves on each of two dinner plates and spoon the potato-salmon mixture on the leaves, leaving room for the bread and the eggplant.

Yield: 2 servings

Eggplant Tahini

1 pound (16 ounces)
   Japanese eggplant or
   other small, long eggplant
1 tablespoon olive oil
1 clove garlic
1 tablespoon water
1 tablespoon tahini
2 teaspoons fresh lemon
   juice

1. Turn on the broiler, if using. Line the broiler pan with aluminum foil.
2. Wash, trim, and cut the eggplant in half lengthwise. Lightly coat the cut sides of the eggplant with oil. Prepare stove-top grill, if using. Grill or broil the eggplant. The eggplant should be very brown and soft, which will take 10 to 15 minutes.
3. Mince the garlic.
4. In a serving bowl beat together the water, tahini, and lemon juice until thoroughly mixed; stir in the garlic.
5. When the eggplant is cooked, remove the flesh from the skin with a spoon and stir into the tahini mixture until thoroughly blended.
6. Spoon the eggplant onto arugula leaves next to the potato salad, and serve with crusty country bread.

Yield: 2 servings

G A M E   P L A N

Cook potatoes.

Grill eggplant.

Make dressing for potato salad.

Prepare salmon, onion, and dill.

Prepare tahini dressing.

Add potatoes to salad.

Prepare arugula.

Add eggplant to tahini.

APPROXIMATE NUTRITION INFORMATION PER SERVING, INCLUDING ONE SLICE OF BREAD: 525 calories, 15 grams fat, 5 milligrams cholesterol, 570 milligrams sodium, 15 grams protein, 85 grams carbohydrate

Grilled Herbed Swordfish

Sunshine Salsa

*S*erve this very simple fish with crusty Italian or French bread. If you can find a flavored bread like rosemary or olive, even better. ❧ As good as the swordfish is without the salsa, the combination of pungent, tart, sweet, and salty flavors in the sauce gives it an added edge. This preparation is good with any strong-flavored fish, so try it, too, with tuna or bluefish or mackerel. The salsa is like a hearty salad, so the meal is complete.

Grilled Herbed Swordfish

1 to 2 sprigs oregano, to
  yield 1 tablespoon
  chopped
5 sprigs cilantro, to yield
  1 tablespoon chopped
1 clove garlic
1½ tablespoons fresh orange
  juice
1½ teaspoons fresh lime
  juice
⅛ teaspoon hot pure chili
  powder
2 (5-ounce) swordfish steaks

1. If using a broiler, preheat. Line the broiler pan with aluminum foil.
2. Wash, dry, and chop the oregano and cilantro. Mince the garlic. Combine all the ingredients but the swordfish in a deep dish. Place the swordfish in the dish and spoon the mixture over it.
3. If using a top-of-the-stove grill, prepare it.
4. Grill or broil the swordfish steaks according to the Canadian rule: measure the fish at its thickest part and cook the fish 8 to 10 minutes per inch. Baste the fish several times on both sides. Serve topped with salsa.

Yield: 2 servings

Sunshine Salsa

5 ounces whole yellow,
  orange, or red bell pepper
  or 4 ounces ready-cut
  diced yellow, orange, or
  red bell pepper (1 cup)
4 ounces (¼ pound) yellow
  tomatoes (cherry or pear
  tomatoes can be
  substituted)
4 ounces red tomatoes
  (cherry or pear tomatoes
  can be substituted)
2 sprigs basil, to yield ¼ cup
  minced
6 or 7 sprigs parsley, to yield
  2 tablespoons minced
4 Italian, French, or Greek
  olives
½ teaspoon capers
2 teaspoons fresh lime juice
1½ teaspoons balsamic
  vinegar

1. Wash, trim, seed, and dice whole peppers.
2. Wash, trim, and dice the yellow and red tomatoes.
3. Wash and dry the basil and parsley; mince.
4. Pit the olives. Rinse and drain the capers.
5. Combine all ingredients and serve with swordfish.

Yield: 2 servings

GAME PLAN

Prepare broiler, if using.

Prepare marinade for fish.

Prepare stove-top grill, if using.

Prepare peppers, tomatoes, basil, and parsley for salsa.

Grill or broil swordfish.

Finish salsa.

APPROXIMATE NUTRITION INFORMATION PER SERVING,
WITHOUT BREAD: 350 calories, 10 grams fat, 65 milligrams
cholesterol, 580 milligrams sodium, 40 grams protein,
30 grams carbohydrate

Grilled Pineapple Ginger Swordfish

Pineapple Cucumber Salsa
Asian Rice

*T*he swordfish can be marinated for up to an hour, if that is convenient, but don't marinate it longer or the fish will become too mushy. The sweetness comes from the salsa, along with an edge of sharpness from vinegar and shallot. ❧ Even with three components to this meal, it will take you less than half an hour to prepare it.

Grilled Pineapple Ginger Swordfish

10 ounces swordfish steak
Fresh or frozen ginger, to
   yield 1½ teaspoons
   coarsely grated
1 clove garlic
¼ cup unsweetened
   pineapple juice
¼ cup dry white wine

1. Preheat the broiler, if using. Line the broiler pan with aluminum foil.
2. Wash and dry the fish.
3. Grate the ginger and mince the garlic; combine with the pineapple juice and wine. Add the swordfish and marinate at least 10 minutes or up to 1 hour.
4. If using stove-top grill, prepare.
5. Broil or grill the swordfish according to the Canadian rule: Measure at its thickest part and cook for 8 to 10 minutes per inch, basting occasionally with marinade. Serve with pineapple cucumber salsa.

Yield: 2 servings

Pineapple Cucumber Salsa

1 teaspoon sugar
1 teaspoon rice vinegar
½ fresh pineapple, to yield
   1 cup fresh, very ripe,
   finely diced peeled
   pineapple
4 ounces Kirby cucumber,
   diced (1 cup)
1 shallot

1. Combine the sugar and vinegar in a serving dish.
2. Peel and cut the pineapple into very small dice.
3. Wash, trim, but do not peel the cucumber. Cut into tiny dice.
4. Mince the shallot and combine with the pineapple, cucumber, and dressing.

Yield: 2 servings

Food Note ❧ Purchasing whole pineapples is chancy, since you can never be quite sure of their sweetness and ripeness. So, look for fresh pineapple slices, pineapple chunks, or peeled fresh pineapple for a better shot at sweet, ripe pineapple. Ripe pineapple is generally yellower in color then unripe pineapple.

Asian Rice

¼ pound (4 ounces) whole onion or 3 ounces diced ready-cut onion (1 cup)

1 teaspoon Asian sesame oil

½ cup long-grain rice

1 cup no-salt-added chicken stock or broth

1 teaspoon reduced-sodium soy sauce

1. Dice whole onion. Heat the oil in a heavy-bottomed pot for a few minutes, add the onion, and sauté until it begins to brown.
2. Add the rice, stock, and soy sauce, bring to a boil, reduce heat, cover, and simmer until the rice is tender and the liquid has been absorbed, about 17 minutes.

Yield: 2 servings

GAME PLAN

Preheat broiler, if using.

Prepare and sauté onion in sesame oil for rice.

Prepare swordfish and marinade and combine.

Add rice, stock, and soy sauce to onion and cook.

Combine sugar and vinegar for salsa.

Prepare remaining salsa ingredients.

Prepare stove-top grill, if using; grill or broil swordfish, basting.

Finish salsa preparation.

APPROXIMATE NUTRITION INFORMATION PER SERVING: 495 calories, 10 grams fat, 60 milligrams cholesterol, 265 milligrams sodium, 35 grams protein, 60 grams carbohydrate

Grilled Swordfish on Black Bean and Pineapple Salsa

*S*alsas, relishes, and chutneys have long since taken over from beurre blanc and other high-fat sauces, proving that low-fat can be just as flavorful and satisfying. ❧ The black bean and pineapple salsa served with swordfish here would be just as delicious for grilled tuna or grilled chicken.

Grilled Swordfish on Black Bean and Pineapple Salsa

10 ounces swordfish steak
1 (15-ounce) can
   no-salt-added black beans
½ small fresh pineapple
2 ounces onion, to yield
   ⅓ cup finely diced
2 ounces red pepper, to yield
   ½ cup finely diced
2 ounces finely diced yellow
   or orange or purple
   pepper (½ cup)
¼ to ½ jalapeño or serrano
   chile
1 teaspoon ground coriander
1 teaspoon ground cumin
1 tablespoon rice vinegar
A little oil for brushing
¼ cup chopped fresh cilantro
2 slices crusty French or
   Italian bread

1. Preheat the broiler, if using. Line the broiler pan with aluminum foil.
2. Wash and dry the fish.
3. Drain the beans and rinse thoroughly under cold water; drain and set aside.
4. Cut the pineapple into small dice; finely dice onions and peppers. Mince the chile; combine with the coriander, cumin, and vinegar in a nonreactive bowl. Stir in the beans.
5. If using a stove-top grill, prepare. Brush the fish lightly with oil. Grill or broil according to the Canadian rule: Measure the fish at its thickest part and cook for 8 to 10 minutes per inch.
6. Wash, dry, and chop cilantro. Just before serving stir the cilantro into the salsa and arrange some on serving plates. Place the fish on top and then top fish with additional salsa.

Yield: 2 servings

GAME PLAN

Follow recipe directions.

APPROXIMATE NUTRITION INFORMATION PER SERVING,
INCLUDING 1 SLICE OF BREAD: 595 calories, 10 grams fat,
55 milligrams cholesterol, 400 milligrams sodium,
45 grams protein, 80 grams carbohydrate

Grilled Tuna | Eggplant, Tomatoes, and Onion Pasta

*I*f you are fortunate enough to be able to grill a piece of tuna over charcoal, you know that it requires no seasonings at all for spectacular flavor. ❧ The next best alternative is one of those top-of-the-stove grills that provide the moist interior and crusty exterior. ❧ The accompanying pasta and vegetable mélange can certainly be made with canned tomatoes but that version can't compare to the flavor of local tomatoes when they are in season. If you have a choice, select either baby eggplant or white eggplant: They are less likely to be bitter than large purple eggplants.

Grilled Tuna

16 ounces (1 pound) tuna steaks

1. Prepare top-of-the-stove grill.
2. Wash and dry the tuna steaks and cook according to the Canadian rule: Measure the fish at its thickest part and cook 8 to 10 minutes per inch.

Yield: 3 servings

Eggplant, Tomatoes, and Onion Pasta

24 ounces (1½ pounds) baby, white Asian, or regular eggplant

4 teaspoons olive oil

16 ounces (1 pound) whole onion or 14 ounces chopped ready-cut onion (3⅓ cups)

8 ounces (½ pound) fresh shell pasta—multicolored assortment, if possible

16 ounces (1 pound) ripe tomatoes

Fresh or frozen ginger, to yield 1 tablespoon coarsely grated

1 teaspoon sugar

1 tablespoon reduced-sodium soy sauce

Freshly ground black pepper

1. Turn on the broiler and cover the pan with a double thickness of aluminum foil.
2. Bring 2 quarts of water to boil in a covered pot for pasta.
3. Trim the eggplant; slice small ones in half lengthwise; cut regular-size eggplant into ½-inch-thick slices. Place on the broiler pan and brush cut sides very sparingly with oil, using about 2 teaspoons. Broil about 2 inches from the source of heat, turning once, about 7 to 10 minutes altogether, until the outsides are brown and the flesh is soft.
4. Dice whole onion. Heat the remaining 2 teaspoons of oil in a non-stick skillet, add the onion, and sauté until the onion is soft and golden.
5. Cook pasta according to package directions.
6. Wash, trim, and dice the tomatoes; coarsely grate the ginger and add the tomatoes and ginger to the onions. Cut away and discard the eggplant skin. Cut the flesh coarsely and add to the tomato-onion mixture, along with the sugar, soy sauce, and pepper. Cook to meld flavors and heat through, a few minutes.
7. Drain pasta and toss with tomato mixture.

Yield: 3 servings

G A M E   P L A N

Preheat broiler.

Follow recipe for sauce and pasta through Step 5.

Prepare stove-top grill; cook tuna.

Finish pasta recipe.

APPROXIMATE NUTRITION INFORMATION PER SERVING:
740 calories, 20 grams fat, 65 milligrams cholesterol, 435 milligrams sodium, 55 grams protein, 95 grams carbohydrate

Penne with Tuna and Peas in Tomato Sauce

Fennel and Parmigiano

*V*ariations on the Tuscan or Neapolitan dish tuna with peas and tomatoes are found in several Italian cookbooks. Sometimes hot pepper is an ingredient, sometimes onions, sometimes sage. As with many Italian dishes, there is no single "authentic" version. ❧ What's wonderful about American cooking is that we can do whatever sounds good and tastes good. And the sauce here clings nicely to penne. ❧ An Italian salad of fennel and very thin slices of Parmigiano-Reggiano with the lightest of oil and lemon dressings goes well with the simple fish dish.

Penne with Tuna and Peas in Tomato Sauce

1 large clove garlic
2 teaspoons olive oil
¼ teaspoon hot pepper flakes
½ cup dry white wine
2 cups crushed no-salt-added tomatoes
2 tablespoons no-salt-added tomato paste
8 ounces (½ pound) penne-shaped pasta
8 ounces (½ pound) fresh tuna
2 cups frozen peas

1. Bring enough water to boil in a covered pot for the penne.
2. Mince the garlic, heat the oil in a nonstick skillet, and sauté garlic in hot oil about 30 seconds. Add hot pepper flakes and sauté 15 seconds.
3. Add the wine and cook quickly to reduce by half.
4. Add the tomatoes and tomato paste; reduce the heat and simmer gently.
5. When the water boils, add the penne and cook according to package directions.
6. Cut the tuna into bite-size chunks. Add along with the peas to the tomato sauce. Simmer about 5 minutes, until the tuna is just cooked.
7. When the penne is cooked, drain and top with the tuna-pea sauce.

Yield: 2 servings

Fennel and Parmigiano

8 ounces (½ pound) fennel
bulb (1 small)
½ ounce Parmigiano-
Reggiano (2 to
3 tablespoons)
1 teaspoon olive oil
1 teaspoon fresh lemon juice
Freshly ground black pepper

1. Wash the fennel, trim away the top, and slice off the bottom of the bulb. Slice the bulb thinly and then cut into julienne strips. Place the fennel in a serving bowl.
2. Coarsely grate the cheese and add to the fennel in the serving bowl.
3. Sprinkle oil and lemon juice over the fennel and cheese and toss to mix well.
4. Season with pepper.

Yield: 2 servings

GAME PLAN

Prepare penne sauce through Step 3.

Prepare salad through Step 1.

Continue penne sauce through Step 4.

Continue with salad until water boils for penne.

Cook penne.

Cut up tuna.

Finish salad.

Finish penne.

APPROXIMATE NUTRITION INFORMATION PER SERVING:
855 calories, 15 grams fat, 55 milligrams cholesterol,
340 milligrams sodium, 55 grams protein, 130 grams
carbohydrate

Snapper Marinara

Green Noodles
Sesame Broccoli

*P*erch and flounder work as well as snapper in this dish; choose the fish you wish to use according to the market. ❧ Spinach linguine was selected for this menu for its pretty color, but plain linguine or other flat fresh pasta will do as nicely, too.

Snapper Marinara

2 cloves garlic
6 to 8 parsley sprigs, to make 2 tablespoons minced
1 teaspoon olive oil
6 capers
1 (28-ounce) can no-salt-added crushed tomatoes
¼ teaspoon anchovy paste
16 ounces (1 pound) red snapper fillet

1. Mince the garlic. Wash the parsley and mince.
2. Heat the oil in a nonstick skillet; add the garlic and parsley and sauté for 30 seconds.
3. Rinse the capers and add to the skillet with the tomatoes and anchovy paste; stir, reduce heat, and simmer 5 minutes.
4. Cut fish into small chunks and add to sauce, spooning the sauce over; simmer until the fish is cooked, about 5 minutes. Serve with some of the sauce spooned over the noodles.

Yield: 3 servings

Green Noodles

9 ounces fresh spinach linguine

1. Bring 3 quarts of water to boil in a covered pot.
2. Cook the pasta according to package directions; drain and serve topped with some of the marinara sauce.

Yield: 3 servings

Sesame Broccoli

24 ounces (1½ pounds)
  whole broccoli or
  14 ounces ready-cut
  broccoli florets (5 to
  6 cups)
2 teaspoons Asian sesame oil
1 tablespoon rice vinegar
1½ teaspoons sesame seeds
Freshly ground black pepper

1. Remove tough stems from whole broccoli; cut the broccoli into bite-size pieces. Steam over simmering water about 7 minutes, until broccoli is tender but still crisp.
2. Meanwhile, in a serving dish mix together the oil, vinegar, and sesame seeds.
3. When the broccoli is cooked, drain and mix gently with the dressing to coat. Season with pepper.

Yield: 3 servings

G A M E   P L A N

Put water on to boil for noodles.
Prepare sauce for fish and cook.
Prepare broccoli and its sauce.
Cook broccoli.
Cook fish.
Cook noodles.

APPROXIMATE NUTRITION INFORMATION PER SERVING:
615 calories, 10 grams fat, 140 milligrams cholesterol, 185 milligrams sodium, 50 grams protein, 80 grams carbohydrate

Yellow Fruited Rice with Fish

Belgian Endive and Blue Cheese Dressing

This meal is full of enticing elements, and the salad dressing is a triumph of taste and healthful eating. The menu features salmon, tuna, or swordfish, a rice dish flavored with dried cherries and banana, and a salad of endive and Gorgonzola. It is a treat for any family dinner or for last-minute company on a weekday. ❧ Sharp cheeses—Gorgonzola, blue, Roquefort, Parmigiano-Reggiano—have such intense flavors that a little goes a long way, so it's possible to have a pungent dressing for two with no more than an ounce of cheese. Once you have tried this dressing, you will use it for all kinds of salads.

Yellow Fruited Rice with Fish

4 ounces (¼ pound) whole onion or 3 ounces chopped ready-cut onion (1 cup)

1 teaspoon olive oil

¾ cup long-grain rice

1½ cups no-salt-added chicken stock or broth

½ teaspoon turmeric OR ¼ teaspoon saffron threads

1 (10-ounce) piece of salmon, swordfish, or tuna

1 tablespoon fresh lime juice

¼ cup dried cherries

1½ scallions

1 ripe banana

¼ teaspoon salt

Pinch nutmeg

1. Cover the broiler pan with a double thickness of aluminum foil and preheat the broiler.
2. Chop whole onion.
3. In a very hot, nonstick pan, heat the oil; sauté the onion over medium-high heat until it begins to soften and brown.
4. Stir in the rice, stock, and turmeric or saffron; bring to a boil, reduce heat, cover, and cook 17 minutes, until the rice is tender and the liquid has been absorbed.
5. After the rice has been cooking for about 5 minutes, wash and dry the fish and place it in the broiler pan. Cook according to the Canadian rule: Measure the fish at the thickest part and cook 8 to 10 minutes to the inch. For thick cuts, like swordfish or tuna, turn fish halfway through broiling.
6. Squeeze the lime juice over the cherries; set aside.
7. Wash, trim, and slice the scallions; cut the banana into small cubes.
8. When the rice is cooked, stir in the cherries with the lime juice, scallions, banana, salt, and nutmeg, and serve with the fish.

Yield: 2 servings

Belgian Endive and Blue Cheese Dressing

8 ounces (½ pound) Belgian
   endive
1 ounce blue cheese
   (2 tablespoons)
3 tablespoons nonfat plain
   yogurt
1 tablespoon brandy
Pinch cayenne

1. Trim, wash, and dry endive leaves; arrange on two salad plates.
2. In a small bowl, mash the cheese with the yogurt, brandy, and cayenne and mix well.
3. Spoon the dressing over the endive leaves.

Yield: 2 servings

GAME PLAN

Prepare rice and fish dish through Step 5.

Prepare the endive.

Continue with rice and fish through Step 7.

Make salad dressing and spoon over endive.

Finish rice.

APPROXIMATE NUTRITION INFORMATION PER SERVING:
655 calories, 15 grams fat, 40 milligrams cholesterol,
665 milligrams sodium, 35 grams protein, 95 grams
carbohydrate

Halibut with Spiced Vegetables

Braised Fennel and Rice

*F*usion cooking seems to be the newest catchall phrase for dishes with ingredients from more than one part of the world. ❧ This recipe for halibut and spiced vegetables puts an Italian accent on Chinese ingredients. The combination produces a dish with a delicious jolt of flavorings. The accompanying fennel with rice continues the Italian theme.

Halibut with Spiced Vegetables

12 ounces (¾ pound) whole onion or
    11 ounces thin-sliced ready-cut onion
    (2½ to 3 cups)
2 teaspoons olive oil
½ cup plus 2 tablespoons fish stock or
    bottled clam juice
8 ounces (½ pound) whole red bell
    pepper or
    7 ounces thin-sliced ready-cut
    pepper (2 cups)
8 ounces (½ pound) whole green bell
    pepper or
    7 ounces thin-sliced ready-cut
    pepper (2 cups)
Fresh or frozen ginger, to yield
    1 tablespoon coarsely grated
½ teaspoon five-spice powder
16 ounces (1 pound) halibut
15 sprigs cilantro, to yield
    3 tablespoons chopped
3 scallions
2 tablespoons pine nuts
1 tablespoon reduced-sodium soy sauce

1. Cut the whole onion into thin slices.
2. Heat 1 teaspoon of the oil in a nonstick skillet until it is quite hot. Add the onion and sauté over medium heat, stirring occasionally, until the onion begins to soften and take on color. When the onion begins to dry out, stir in 2 tablespoons of the fish stock.
3. Meanwhile, wash, trim, seed, and cut the whole red and green peppers into thin slices and add to the onion. Cook, stirring, until the peppers begin to soften.
4. Grate the ginger, and stir into the peppers along with the five-spice powder.
5. Cut the halibut into 3 pieces; discard the bone. Place the halibut in the pan and cover with vegetables. Cover, and cook according to the Canadian rule: Measure the fish at its thickest part and cook 8 to 10 minutes per inch.
6. Meanwhile, trim, wash, and chop cilantro and scallions and sauté them with pine nuts in the remaining 1 teaspoon olive oil in a small pot for about 1 minute.
7. Add the remaining ½ cup fish stock and the soy sauce to the pine nut mixture and cook until slightly reduced.
8. When the fish is cooked, arrange the vegetables on each of three plates; top with halibut, and spoon pine nut mixture over top of each.

Yield: 3 servings

Braised Fennel and Rice

¾ cup long-grain rice
8 ounces (½ pound) whole
    onion or 7 ounces
    ready-cut onion (1⅔ cups)
1 teaspoon olive oil
1 large clove garlic
16 ounces (1 pound) fennel
¼ cup no-salt-added
    vegetable stock or broth
¾ cup dry white wine
¼ cup no-salt-added tomato
    sauce
¼ teaspoon hot pepper
    flakes
1 teaspoon fennel seed
½ teaspoon ground coriander
½ teaspoon salt
Freshly ground black pepper

1. Combine the rice and 1½ cups water in a heavy-bottomed pot. Bring to a boil, reduce heat, cover, and cook for 17 minutes.
2. Chop whole onion.
3. Heat the oil in a nonstick skillet until it is very hot. Add the onion and sauté over medium heat until it begins to soften and brown.
4. Meanwhile, mince the garlic, and add to the onion as it cooks.
5. Trim the fennel and slice very thin. There should be about 4 cups.
6. When the onion begins to dry out, stir in 1 tablespoon of the vegetable stock.
7. Add the fennel, remaining vegetable broth, wine, tomato sauce, hot pepper flakes, fennel seed, and coriander. Cover, reduce heat, and simmer until the fennel is tender, about 7 minutes.
8. As soon as the rice is cooked, stir it into fennel mixture and continue cooking.
9. When the fennel is cooked, season with salt and pepper to taste.

Yield: 3 servings

GAME PLAN

Cook rice.
Prepare fish through Step 3.
Continue with rice and fennel through Step 5.
Continue with fish through Step 4.
Continue with rice through Step 7.
Finish fish.
Finish rice.

APPROXIMATE NUTRITION INFORMATION PER SERVING:
610 calories, 10 grams fat, 50 milligrams cholesterol,
735 milligrams sodium, 40 grams protein, 75 grams
carbohydrate

"Fried" Potatoes and Fish Vinaigrette

Gingered Carrots and Raisin Salad

*F*rying is not something usually encouraged in a book about healthful eating. But a small amount of oil in a good nonstick pan will brown potatoes very nicely. ❧ Sautéed potatoes add a wonderful contrasting taste and texture to fish braised in a tomato-olive sauce. Because all of the cooking is done in one pan, the effect is similar to that of a more time-consuming baked dish. ❧ Carrot-raisin salad, dressed with yogurt and refreshed with ginger, contrasts with the sharpness of the fish.

"Fried" Potatoes and Fish Vinaigrette

16 ounces (1 pound) new potatoes

1 tablespoon olive oil

16 ounces (1 pound) ripe tomatoes or cherry tomatoes

4 sprigs fresh thyme, to yield 1 tablespoon leaves

6 large Greek, Italian, or French olives

1 teaspoon capers

1 large clove garlic

8 ounces (½ pound) flounder, sole, scrod, or other white fish

1. Scrub but do not peel the potatoes. Cut them in half and slice in the food processor with the medium slicing blade. Sauté in hot oil in a large nonstick skillet, turning occasionally to brown both sides.
2. Meanwhile, wash, trim, and slice the tomatoes in the food processor with the same slicing blade.
3. Wash, dry and chop the thyme; rinse, pit, and cut up the olives. Add the thyme and olives to the tomatoes.
4. Rinse and drain the capers; put the garlic through a garlic press; add capers and garlic to tomatoes. Mix well.
5. Wash the fish, dry, and cut into 2 portions. Arrange over the potatoes; spoon the tomato mixture over the fish, covering it completely; cover the pan. Reduce heat to medium and cook the fish according to the Canadian rule: Measure the fish at its thickest point and cook 8 to 10 minutes per inch.

Yield: 2 servings

Gingered Carrots and Raisin Salad

6 ounces peeled whole or
  shredded ready-cut
  carrots (2 cups shredded)
Fresh or frozen ginger, to
  yield 2 teaspoons coarsely
  grated
½ cup nonfat plain yogurt
3 heaping tablespoons
  raisins

1. Shred the carrots with the shredding blade of food processor.
2. Grate the ginger into a serving bowl.
3. Stir in the yogurt and raisins and mix well. Stir in the carrots and serve.

Yield: 2 servings

G A M E   P L A N

Prepare potatoes and fish through Step 5.
Prepare carrots and raisin salad.

APPROXIMATE NUTRITION INFORMATION PER SERVING:
570 calories, 10 grams fat, 55 milligrams cholesterol,
345 milligrams sodium, 30 grams protein, 95 grams
carbohydrate

Chinese Marinated Broiled Fish

Broccoli Mashed Potatoes

A thin fish fillet, like sole or flounder or scrod, does not need to be marinated for long. The fish absorbs much of the flavor of the marinade within a few minutes. So even for those meals that have to be on the table in less than half an hour, seasoning fish with a simple, intense marinade is worth the minute or two it takes to put one together. In fact, marinating some fish for too long can ruin its texture. ❧ The most delicious and interesting part of this menu may not be the fish but the broccoli and mashed potatoes, which have a wonderful green color and distinctive flavor from sautéed onions. No one can get enough of these.

Chinese Marinated Broiled Fish

3 tablespoons dry sherry
1 teaspoon (Asian) sesame oil
Fresh or frozen ginger, to yield 1 tablespoon coarsely grated
10 ounces fillet of scrod or other firm white fish fillet

1. Turn on the broiler. Cover the broiler pan with aluminum foil.
2. Combine the sherry and sesame oil; grate the ginger and add to the mixture.
3. Wash and dry the fish and coat with the marinade.
4. When it is time to cook the fish, remove it from the marinade and broil according to the Canadian rule: Measure the fish at its thickest part and cook 8 to 10 minutes per inch. (A piece of filleted scrod will be less than 1 inch thick and will take about 5 minutes.) Brush with marinade once.

Yield: 2 servings

Broccoli Mashed Potatoes

12 ounces (¾ pound) tiny whole new potatoes (or larger potato, cut up)

8 ounces (½ pound) whole onion or 7 ounces chopped ready-cut onion (1⅔ cups)

2 teaspoons canola oil

8 ounces (½ pound) whole broccoli—1 large stalk

3 tablespoons light sour cream

¼ teaspoon salt

Freshly ground black pepper

1. Scrub but do not peel the potatoes. Cover with water and boil in a covered pot until they are done, about 20 minutes.
2. Chop whole onions. Heat the oil in a nonstick pan; add the onions and sauté until they soften and start to brown.
3. Trim away about ⅓ of broccoli stem and wash. Cut remaining stem into ¼-inch-thick slices and the head into small chunks. Six to 8 minutes before the potatoes will be finished, add the broccoli to the pan and continue cooking until both are done.
4. Place sour cream, onions, drained broccoli, and potatoes in a food processor and process until the mixture is smooth. Season with salt and pepper to taste.

Yield: 2 servings

GAME PLAN

Cook potatoes.

Turn on broiler or toaster oven.

Marinate fish.

Prepare onion and sauté.

Prepare broccoli.

Cook broccoli.

Cook fish.

Process potatoes and broccoli with onions, broccoli, and sour cream; season.

APPROXIMATE NUTRITION INFORMATION PER SERVING:
465 calories, 10 grams fat, 65 milligrams cholesterol, 405 milligrams sodium, 35 grams protein, 50 grams carbohydrate

Fish Steamed Chinese-Style | Green Rice and Asparagus

*T*he original version of this menu was created after a trip to the Union Square Greenmarket, one of New York's fabulous farmers' markets. On that spring day I bought local asparagus, scallions, and what the vendor called black fish. ❧ Black fish is similar to bass, but firmer. The recipe has also been made with halibut, but any white fish takes well to steaming Chinese-style. ❧ The seasoning for the rice could be described as a very thick salad dressing. It gives the rice a lovely green cast, which is further accented by the bright green of the asparagus. ❧ To save pots the asparagus are added to the rice a few minutes before it is ready and the two cook together.

Fish Steamed Chinese-Style

10 ounces any white fish
    fillets or steaks
Fresh or frozen ginger, to
    yield 1 tablespoon
    coarsely grated
1 scallion
1 tablespoon dry sherry
2 teaspoons reduced-sodium
    soy sauce
¼ teaspoon sugar

1. Cut the fish in half and arrange on a rack in a steamer over water.
2. Coarsely grate the ginger; wash, trim, and julienne the white part of the scallion; mix the ginger and scallion with the sherry, soy, and sugar; spoon carefully over the fish. Cover and steam, following the Canadian rule: Measure the fish at its thickest part and cook 8 to 10 minutes per inch.

Yield: 2 servings

Green Rice and Asparagus

¾ cup long-grain rice
10 medium asparagus spears
3 scallions
4 or 5 large basil leaves, to
    yield ½ cup chopped
1 clove garlic
1 tablespoon olive oil
2 tablespoons balsamic
    vinegar
⅛ teaspoon hot pepper
    flakes
Freshly ground black pepper
3 tablespoons pine nuts

1. Combine the rice with 1½ cups water in a heavy-bottomed pot. Bring to a boil; reduce heat, cover, and cook for a total of 17 minutes.
2. Wash and break the asparagus at the point where the woody part of the stem and the tender stalk meet. Cut the asparagus just below the tips; then cut the remaining stalks into ½-inch lengths. Five to 7 minutes before rice is cooked, stir the asparagus in with the rice, cover, and continue cooking. (The cooking time will depend on the thickness of the asparagus stalks.)
3. Wash, trim, and cut the scallions into thirds; wash and dry the basil leaves; mince the garlic and put the basil and garlic in the food processor along with olive oil, vinegar, hot pepper flakes, and black pepper to taste, and blend only until the basil is roughly chopped.
4. When the rice and asparagus are cooked, stir in the basil mixture and then the pine nuts and serve.

Yield: 2 servings

GAME PLAN

Cook rice.

Prepare fish.

Prepare asparagus, scallions, and basil.

Cook fish.

Cook asparagus.

Prepare seasonings for rice and asparagus.

Finish rice and asparagus.

APPROXIMATE NUTRITION INFORMATION PER SERVING:
555 calories, 15 grams fat, 65 milligrams cholesterol,
300 milligrams sodium, 35 grams protein, 65 grams
carbohydrate

Fish in Warm Vinaigrette

Potatoes with Italian Peppers and Onions

oaching is one of the simplest methods for cooking. Here, a mild vinaigrette makes a typical poaching liquid even more flavorful and the flavors suffuse the fish nicely.

Fish in Warm Vinaigrette

2 to 3 sprigs fresh oregano, to yield 2 tablespoons chopped, or 2 teaspoons dried oregano
½ cup water
½ cup dry vermouth
1 tablespoon olive oil
1 tablespoon white wine vinegar
24 ounces (1½ pounds) black bass fillet or other fillet of firm fish

1. Chop the oregano. Combine with water, vermouth, oil, and vinegar in a sauté pan large enough to hold the fish.
2. Add the fish to the liquid. Cover and cook over medium heat, following the Canadian rule: Measure the fish at its thickest point and cook 8 to 10 minutes per inch.

Yield: 3 servings

Potatoes with Italian Peppers and Onions

12 ounces (¾ pound) baking
   potatoes
12 ounces (¾ pound) Italian
   peppers
10 ounces whole onion or
   9 ounces sliced or
   chopped ready-cut onion
   (2 cups)
1 tablespoon olive oil
½ teaspoon dried thyme
Freshly ground black pepper
¼ teaspoon salt (optional)

1. Peel and slice the potatoes on the thick slicing blade of the food processor. Cut the slices into small cubes.
2. Core and seed the peppers and slice with the thin slicing blade of the processor.
3. Peel and slice whole onions in the processor. Drain any accumulated liquid from the peppers and onions.
4. Heat the olive oil in a nonstick skillet. Add the potatoes, peppers, onion, and thyme. Cook over medium-high heat until the vegetables begin to brown. Stir and turn to brown all over.
5. Season with pepper and salt (if desired) to taste.

Yield: 3 servings

Food Note ❧ Italian peppers are slender, light green in color, and mild to the taste. If you want a bit of heat, a poblano chile or two, or a half of a jalapeño or serrano, is a nice touch.

G A M E   P L A N

Prepare potatoes, peppers, and onions and cook with thyme.
Prepare ingredients in which to cook fish; poach fish.
Season potato dish.

APPROXIMATE NUTRITION INFORMATION PER SERVING,
WITHOUT SALT: 500 calories, 20 grams fat, 155 milligrams
cholesterol, 170 milligrams sodium, 45 grams protein,
30 grams carbohydrate

Fish in Curried Yogurt Sauce

Warm Broccoli and Potato Salad

*F*ans of Indian food will find much to admire in this simple method for braising fish. Because the fish is enrobed by the sauce, it is richly imbued with the flavors. The spiciness will be determined by the amount of hot pepper used.

Fish in Curried Yogurt Sauce

12 ounces (¾ pound) whole onion or 11 ounces chopped ready-cut onion (2½ cups)
1 large clove garlic
1 teaspoon olive oil
1 cup nonfat plain yogurt
1 tablespoon cornstarch
½ teaspoon ground cumin
¼ teaspoon ground ginger
⅛ teaspoon ground cinnamon
¼ teaspoon ground turmeric
⅛ to ¼ teaspoon hot pepper flakes
8 ounces (½ pound) scrod or flounder fillets
10 sprigs cilantro, to yield 2 tablespoons chopped

1. Chop whole onion and mince the garlic; sauté in hot oil in a nonstick skillet until the onion begins to soften.
2. Blend a little yogurt with the cornstarch to make a smooth paste and combine with the remaining yogurt.
3. Add the spices to the onion and stir. Remove from heat; stir in the yogurt and process in the blender.
4. If the fish is one large piece, cut it in half.
5. Return the yogurt mixture to the skillet and add the fish; spoon the yogurt over the fish. Cover and cook over medium heat, following the Canadian rule: Measure the fish at its thickest part and cook 8 to 10 minutes per inch. The sauce will take on a beautiful dark mustard color.
6. Wash, dry, and chop cilantro; sprinkle on top.

Yield: 2 servings

Warm Broccoli and Potato Salad

12 ounces (¾ pound) new
  potatoes
12 ounces (¾ pound) whole
  broccoli or 6 ounces
  ready-cut broccoli florets
  (2½ to 3 cups)
1 tablespoon olive oil
1 tablespoon balsamic
  vinegar
1 teaspoon Dijon mustard

1. Scrub but do not peel the potatoes; cut into 1-inch pieces and cook in water to cover about 10 to 12 minutes.
2. Trim tough stems off the broccoli; cut the remaining broccoli into bite-size pieces. When the potatoes have been cooking for about 5 minutes, place the broccoli in a steamer basket and set it in the pot. Cook broccoli 5 to 7 minutes. (If one vegetable is finished before the other, remove it and continue cooking the remaining vegetable.)
3. In a serving bowl whisk together the oil, vinegar, and mustard. When the vegetables are cooked, drain and mix thoroughly with dressing.

Yield: 2 servings

G A M E   P L A N

Prepare and cook potatoes.

Sauté onion and garlic.

Blend yogurt and cornstarch.

Add spices to onion; add yogurt and process in blender.

Prepare broccoli and cook.

Cook fish.

Make dressing for potatoes and broccoli.

Chop cilantro.

Finish fish.

Finish broccoli and potatoes.

APPROXIMATE NUTRITION INFORMATION PER SERVING:
520 calories, 10 grams fat, 50 milligrams cholesterol, 265 milligrams sodium, 35 grams protein, 70 grams carbohydrate

Mediterranean Fish with Potatoes

*V*ersions of this fish dish with potatoes and tomatoes are found throughout the Mediterranean. Most are far more time-consuming, requiring more initial preparation as well as the final baking. ❧ Here the recipe has been turned into a one-dish meal, complete with protein—the fish; starch—the potatoes; and the vegetables—tomatoes and green pepper. And the cooking is done on top of the stove. In revising the dish, I've added fresh ginger to the traditional garlic, onion, cumin, and cilantro, which gives it a slight sweetness and piquancy. ❧ Italian parsley can be substituted for the fresh cilantro. ❧ Some very crusty bread would go along nicely.

Mediterranean Fish with Potatoes

16 ounces (1 pound) new potatoes
1 tablespoon olive oil
10 ounces whole onion or 9 ounces
    sliced ready-cut onion (2 cups)
Fresh or frozen ginger to yield
    1 tablespoon coarsely grated
1 clove garlic
1 teaspoon ground cumin
9 ounces whole green pepper or
    8 ounces sliced ready-cut pepper
    (1¾ cups)
4 small or 3 large plum tomatoes
2 tablespoons no-salt-added tomato
    paste
2 tablespoons balsamic vinegar
⅛ teaspoon salt (optional)
12 ounces (¾ pound) scrod or other
    firm white fish fillets
About 15 sprigs fresh cilantro, to yield
    ⅓ cup chopped

1. Scrub but do not peel the potatoes, and slice them ⅛ inch thick.
2. Heat the oil in a nonstick skillet large enough to hold all the ingredients; add the potatoes and brown on both sides.
3. Slice whole onions, grate the ginger, and mince the garlic; add with the cumin to the potatoes and stir well. Sauté for 3 or 4 minutes, until the onions begin to soften.
4. Cut whole pepper into small chunks and add; cook 3 or 4 minutes longer.
5. Wash, trim, and slice the tomatoes about ⅛ inch thick.
6. Stir in tomato paste, vinegar, and optional salt. Arrange the fish over the vegetable mixture and top with tomatoes. Cover and cook fish according to the Canadian rule: Measure the fish at its thickest point and cook 8 to 10 minutes per inch.
7. Wash, dry, and chop cilantro.
8. Arrange vegetables and fish on plates and sprinkle with cilantro.

Yield: 2 servings

GAME PLAN

Follow recipe.

APPROXIMATE NUTRITION INFORMATION PER SERVING (DOES NOT INCLUDE SALT): 615 calories, 10 grams fat, 75 milligrams cholesterol, 385 milligrams sodium, 40 grams protein, 90 grams carbohydrate

Speedy Fish Stew Scented with Orange and Fennel | Boiled Potatoes

*I*f the mention of fish stew conjures up images of fish heads and bones and shells—in other words a big, smelly mess in the kitchen—this speedy simplified version will entice you to try the genre. ❧ But "simplified" does not mean thin flavor. Taking its cue from Mediterranean fish stews, this one is seasoned with the bittersweetness of orange peel and the hint of licorice from fennel seeds. ❧ The most time-consuming part of the meal comes from waiting for the potatoes to cook. If you cannot find tiny new potatoes that cook in 20 minutes or less, cut larger ones in half or into quarters. ❧ Add a green salad for a more elaborate meal.

Speedy Fish Stew Scented with Orange and Fennel

8 ounces (½ pound) whole onion or
   7 ounces thinly sliced ready-cut
   onions (1⅔ cups)
1 clove garlic
1 tablespoon olive oil
Grated rind of 1 orange
4 sprigs fresh thyme, to yield
   1 tablespoon leaves, or 1 teaspoon
   dried thyme
¾ cup dry white wine
½ a 28-ounce can no-salt-added crushed
   tomatoes in sauce
3 tablespoons no-salt-added tomato
   paste
½ to 1 teaspoon fennel seeds
1 small bay leaf
12 ounces (¾ pound) fish fillets or
   steaks such as grouper, snapper, sea
   bass, swordfish

1. Slice whole onion and the garlic. Heat the oil in a deep nonstick skillet or a pot, add the onion and garlic, and sauté until the onion softens and begins to brown.
2. Grate the orange peel. Remove thyme leaves from stems. Add the orange peel, thyme, wine, tomatoes, tomato paste, fennel seeds, and bay leaf to the pan; cover and cook 10 minutes.
3. Cut the fish into 1½- to 2-inch chunks. Add the fish and cook 3 or 4 minutes, just until it is done. Remove the bay leaf. Serve over boiled potatoes.

Yield: 2 servings

Boiled Potatoes

12 ounces (¾ pound) tiny new potatoes
Water

1. Scrub but do not peel the potatoes.
2. Cover with cold water; cover the pot and bring to a boil; boil until the potatoes are done, 15 to 20 minutes.
3. Drain and place on two dinner plates; cut in quarters and top with fish stew.

G A M E   P L A N

Cook potatoes.

Follow recipe for fish stew.

APPROXIMATE NUTRITION INFORMATION PER SERVING (DOES NOT INCLUDE SALAD): 525 calories, 10 grams fat, 60 milligrams cholesterol, 150 milligrams sodium, 40 grams protein, 55 grams carbohydrate

Summer Fish Stew

his is a perfect late-summer dinner, when all the vegetables can be local and don't require much to bring out their wonderful taste. Choose a good hearty bread for dunking.

Summer Fish Stew

6 ounces whole onion or 5 ounces thinly sliced ready-cut onion (about 1⅓ cups)

1 large clove garlic

1 tablespoon olive oil

16 ounces (1 pound) new potatoes

8 ounces (½ pound) whole zucchini or 7 ounces sliced ready-cut zucchini (1⅓ to 1½ cups)

8 ounces (½ pound) plum tomatoes

4 sprigs fresh thyme, to yield 1 tablespoon chopped leaves

3 tablespoons tomato paste

1 (6-ounce) can no-salt-added tomato-vegetable juice

¼ cup dry white wine or dry vermouth

1 ear corn

4 large shrimp

4 ounces (¼ pound) white fish

4 ounces (¼ pound) scallops

⅛ teaspoon salt (optional)

Freshly ground black pepper

2 slices good crusty bread

1. Slice whole onion thinly and mince the garlic. Heat the oil in a nonstick pan large enough to hold all the ingredients. Add the onions and garlic and sauté until the onions begin to soften and brown.
2. Scrub, halve, and slice the potatoes very thinly. Add to the onions and continue to sauté for about 5 minutes.
3. Scrub, trim, and slice the zucchini ⅛ inch thick. Wash, trim, and coarsely chop the tomatoes. Wash, dry, and chop the thyme leaves. Add the zucchini, tomatoes, and thyme to the potatoes, along with the tomato paste, tomato-vegetable juice, and wine; reduce heat to medium and cook until the zucchini begins to soften, 4 or 5 minutes.
4. Shuck the corn and scrape off the kernels. Shell shrimp. Add corn and shrimp to vegetables and cook 2 minutes.
5. Wash the fish and cut into chunks. Add the fish and scallops to the stew; season with salt, if desired, and the pepper, and continue cooking about 3 more minutes, just until the fish is cooked through. Serve with bread.

Yield: 2 servings

GAME PLAN

Follow recipe.

APPROXIMATE NUTRITION INFORMATION PER SERVING, INCLUDING 1 SLICE OF BREAD (DOES NOT INCLUDE SALT): 490 calories, 10 grams fat, 90 milligrams cholesterol, 510 milligrams sodium, 30 grams protein, 65 grams carbohydrate

Soft-Shell Crabs with Pineapple-Mango Salsa

Corn on the Cob

*C*hefs looking for novel ways of presenting soft-shell crabs can do awful things to them, sometimes smothering them with flavors that overwhelm their delicate sweetness. ❧ I had my doubts about a pineapple-mango salsa to accompany some grilled soft-shells, but the combination works, especially with simply steamed fresh corn as the accompanying dish. ❧ If you don't have a stove-top grill, sauté the crabs in a nonstick pan with just a couple of teaspoons of oil.

Soft-Shell Crabs with Pineapple-Mango Salsa

4 cleaned soft-shell crabs
2 egg whites
3 tablespoons flour
½ a large ripe pineapple
1 ripe mango
½ jalapeño pepper
½ small red onion, to yield
   2 tablespoons finely
   chopped
1 tablespoon fresh lime juice
10 sprigs cilantro, to yield
   2 tablespoons chopped
Freshly ground black pepper

1. Wash the crabs, drain, and dry.
2. Beat the egg whites until slightly foamy; dip the crabs in the egg whites and then in flour to coat lightly, and set aside on a piece of wax paper.
3. Trim, peel, and dice the pineapple and mango and place them in a serving bowl.
4. Mince the jalapeño, finely chop the onion, and add them to the bowl.
5. If using a stove-top grill, prepare it. Grill the crabs about 3 minutes on each side over medium-high heat. To sauté use a nonstick pan and 2 teaspoons of oil.
6. Squeeze the lime juice into the pineapple mixture.
7. Wash, dry, and chop the cilantro and add it to the bowl; season with pepper.
8. Serve the crabs with salsa on the side.

Yield: 2 servings

Corn on the Cob

2 to 4 ears corn

Shuck corn and steam or boil for about 3 minutes. Drain and serve.

Yield: 2 servings

G A M E   P L A N

Boil water for corn.

Prepare crabs and salsa through Step 5.

Cook corn.

Finish crabs and salsa.

APPROXIMATE NUTRITION INFORMATION PER SERVING, INCLUDING 2 EARS OF CORN: 615 calories, 5 grams fat, 130 milligrams cholesterol, 635 milligrams sodium, 45 grams protein, 110 grams carbohydrate

Cornmeal-Crusted Soft-Shell Crabs with Bean Papaya Salsa

*S*ometimes cooks look over one-dish menus and say, "Too many ingredients." But combining the crab and salsa recipes into one—admittedly with 11 ingredients—produces a complete meal. The directions make it easy to have all the parts ready at the same time; ease is the name of the game. ❧ Certain shortcuts are taken: Canned beans replace freshly cooked ones, and if your market sells fresh pineapple already cut up into chunks, you will cut down further on preparation time. ❧ Coating the crabs with a little egg white and a little cornmeal is all you need to bring out their sweetness.

Cornmeal-Crusted Soft-Shell Crabs with Bean Papaya Salsa

1 egg white
4 cleaned soft-shell crabs
¼ cup cornmeal
1 (15-ounce) can
    no-salt-added black beans
2 papayas
¼ a fresh ripe pineapple
1 tablespoon canola oil
½ jalapeño pepper
Fresh or frozen ginger, to
    yield 1 tablespoon
    coarsely grated
1 teaspoon brown sugar
1 tablespoon fresh lime juice
10 sprigs cilantro, to yield
    2 tablespoons chopped

1. Beat the egg white slightly. Wash and dry the crabs and dip them into the egg white and then into cornmeal.
2. Drain and rinse the beans under cold running water; drain again.
3. Cut the papayas and pineapple into small chunks and place in a mixing bowl large enough to hold all the ingredients but the crabs.
4. Heat the oil in a nonstick pan and sauté the crabs until they turn red and the crust turns golden brown on both sides, about 5 minutes, depending on size.
5. Mince the jalapeño; coarsely grate ginger and add both to fruit.
6. Stir in the brown sugar and lime juice; add the beans.
7. Wash, dry, and chop the cilantro and stir in.
8. Arrange salsa on each of two dinner plates and top with the crabs.

Yield: 2 servings

Follow recipe directions.

APPROXIMATE NUTRITION INFORMATION PER SERVING:
670 calories, 10 grams fat, 160 milligrams cholesterol,
520 milligrams sodium, 50 grams protein, 95 grams
carbohydrate

Mussel, Tomato, and Potato Salad with Olive Dressing

A little smoked seafood, whether mussels, as here, or scallops, clams, oysters, smoked tuna, or salmon, goes a very long way. This meal for two has just 6 ounces but its pronounced flavor permeates the salad. ❧ The meal is cooked in 20 minutes, with time to clean up while you wait for the potatoes to cook. ❧ Serve with some good crusty bread.

Mussel, Tomato, and Potato Salad with Olive Dressing

16 ounces (1 pound) tiny new potatoes

1 tablespoon olive oil

1 tablespoon balsamic vinegar

2 teaspoons Dijon mustard

5 large Greek, French, or Italian black olives packed in brine

1 small bulb fennel (1 cup chopped)

2 medium-large ripe tomatoes

4 large leaves basil, to yield 1 tablespoon chopped

10 sprigs fresh cilantro, to yield 2 tablespoons chopped

6 ounces smoked mussels

Freshly ground black pepper

2 slices densely textured country bread

1. Scrub but do not peel the potatoes, and cook in water to cover in a covered pot for 10 to 20 minutes, depending on their size.
2. In a serving bowl, whisk together the oil, vinegar, and mustard. Pit and cut up the olives and add them to dressing.
3. Wash, trim, and chop the fennel into small dice, and add to the bowl.
4. Wash, trim, and cut the tomatoes into small chunks; add.
5. Wash the basil and cilantro and finely chop; add to the bowl.
6. If the mussels are packed in a lot of oil, rinse and pat dry. Stir in the mussels.
7. When the potatoes are cooked, drain and cut them into bite-size pieces; add to the salad and season to taste with pepper. Serve with densely textured country bread.

Yield: 2 servings

Follow recipe.

APPROXIMATE NUTRITION INFORMATION PER SERVING, WITH
BREAD: 540 calories, 10 grams fat, 50 milligrams
cholesterol, 690 milligrams sodium, 25 grams protein,
85 grams carbohydrate

Mussels Provençale

For those with a culinary bent, Belgium means mussels. Americans tend to eat their mussels one way—steamed with some wine and parsley—while Belgians eat theirs a dozen different ways. On a recent trip to Bruges, I had the best-tasting mussels I have ever eaten—though they were prepared Provençale-style, which of course is French, not Belgian. ❧ For those who like one-dish meals, this one ranks right up there with the best. All the vegetables are included and all you'll need to finish off the meal is some crusty bread to dip into the wonderful sauce. ❧ One reason more mussels aren't sold in this country probably has to do with the time-consuming task of cleaning them. Now, though, some supermarkets and fish stores sell mussels that have already been scrubbed clean of grit and debearded. ❧ Of course any fresh mussels will do; the cleaning will just add a little time.

Mussels Provençale

12 ounces (¾ pound) whole onion or 11 ounces finely chopped ready-cut onion (2¼ cups)

3 teaspoons olive oil

12 ounces (¾ pound) whole red and yellow peppers or 11 ounces finely chopped ready-cut peppers (2¾ cups)

1 large clove garlic

32 ounces (2 pounds) mussels

12 ounces (¾ pound) whole zucchini or 11 ounces finely chopped ready-cut zucchini (2½ cups)

1 (28-ounce) can no-salt-added chopped tomatoes

1 cup dry white wine

1. Finely chop the whole onion.
2. Heat 2 teaspoons of the oil in a nonstick pot large enough to hold all the ingredients. Sauté the onion over medium heat.
3. Meanwhile, wash, trim, seed, and finely chop whole peppers, mince the garlic, and add both to the onion. Continue to sauté.
4. Wash and debeard the mussels if necessary.
5. Wash, trim, and finely chop whole zucchini; add to the pot, along with the tomatoes, wine, and mussels. Mix well and cover the pot. Cook about 4 minutes, just until the mussels open. Any mussels that do not open should be discarded. Stir in the remaining teaspoon of oil. Serve with good crusty bread for dunking.

Yield: 2 large servings

Follow recipe directions.

APPROXIMATE NUTRITION INFORMATION PER SERVING:
505 calories, 10 grams fat, 95 milligrams cholesterol,
555 milligrams sodium, 30 grams protein, 55 grams
carbohydrate

Mussels and Pasta | Fennel with Parmesan Chips

*T*his simple recipe finds its flavor in the reduction of the liquid in which the mussels have been cooked. The brininess of the sea combines with the garlic and tomatoes to provide a richness that belies the lack of more than a touch of olive oil. ❧ Crisp fennel offers a contrast to the mussel and pasta dish, and its licorice flavor is made more mellow by the cheese.

Mussels and Pasta

32 ounces (2 pounds) mussels
3 large cloves garlic
½ cup dry white wine
16 ounces (1 pound) fresh, ripe tomatoes or 1 (28-ounce) can no-salt-added whole tomatoes
2 teaspoons olive oil
8 ounces (½ pound) fresh eggless fettuccine

1. If the mussels have not been washed, cleaned, and debearded, scrub them with a firm brush and remove the beards; otherwise rinse.
2. Combine the mussels with 2 cloves of the garlic and the white wine in a pot; cover and cook 4 to 5 minutes, until the mussels open. Discard any that do not open. Strain and reserve the liquid.
3. Bring 3 quarts water to boil in a covered pot for fettuccine.
4. Wash, trim, and cut the fresh tomatoes in half. Squeeze some of the juice and seeds out of the tomatoes; dice. If using canned tomatoes, drain them well and crush with your fingers.
5. Coarsely chop the remaining clove of garlic. Heat the oil in a sauté pan; sauté the garlic for 30 seconds. Add the tomatoes and reserved cooking liquid from mussels. Over medium-high heat boil the mixture until it is reduced by half.
6. Cook the fettuccine in boiling water according to package directions.
7. Remove the mussels from their shells and stir them into the sauce just to heat through.
8. Drain the fettuccine and serve topped with sauce.

Yield: 2 servings

Food Note ❧ The way many mussels are sold today makes them a cinch to prepare. They have been washed, cleaned, and debearded and packaged in plastic bags. All you have to do is rinse and cook.

Fennel with Parmesan Chips

**6 ounces whole fennel bulb
(about 1½ cups diced)**
**½ ounce thin strips
Parmigiano-Reggiano
(about 2 tablespoons)**
1 teaspoon olive oil

1. Wash, trim, and thinly slice the fennel. Arrange the fennel slices on two salad plates.
2. Slice the Parmigiano and arrange on top of fennel; sprinkle on the oil.

Yield: 2 servings

GAME PLAN

Follow directions for mussels through Step 5.

Prepare fennel.

Cook pasta.

Slice Parmigiano and dress salad.

Finish pasta dish.

APPROXIMATE NUTRITION INFORMATION PER SERVING:
590 calories, 15 grams fat, 175 milligrams cholesterol, 595 milligrams sodium, 35 grams protein, 80 grams carbohydrate

Scallops and Peppers with Black Bean Sauce

Orange Rice

Chinese black beans are popular in Cantonese cooking. They have been processed to preserve them and have such an intense flavor that small quantities characterize a dish. Sometimes they are called fermented black beans, sometimes salted black beans. You will have to get yourself to a Chinese market to find them, but once you have a bag or jar on hand they will keep for months, even years. ❧ The combination of tastes in this dish—sweet, sour, salt, and hot—typifies the appeal of Chinese food. ❧ Steamed rice is the usual Chinese accompaniment: Here it has been given a slightly different slant with orange juice and orange rind.

Scallops and Peppers with Black Bean Sauce

16 ounces (1 pound) whole
    red, yellow, or orange
    peppers or 14 ounces
    thinly sliced ready-cut
    peppers (4 cups)
1 tablespoon canola oil
2 tablespoons salted black
    beans
1 tablespoon dry sherry
1 clove garlic
Fresh or frozen ginger, to
    yield 1 tablespoon
    coarsely grated
4 scallions
10 ounces sea or bay
    scallops
½ teaspoon sugar

1. Wash, trim, seed, and thinly slice whole peppers.
2. Heat the oil in a wok or nonstick skillet; add the peppers and sauté while preparing the rest of the dish.
3. Rinse the black beans under running water, drain, then mash them slightly with the sherry.
4. Mince the garlic, grate the ginger, and wash, trim, and slice the scallions.
5. Add the beans, garlic, and ginger to the peppers and stir for 10 seconds.
6. Add the scallops and cook tiny scallops about 1 minute; cook large ones 2 or 3 minutes. Stir in the sugar and scallions and serve.

Yield: 2 servings

Orange Rice

¾ cup long-grain rice
¾ cup fresh orange juice
¾ cup no-salt-added chicken
stock or broth
Grated rind of 1 orange

1. Combine the rice, orange juice, and stock in a heavy-bottomed pot and bring to a boil.
2. Grate the rind of the orange and stir into the rice.
3. When the rice boils, reduce heat, cover, and simmer, stirring once in a while, for a total of 17 minutes.

Yield: 2 servings

G A M E   P L A N

Start rice.
Make scallop dish, following recipe.

APPROXIMATE NUTRITIONAL ANALYSIS PER SERVING:
575 calories, 10 grams fat, 45 milligrams cholesterol,
346 milligrams sodium, 30 grams protein, 85 grams
carbohydrate

Asian Scallop Salad

Couscous with Tomato and Shallots

*N*ames given to recipes often have more to do with the delights and prejudices of the creator than an obvious connection with the ingredients. This Asian scallop salad might as easily have been called Caribbean salad. ❧ In truth there are many distinctive ingredients common to Caribbean and Far East cooking—ginger, coconut, and cilantro among them.

Asian Scallop Salad

Fresh or frozen ginger, to yield
    1 tablespoon plus 1 teaspoon
    coarsely grated
1 large clove garlic
1 stalk lemon grass
1 teaspoon canola oil
12 ounces (¾ pound) bay or calico
    scallops
2 scallions
5 sprigs fresh cilantro, to yield
    1 tablespoon chopped
1 tablespoon fresh lime juice
1 tablespoon brown sugar
2 teaspoons reduced-sodium soy sauce
¼ teaspoon hot Chinese chili sauce
1 mango
2 medium Kirby cucumbers (about 6
    ounces)
8 ounces (½ pound) whole red pepper
    or 6 ounces chopped ready-cut red
    pepper (1½ cups)
3 cups mixed greens such as arugula,
    Bibb or limestone lettuce, and red
    leaf lettuce, washed and dried

1. Grate the ginger and crush the garlic in a press; mince the lemongrass to yield 2 teaspoons.
2. Heat the oil in a nonstick skillet and sauté 1 tablespoon of the ginger, the garlic, and the lemon grass for about 1 minute.
3. Wash and dry the scallops and add them to pan, cooking for a couple of minutes, just until the scallops are firm; remove the mixture from the heat and set aside in a serving dish.
4. Wash, dry, trim, and finely chop the scallions and cilantro. Combine with the lime juice, sugar, soy sauce, chili sauce, and remaining 1 teaspoon ginger. Blend thoroughly.
5. Cut the mango into ¼-inch dice.
6. Scrub, trim, and cut cucumbers into ¼-inch dice.
7. Wash, trim, seed, and cut whole red pepper into ¼-inch dice.
8. Add the mango, cucumber, red pepper, and the scallion mixture to the scallops and combine well.
9. Wash, dry, and arrange the greens on a serving plate and top with the scallop mixture.

Yield: 2 servings

Couscous with Tomato and Shallots

1 large shallot

Chicken stock or broth

¾ cup whole-wheat couscous

6 red or yellow cherry or pear tomatoes

5 sprigs fresh cilantro, to yield
　1 tablespoon chopped

1 teaspoon Asian sesame oil

1. Mince the shallot.
2. Following the couscous package directions for the amount of liquid, boil the chicken stock with the shallot in a covered pot.
3. Stir in the couscous; cover and finish according to the package directions.
4. Wash and quarter the tomatoes, and wash, dry, and chop the cilantro; stir into the couscous along with the sesame oil.

Yield: 2 servings

G A M E　P L A N

Follow scallop recipe through step 4.

Chop shallot for couscous and bring stock to boil.

Prepare mango.

Cook couscous.

Prepare cucumbers and pepper and combine with other ingredients.

Chop tomatoes and cilantro.

Prepare greens.

Add tomatoes, cilantro, and sesame oil to couscous.

APPROXIMATE NUTRITION INFORMATION PER SERVING:
605 calories, 10 grams fat, 55 milligrams cholesterol, 505 milligrams sodium, 40 grams protein, 95 grams carbohydrate

Shrimp, Chicken, Bean Stew

*T*his one-dish meal could have been called a gumbo if it had been thickened with a roux (butter or oil-flour mixture) and/or okra. Since it has neither, it will have to do with the less interesting name of stew. ❧ But gumbo fanciers will recognize some of gumbo's characteristic flavors: thyme, oregano, and hot pepper. ❧ If you want to keep up with the Louisiana theme get yourself some corn muffins and warm them up to serve with this hearty, gutsy gumbolike soup-stew.

Shrimp, Chicken, Bean Stew

1 cup long-grain rice
16 ounces (1 pound) whole onion or 14 ounces chopped ready-cut onion (3½ cups)
2 teaspoons canola oil
2 large stalks celery or 7 ounces chopped ready-cut celery (1 cup)
2 cloves garlic
16 ounces (1 pound) whole green peppers or 14 ounces chopped ready-cut green peppers (4 cups)
1 small dried hot red pepper
1 (28-ounce) can no-salt-added crushed tomatoes
2 cups no-salt-added vegetable or chicken stock or broth
1½ teaspoons dried thyme
1½ teaspoons dried oregano
Freshly ground black pepper
1 (15-ounce) can no-salt-added kidney beans
6 ounces jumbo shrimp in the shell
8 ounces skinless, boneless chicken breasts
¼ teaspoon salt (optional)

1. Bring the rice and 2 cups of water to boil in a heavy-bottomed pot. Cover and simmer, cooking a total of 17 minutes.
2. Chop whole onion. Heat the oil in a nonstick pot. Add the onion and sauté over medium-high heat.
3. Wash, trim, and chop whole celery; mince the garlic. Add them to onion.
4. Wash, trim, seed, and chop green pepper and add to onion.
5. Chop hot pepper and add to the mixture; cook a total of 10 minutes.
6. Add the tomatoes, stock, thyme, oregano, and freshly ground black pepper and bring to boil. Lower the heat and let the mixture continue to simmer.
7. Drain and rinse the beans thoroughly.
8. Shell the shrimp and cut into halves or thirds, depending on their size.
9. Cut the chicken into small dice and add with the shrimp and beans to the stew; cook for about 3 minutes, just until shrimp and chicken are cooked through. Do not overcook.
10. Stir the cooked rice into the stew. Season to taste with pepper, and salt if you wish. Serve with corn muffins, if desired.

Yield: 4 servings

GAME PLAN

Follow recipe.

APPROXIMATE NUTRITION INFORMATION PER SERVING (WITHOUT SALT OR MUFFIN): 485 calories, 5 grams fat, 100 milligrams cholesterol, 195 milligrams sodium, 35 grams protein, 75 grams carbohydrate

Shrimp, Turkey Ham, and Rice Casserole

*H*ere is an exercise in surgical fat removal—surgical because you will not miss the butter and the Italian sausages in this version of jambalaya. ❧ Turkey "ham" has been substituted for real ham because it is lower in fat but has the same smoky flavor that contributes an important note to this one-dish meal. ❧ Add a warm crusty bread to dip into the terrific sauce.

Shrimp, Turkey Ham, and Rice Casserole

6 ounces whole onion or
   5 ounces chopped
   ready-cut onions
   (1⅓ cups)
1 tablespoon canola oil
1 clove garlic
4 ounces (¼ pound) whole
   carrots or 3 ounces thinly
   sliced ready-cut carrots
   (½ cup)
6 ounces whole green pepper
   or 5 ounces ready-cut
   green pepper cut into thin
   strips (1¼ cups)
¾ cup long-grain rice
3 cups no-salt-added chicken
   stock or broth
1 cup crushed or puréed
   canned no-salt-added
   tomatoes
½ teaspoon ground turmeric
1 small bay leaf
1 teaspoon dried thyme
Freshly ground black pepper
4 ounces (¼ pound) low-fat
   turkey "ham"
8 ounces (½ pound) raw
   peeled shrimp

1. Coarsely chop whole onion. Heat the oil in a heavy-bottomed non-stick pot large enough to hold all the ingredients; add the onion. Mince the garlic. When the onion begins to soften, add the garlic and sauté for 30 seconds.
2. Peel and slice whole carrots into thin rounds in a food processor.
3. Wash, stem, seed, and cut whole pepper into thin strips in the food processor.
4. Stir the carrots, green pepper, rice, chicken stock, tomatoes, turmeric, bay leaf, thyme, and pepper into the pot. Bring to a boil, reduce the heat, cover, and cook until about 3 minutes before the rice is ready—about 13 minutes.
5. Julienne the turkey ham. Add the turkey ham and shrimp to the pot and continue cooking until the shrimp is done, about 3 minutes. Remove the bay leaf and serve.

Yield: 3 servings

APPROXIMATE NUTRITION INFORMATION PER SERVING, INCLUDING SLICE OF BREAD: 515 calories, 10 grams fat, 150 milligrams cholesterol, 785 milligrams sodium, 35 grams protein, 65 grams carbohydrate

Sesame Shrimp with Angel Hair Pasta | Asparagus with Pimiento

*S*esame shrimp with angel hair pasta probably is not a dish ever seen in China, but it has a Chinese sensibility and a Chinese flavor.

Sesame Shrimp with Angel Hair Pasta

3 stalks celery, or 5 ounces, to yield about 1 cup chopped

1 clove garlic

1 teaspoon Asian sesame oil

3 scallions

4 ounces (¼ pound) pork tenderloin

1¼ cups no-salt-added chicken stock or broth

Fresh or frozen ginger, to yield 1 tablespoon coarsely grated

3 tablespoons dry sherry

1 tablespoon cornstarch

1 tablespoon reduced-sodium soy sauce

½ teaspoon or more hot sesame oil

8 ounces (½ pound) fresh angel hair pasta

8 ounces (½ pound) cooked peeled shrimp

1. Bring 4 quarts of water to boil in a covered pot for the pasta.
2. Finely chop whole celery; mince garlic. Heat the oil in a nonstick skillet, and add the celery and garlic.
3. Thinly slice the scallions; grind the pork in the food processor. Add ⅔ of the scallions and all the pork to the celery and cook over medium heat until the pork browns.
4. Add the stock to the pork and celery.
5. Grate the ginger. Mix the sherry with cornstarch to make a smooth paste; stir into the pan along with the soy sauce, ginger, and hot sesame oil. Cook, stirring, until the mixture begins to thicken.
6. Cook the pasta.
7. Coarsely chop the shrimp, add to the pork mixture, and cook just until the shrimp are heated through, about 1 minute; mix in remaining sliced scallion.
8. Drain the pasta and spoon the sauce over.

Yield: 2 servings

Food Note ❧ For the leanest ground pork, buy some pork tenderloin and grind it yourself. The ground pork at the meat counter comes from other cuts and is loaded with fat.

Asparagus with Pimiento

16 spears asparagus
¼ cup julienned strips of
pimiento (about 2 whole)

1. Boil water in the bottom of a steamer for the asparagus.
2. Wash and trim asparagus by breaking at the point where the tough stems meet the tender upper part; the stalks will break easily. Discard tough stems.
3. Add the asparagus to the steamer and steam 5 to 7 minutes.
4. Rinse and drain pimiento and julienne.
5. Arrange asparagus on salad plates and top with the pimiento.

Yield: 2 servings

G A M E   P L A N

Boil water for pasta.

Prepare and cook celery, garlic, pork, and scallions.

Boil water for asparagus.

Prepare asparagus.

Add stock to pork.

Cook asparagus.

Grate ginger.

Finish sauce for pasta.

Cook pasta.

Prepare pimiento for asparagus.

Prepare shrimp and add to pasta sauce.

Drain pasta; add scallion to sauce and spoon it over pasta.

Drain asparagus and decorate with pimiento.

APPROXIMATE NUTRITION INFORMATION PER SERVING:
685 calories, 10 grams fat, 400 milligrams cholesterol,
710 milligrams sodium, 55 grams protein, 85 grams
carbohydrate

Grilled Shrimp with Papaya Salsa

Whole-Wheat Couscous Salad

A couple of years ago a friend pointed out that it is just as easy to make whole-wheat instant couscous as it is the ordinary kind. And, he assured me, it is just as easy to find the whole-wheat variety. ❧ It's easy for him because he shops regularly in a health-food store. ❧ Nevertheless, it is worth making an occasional trip to a specialty market to get the whole-wheat variety, which offers more fiber and more flavor with no more effort. ❧ The sweet-tart salsa here will provide just as appropriate a foil for the grilled shrimp if mango or pineapple is substituted for the papaya.

Grilled Shrimp with Papaya Salsa

1 large papaya
1 ounce red onion to yield
⅓ cup finely chopped
4 ounces (¼ pound) whole
red bell pepper or
3 ounces chopped
ready-cut pepper (¾ cup)
¼ to ½ jalapeño pepper
5 sprigs cilantro, to yield
1 tablespoon chopped
12 jumbo shrimp in the shell
Juice of ½ lime
2 teaspoons rice vinegar

1. Preheat broiler, if using. Cover broiler pan with aluminum foil.
2. Dice the papaya; finely chop the red onion.
3. Wash, stem, seed, and chop whole red pepper; wash, stem, seed, and finely mince the jalapeño.
4. Wash, dry, and chop the cilantro.
5. Prepare stove-top grill, if using.
6. Shell the shrimp and grill on a stove-top grill or in the preheated broiler. Allow about 4 to 5 minutes total.
7. Combine papaya, onion, red pepper, jalapeño, cilantro, lime juice, and vinegar in a serving bowl and mix well. Arrange salsa on each of two dinner plates and surround with the shrimp.

Yield: 2 servings

Whole-Wheat Couscous Salad

¾ cup whole-wheat couscous

½ teaspoon ground cumin

3 sun-dried tomatoes packed in oil

½ large, ripe, flavorful tomato

2 scallions

1. Follow package directions for proper amount of water for couscous. Bring to a boil, add the couscous and cumin, cover, and remove from heat. Allow to sit about 5 minutes, until the water has been absorbed.
2. Rinse, dry, and cut sun-dried tomatoes in fine julienne strips.
3. Wash, trim, and cut fresh tomato into small cubes.
4. Wash, trim, and thinly slice scallions into rounds.
5. Stir sun-dried tomatoes, ripe tomato, and scallions into couscous and serve.

Yield: 2 servings

G A M E   P L A N

Prepare broiler, if using.

Prepare papaya, onion, red pepper, jalapeño, and cilantro.

Shell shrimp.

Cook couscous.

Prepare stove-top grill, if using.

Cook shrimp.

Prepare sun-dried and fresh tomatoes and scallions for couscous; mix with couscous.

Finish salsa and arrange with shrimp on plates.

APPROXIMATE NUTRITION INFORMATION PER SERVING:
560 calories, 5 grams fat, 175 milligrams cholesterol, 275 milligrams sodium, 35 grams protein, 95 grams carbohydrate

Indian Shrimp with Apples | Couscous with Raisins and Pine Nuts

*C*urries are usually accompanied by an array of sweet condiments, but for this curried shrimp, some of the sweetness is found in the couscous with its raisins. If you wish to make the dinner a little more festive, add one of the excellent chutneys on the market now. You are no longer restricted to one manufacturer of one variety, namely mango.

Indian Shrimp with Apples

½ pound (8 ounces) whole onion or 7 ounces chopped ready-cut onion (1⅔ cups)

1 tablespoon canola oil

1 teaspoon ground coriander

1 teaspoon cumin

½ teaspoon turmeric

⅛ to ¼ teaspoon cayenne

2 apples

4 ounces (¼ pound) cabbage, whole or shredded (ready-cut)

12 ounces (¾ pound) raw shrimp in the shell

1 cup nonfat plain yogurt

1 tablespoon cornstarch

1. Chop whole onion. Heat the oil in a nonstick skillet large enough to hold all the ingredients. Add the onion and sauté with the coriander, cumin, turmeric, and cayenne until the onion begins to brown.
2. Wash but do not peel the apples; cut into chunks. Shred the whole cabbage. Add the apples and cabbage to the onion and cook over medium heat until the apples begin to soften.
3. Peel the shrimp, stir into the skillet, and cook for 3 to 5 minutes, just until the shrimp are cooked.
4. Blend a little of the yogurt with the cornstarch, then stir the mixture into the remaining yogurt. Add the yogurt to skillet and cook, stirring, until hot.

Yield: 3 servings

Couscous with Raisins and Pine Nuts

Chicken stock or broth
1 cup whole-wheat couscous
¼ cup raisins
2 tablespoons pine nuts

1. Bring the chicken stock to a boil in a covered pot, following directions on package of couscous for the amount of liquid.
2. Stir the couscous and raisins into the boiling liquid. Turn off heat; cover and allow to sit for about 5 minutes, until the liquid is absorbed.
3. Stir in pine nuts and serve.

Yield: 3 servings

G A M E   P L A N

Prepare onion and cook with spices.

Prepare apple and cabbage and cook with onion.

Peel shrimp.

Boil stock for couscous.

Cook shrimp.

Cook couscous.

Mix yogurt with cornstarch and add to shrimp.

APPROXIMATE NUTRITION INFORMATION PER SERVING:
640 calories, 15 grams fat, 180 milligrams cholesterol,
330 milligrams sodium, 40 grams protein, 90 grams
carbohydrate

Steamed Sushi

*T*here used to be a tiny carry-out sushi counter at the back of the little fish store in my Bethesda, Maryland, neighborhood. ❧ One of the dishes, apparently created in response to concerns about parasites in raw fish, and an urge to do something different, was warm sushi. Now the sushi parlor has taken over the shop and the steamed sushi that inspired this dish has disappeared. ❧ It consisted of sushi rice—rice seasoned with mirin or sweet rice wine, rice vinegar, and a bit of sugar—plus bits of cooked seafood and vegetables, fried bean curd, egg, flying fish roe, and sesame seeds. Pickled ginger and soy sauce were the condiments. ❧ Since most of us lack easy access to fried bean curd and flying fish roe and might feel challenged to make a Japanese omelet, those ingredients are not included here, though they certainly could be. ❧ This version has far more seafood and vegetables in relation to the rice and makes a complete and filling meal.

Steamed Sushi

¾ cup long-grain rice

1 small Kirby cucumber or
⅓ an English seedless
cucumber

6 thin asparagus spears

1 tablespoon pickled ginger,
plus additional slices for
garnish

4 ounces (¼ pound) calico
or bay scallops, or sea
scallops

4 ounces (¼ pound) shelled
uncooked shrimp

3½ tablespoons mirin or dry
sherry

¼ cup rice vinegar

½ teaspoon sugar

1 tablespoon sesame seeds

1½ teaspoons reduced-
sodium soy sauce

1. Combine the rice with 1½ cups water and bring to a boil in the bottom of a steamer or in another heavy-bottomed pot large enough to hold a steamer rack and all the other ingredients to be cooked. Cover and cook for 17 minutes total, until the rice is tender and all the water has been absorbed.
2. Meanwhile wash, trim, and cut the cucumber into ⅛-inch pieces.
3. Break off the tough ends of the asparagus; cut the tips off and cut the rest of the remaining stems into ⅛-inch-thick pieces.
4. Mince enough ginger to make 1 tablespoon. Cut large scallops up into quarters and cut shrimp into bite-size pieces.
5. When the rice is cooked add 2 tablespoons mirin, 2 tablespoons rice vinegar, and the sugar, stirring well. Taste for seasoning. Stir in the scallops, shrimp, and the minced ginger. Place the rice mixture in a steamer over boiling water and steam for about 5 minutes, just until shrimp and scallops are cooked. Do not overcook or the vegetables will turn gray green.
6. Toast the sesame seeds in toaster oven.
7. Spoon the rice mixture into a serving bowl and season it with the remaining 1½ tablespoons mirin, 2 tablespoons vinegar, and with the soy sauce. Sprinkle with sesame seeds and serve with the slices of pickled ginger.

Yield: 2 servings

Food Note ❧ Mirin and pickled ginger can be found in specialty food stores and Asian markets, and even in some supermarkets.

G A M E   P L A N

Follow recipe.

APPROXIMATE NUTRITION INFORMATION PER SERVING:
450 calories, 5 grams fat, 105 milligrams cholesterol,
315 milligrams sodium, 65 grams carbohydrate, 30 grams
protein

Soft Grilled Fish Tacos | Beans Salsa

$\int$oft fish tacos are a recent trend from California. Before guffawing at the notion, try this version. ❧ When you think about it, what could be bad about swordfish with black beans and mango salsa? What's new is that everything is wrapped up in a tortilla. It's a little messy because the tortillas are so crammed, but the mess is delicious. Once you've made swordfish tacos you will want to try red snapper tacos and tuna tacos and shrimp tacos and crabmeat tacos. ❧ If you cannot find whole-wheat tortillas, use white flour tortillas. ❧ There are three elements to this meal, but it still comes in under 30 minutes.

Soft Grilled Fish Tacos

10 ounces swordfish, red
  snapper, or other
  firm-fleshed fish
1 to 2 sprigs fresh marjoram,
  to yield 1 tablespoon
  chopped, OR
  1 teaspoon dried
  marjoram
1 clove garlic
¼ cup dry white wine

1. If using the broiler, turn it on. Cover the broiler pan with aluminum foil.
2. Wash and dry the fish.
3. Wash, dry, and chop fresh marjoram; mince the garlic. Combine the marjoram and garlic with wine and pour over the fish, coating both sides.
4. If using a stove-top grill, prepare it. Broil or grill the fish following the Canadian rule: Measure the fish at its thickest part and cook a total of 8 to 10 minutes to the inch. Brush the fish with marinade a couple of times. When the fish is cooked, cut it into thin strips.

Yield: 2 servings

Beans

1 cup frozen corn kernels
1 (15-ounce) can
   no-salt-added black beans
1 small red onion, to yield
   ¼ cup chopped
1 small red pepper, to yield
   ½ cup chopped
1 jalapeño pepper
1 small bunch cilantro, to
   yield ½ cup chopped
2 tablespoons fresh lime
   juice
⅛ teaspoon salt
Freshly ground black pepper

1. Add a tablespoon or two of water to the corn and cook a couple of minutes.
2. Drain the beans and rinse thoroughly.
3. Chop the onion and red pepper; wash, seed, and mince the jalapeño.
4. Wash, dry, and chop cilantro.
5. Drain the corn and combine it with the beans, onion, red pepper, ½ of the jalapeño, ¼ cup of the chopped cilantro, and the lime juice. Season with salt and pepper. Reserve remaining jalapeño and cilantro for salsa.

Yield: 2 servings

Salsa

2 mangos
½ the minced jalapeño
   reserved from beans
¼ cup chopped cilantro
   reserved from beans
1 tablespoon fresh lime juice

1. Peel the mangos and cut the flesh into bite-size pieces.
2. Combine the mango with the reserved jalapeño and cilantro, and add the lime juice.

Yield: 2 servings

To ASSEMBLE:

4 whole-wheat tortillas
4 tablespoons light sour
   cream

1. Wrap 2 tortillas in foil and heat in toaster oven. Spread 1 tablespoon of sour cream over each of the 2 warmed tortillas. Top each with ¼ of beans; place ¼ of fish on top of the beans and top with ¼ of the salsa. Roll and serve.
2. While eating the 2 tacos, heat the remaining 2 tortillas and fill with the remaining filling ingredients.

GAME PLAN

Marinate fish.

Cook corn.

Prepare beans.

Cook fish.

Start salsa.

Heat tortillas.

Finish salsa.

Assemble tacos.

APPROXIMATE NUTRITION INFORMATION PER SERVING:
865 calories, 15 grams fat, 70 milligrams cholesterol,
835 milligrams sodium, 50 grams protein, 130 grams
carbohydrate

Chicken
and
Turkey

Chicken with Spiced Tomato Sauce | Rice Cucumber Olive Salad

*T*he use of pickling spices, more commonly found in a jar of pickles than in a sauce for chicken, is a handy way to add many different flavors to a dish quickly. Along with vinegar, the spices give the tomato sauce for this chicken dish a lift quite different from an Italian version, where oregano and basil would be more predictable. In a French dish tarragon would be the predominant seasoning, and in a Chinese version ginger and soy sauce would be the likely choices. ❧ Serve this simple and easily prepared dish over rice and with a salad of cucumbers flavored with well-seasoned olives.

Chicken with Spiced Tomato Sauce

8 ounces (½ pound) whole or 7 ounces chopped ready-cut onion (1⅔ cups)

2 teaspoons olive oil

1 clove garlic

8 ounces (½ pound) skinless, boneless chicken breast

½ teaspoon mixed pickling spices

1 cup no-salt-added chicken stock or broth

1½ tablespoons white wine vinegar

3 ounces tomato paste (½ a 6-ounce can)

Freshly ground black pepper

1. Chop whole onion. Heat the oil in a nonstick pan large enough to hold all the ingredients. Add the onion and sauté until it is soft.
2. Meanwhile mince the garlic and add to onion.
3. Wash and dry the chicken and cut it into bite-size chunks. When the onion is soft, add the chicken and brown lightly on both sides.
4. Tie the pickling spices in a little bit of cheesecloth or other porous fabric. Add the spices with the stock, vinegar, tomato paste, and pepper to taste. Reduce heat and simmer, stirring occasionally, until the chicken is cooked and the flavors are melded, 7 to 10 more minutes. If the sauce begins to stick, add a little more stock.
5. Remove and discard the bag of spices and serve the chicken and sauce over rice.

Yield: 2 servings

Food Note ✱ When I started to prepare this chicken in spiced tomato sauce I realized I had no cheesecloth in which to wrap the pickling spices. A friend who was watching and kibitzing suggested opening a tea bag and replacing the contents with the pickling spice. It turned out to be a brilliant idea. I closed the bag with a plastic-bag tie to keep the little package together.

Rice

¾ cup long-grain rice

Combine rice and 1½ cups water in a heavy-bottomed pot and bring to a boil. Reduce heat, cover, and simmer a total of 17 minutes, until liquid is absorbed and the rice is cooked.

Yield: 2 servings

Cucumber Olive Salad

2 small Kirby cucumbers
6 kalamata or other large
    Italian, French, or Greek
    black olives
1 teaspoon olive oil
1 teaspoon balsamic vinegar

1. Wash, dry, trim, and thinly slice the cucumbers; place in a serving bowl.
2. Pit and chop the olives and add to the bowl.
3. Add oil and vinegar to the salad and stir to mix well.

Yield: 2 servings

G A M E   P L A N

Cook rice.
Prepare chicken through Step 4.
Make salad.
Finish chicken and serve.

APPROXIMATE NUTRITION INFORMATION PER SERVING:
565 calories, 10 grams fat, 70 milligrams cholesterol, 270 milligrams sodium, 35 grams protein, 75 grams carbohydrate

Orange Apricot Chicken | Curried Bulgur, Corn, and Peas

*C*hicken takes very kindly to almost any flavoring because it has such a mild taste. This sweet orange-apricot marinade is equally good with any chicken part. Breasts are used here because they cook so quickly. Boneless chicken thighs—sometimes available in the market—can be substituted; they also cook quickly. They do have a little more fat than breasts, but in 4-ounce portions, the difference is not significant. ❧ Navel oranges are suggested because they peel easily. If they are not available use any eating orange.

Food Note ❧ Bulgur, or cracked wheat, is best known to Americans as tabbouleh, a cold dish of bulgur with tomatoes, parsley, mint, olive oil, and lemon juice.

But bulgur is used in dozens of Middle Eastern dishes and makes an especially nutritious alternative to recipes that ordinarily call for rice or pasta. It has an additional advantage: It cooks very quickly.

Bulgur comes in coarse, medium-fine, and fine grinds. Here, there is time enough to cook the coarse grains, which have more texture, but you can use any form of bulgur you can find.

Orange Apricot Chicken

Fresh or frozen ginger to
   yield 1 tablespoon
   coarsely grated
1- by 1-inch strip orange rind
1- by 1-inch strip lemon rind
½ cup fresh orange juice
⅓ cup apricot preserves
   sweetened with fruit juice
2 teaspoons Dijon mustard
8 ounces (½ pound) skinless,
   boneless chicken breasts
2 navel oranges
1 teaspoon olive oil

1. With the food processor running, put the ginger, orange rind, and lemon rind through the feed tube and chop fine.
2. Add the orange juice, apricot preserves, and mustard and process to mix well.
3. Wash and dry the chicken breasts and place in a small bowl; pour orange mixture over. Set aside to marinate (see Game Plan).
4. Peel and cut the oranges into small segments.
5. Heat the oil in a nonstick skillet; Remove the chicken from the marinade and brown it on both sides; add the marinade mixture and orange pieces and simmer briskly until the chicken is cooked through and the marinade has been slightly reduced.

Yield: 2 servings

Curried Bulgur, Corn, and Peas

8 ounces (½ pound) whole onion or 7 ounces chopped ready-cut onion (1⅔ cups)

2 teaspoons sesame oil

1 teaspoon curry powder

½ cup bulgur

1 cup no-salt-added chicken stock or broth

½ cup frozen peas

½ cup frozen corn kernels

1. Chop whole onion.
2. Heat the oil in a nonstick skillet or pot. Add the onion and sauté over medium-high heat until it begins to soften but not brown. Stir in the curry powder and bulgur and mix for about 30 seconds.
3. Stir in the stock; reduce heat and simmer about 10 minutes, until bulgur is cooked.
4. A few minutes before the bulgur is ready, stir in the peas and corn and cook until they are heated through and the bulgur is done.

Yield: 2 servings

G A M E   P L A N

Prepare chicken through Step 3.
Prepare bulgur through Step 3.
Prepare oranges.
Brown chicken.
Cook peas and corn.
Finish chicken.

APPROXIMATE NUTRITION INFORMATION PER SERVING:
680 calories, 10 grams fat, 65 milligrams cholesterol, 285 milligrams sodium, 40 grams protein, 115 grams carbohydrate

Hungarian Chicken with Peppers, Tomatoes, and Yogurt

Polenta

Cross-culinary dishes abound around the world, but most especially in the United States. Here, paprika and caraway give the Hungarian accent to this chicken dish that is served not with the traditional noodles but over polenta. ❧ Long, pale green Italian peppers are often recommended in Hungarian-American cookbooks. ❧ The cornstarch keeps the yogurt from separating.

Hungarian Chicken with Peppers, Tomatoes, and Yogurt

1 large clove garlic
12 ounces (¾ pound) whole onion or 11 ounces chopped ready-cut onion (2¼ to 2¾ cups)
1 tablespoon canola oil
24 ounces (1½ pounds) Italian peppers
12 ounces (¾ pound) skinless, boneless chicken breasts
1 (28-ounce) can no-salt-added crushed tomatoes
1½ teaspoons caraway seeds
2 teaspoons sugar
1½ teaspoons Hungarian sweet paprika
1 cup nonfat plain yogurt
2 teaspoons cornstarch
Freshly ground black pepper

1. With the food processor on, put the garlic through the feed tube to mince.
2. Cut whole onion into eighths; add to processor to chop; do not overprocess. If necessary, squeeze out excess liquid before sautéing.
3. Heat the oil in a nonstick skillet, add the onion and garlic, and sauté until the onion begins to brown.
4. Wash, trim, seed, and coarsely dice the peppers. Add to the onion.
5. Wash, dry, and cut the chicken into strips about ½ inch wide and add to the skillet along with the tomatoes, caraway seeds, sugar, and paprika. Cover and cook over medium heat for about 10 minutes, until the chicken is cooked and the peppers are soft.
6. Mix a little of the yogurt with the cornstarch to make a smooth paste; stir into the remaining yogurt. A minute or two before the dish is ready, stir in the yogurt mixture and cook over medium-high heat just until the sauce thickens. Season with pepper. Serve over polenta.

Yield: 3 servings

Polenta

¾ cup quick-cooking polenta
⅛ teaspoon salt (optional)

1. Bring 3½ cups water to the boil in a covered pot.
2. Slowly stir in the polenta and continue to stir until the mixture thickens. Season with salt to taste, if desired.

Yield: 3 servings

G A M E   P L A N

Prepare chicken through Step 5.

Boil water for polenta.

Mix yogurt with cornstarch and add to chicken.

Finish polenta.

APPROXIMATE NUTRITION INFORMATION PER SERVING, WITHOUT SALT: 510 calories, 10 grams fat, 65 milligrams cholesterol, 175 milligrams sodium, 40 grams protein, 70 grams carbohydrate

Pacific Rim Chicken with Greens and Mushrooms

Lemony Potatoes

*M*ost recipes that call for grilling can be done indoors on a stove-top grill. Broiling is a less satisfactory alternative method, because it does not produce that distinctive flavor that comes from cooking over an open flame.

Pacific Rim Chicken with Greens and Mushrooms

2 tablespoons minced onion

Fresh or frozen ginger, to yield 1 tablespoon coarsely grated

1 tablespoon reduced-sodium soy sauce

2 tablespoons dry sherry

¼ teaspoon ground cumin

¼ teaspoon ground cinnamon

¼ teaspoon hot pepper flakes

8 ounces (½ pound) skinless, boneless chicken breasts (2 small)

4 ounces (¼ pound) frisée or curly endive (to yield 2 cups)

4 ounces (¼ pound) bok choy (to yield 2 cups)

4 ounces (¼ pound) shiitake or ordinary white mushrooms

1½ tablespoons white wine vinegar

1. Preheat the broiler, if using. Cover broiler pan with aluminum foil.
2. Mince onion; grate the ginger and combine the onion and ginger with the soy sauce, sherry, cumin, cinnamon, and pepper flakes.
3. Wash and dry the chicken and combine with the marinade, turning to coat the meat well.
4. Prepare stove-top grill, if using. Remove the chicken from the marinade and broil or grill 10 to 15 minutes, until it is cooked through but still tender; turn occasionally. Reserve the marinade.
5. Wash and break up the frisée; wash and slice the bok choy; wash, stem, and slice the mushrooms.
6. Combine the remaining marinade with the vinegar, place it in a skillet with the frisée, bok choy, and mushrooms, and cook quickly —just a minute or two—until the greens are wilted.
7. Serve the chicken on a bed of the greens and mushrooms.

Yield: 2 servings

Lemony Potatoes

12 ounces (¾ pound) tiny
   new potatoes
½ lemon
½ medium onion
1 clove garlic
⅛ teaspoon salt (optional)

1. Scrub the potatoes and place in a pot with water to cover.
2. Cut the lemon half into 4 pieces; cut the onion into 4 pieces; crush the garlic and add these seasonings to the water. Bring the potatoes to boil in a covered pot and continue to cook at a low boil until the potatoes are tender, about 20 minutes.
3. Drain; discard seasonings, and serve, seasoned with salt, if desired.

Yield: 2 servings

G A M E   P L A N

Turn on broiler, if using.

Cook potatoes with seasonings.

Make marinade for chicken and add chicken.

Prepare stove-top grill, if using.

Grill or broil chicken.

Prepare frisée, bok choy, and mushrooms and cook.

Finish potatoes.

Finish chicken.

APPROXIMATE NUTRITION INFORMATION PER SERVING,
WITHOUT OPTIONAL SALT: 350 calories, 2 grams fat,
65 milligrams cholesterol, 260 milligrams sodium,
35 grams protein, 50 grams carbohydrate

Chinese "Carry-Out" Noodles

On a recent Saturday afternoon I had an urge for the kind of noodle dish you usually carry out from Chinese restaurants. They sometimes seem the perfect comfort food. I'm not talking about trendy, cutting-edge Asian noodles, but the old-fashioned kind you might have had in a chop suey parlor forty years ago: lots and lots of very thin or very fat noodles with bits of chicken, onion, and bok choy added. The ratio of noodles to other ingredients was about 500 to 1. ❥ To satisfy my yen, I created a slightly more expensive version, with more chicken, more onion, and more bok choy, reducing the ratio of noodles to other parts to about 50 to 1. It still hit the spot and can be put together in very short order using two pots. This version probably also has less fat but more flavor than the oilier original.

Chinese "Carry-Out" Noodles

4 ounces (¼ pound) whole onion or
   3 ounces chopped ready-cut onion
   (1 cup)
1 teaspoon canola oil
1 teaspoon Asian sesame oil
1 clove garlic
4 ounces (¼ pound) skinless, boneless
   chicken breast (about 1 small
   breast)
Fresh or frozen ginger, to yield
   1 tablespoon coarsely grated
2 large stalks bok choy (or 1 stalk
   celery)
8 ounces (½ pound) fresh angel hair
   pasta
¼ cup no-salt-added chicken stock or
   broth
2 tablespoons dry sherry
1 tablespoon reduced-sodium soy sauce
1½ tablespoons hoisin sauce
2 scallions
⅛ teaspoon salt

1. Bring water to boil in a covered pot for the pasta.
2. Chop whole onion. Heat the canola and sesame oils in a large nonstick skillet until very hot; add the onion and sauté.
3. Mince the garlic, add it to the onion, and continue cooking.
4. Wash, dry, and cut the chicken into bite-size pieces; add to the onion and continue cooking until the chicken browns.
5. Grate the ginger and add to the skillet.
6. Wash, trim, and cut the bok choy into small pieces; add to the skillet and stir.
7. Cook the pasta according to package directions.
8. Add chicken stock, sherry, soy sauce, and hoisin sauce to the skillet and stir well; reduce heat and continue cooking.
9. Wash, trim, and slice the scallions.
10. Drain the pasta and stir it into the chicken mixture until it is well coated. Season with salt. Sprinkle with scallions and serve.

Yield: 2 servings

GAME PLAN

Follow recipe.

Parmesan Chicken with Capers

Sweet Potato and Apple Purée

By the standards most of us grew up with, the proportion of meat to potatoes in this meal may seem a little backward. It calls for only about 5 ounces of chicken per person but a hefty serving of potatoes and apples. However, it reflects today's notion of a well-balanced diet. ❧ The seasoning for the sweet potatoes and apples will be determined largely by the flavor of the apples—more or less lemon juice. Crystallized ginger adds a wonderful sharp-sweet note, but ground ginger can be substituted.

Parmesan Chicken with Capers

16 ounces (1 pound) skinned and boned chicken breasts
1 teaspoon olive oil
1 clove garlic
1 ounce Parmigiano-Reggiano (⅓ cup coarsely grated)
2 teaspoons capers
¼ cup dry white wine
Freshly ground black pepper

1. Wash and dry the chicken. Heat the oil in a nonstick pan; add the chicken and sauté. Mince the garlic. When the chicken is brown on both sides, add the garlic and cook for 10 seconds.
2. Grate the cheese.
3. Rinse the capers. Add the wine, capers, and pepper to taste to the chicken; cover and simmer 8 to 10 minutes, until the chicken shows no pink at the center.
4. Sprinkle the cheese over the breasts; cover to melt the cheese, about 1 minute.

Yield: 3 servings

Sweet Potato and Apple Purée

24 ounces (1½ pounds)
   sweet potatoes
24 ounces (1½ pounds)
   full-flavored apples
Candied ginger to yield
   1 tablespoon chopped, or
   ½ teaspoon ground ginger
½ cup fresh orange juice
1 tablespoon fresh lemon
   juice
½ teaspoon ground cinnamon

1. Peel and thinly slice the potatoes; cover with water, cover the pot, and boil the potatoes until tender, 10 to 15 minutes.
2. Peel, quarter, and thinly slice the apples. Chop the crystallized ginger. Sauté the apples in 3 tablespoons orange juice and the ginger in a skillet until the apple slices are tender.
3. When the potatoes are cooked, drain and purée in a food processor with the apples, lemon juice, remaining orange juice, and cinnamon.

Yield: 3 servings

G A M E   P L A N

Prepare sweet potatoes and cook.

Prepare apples.

Brown chicken.

Prepare garlic and add to chicken.

Chop crystallized ginger.

Grate cheese.

Add wine, capers, and pepper to chicken.

Sauté apples, orange juice, and ginger for potatoes.

Add cheese to chicken and finish cooking.

Purée potatoes and apples and finish dish.

APPROXIMATE NUTRITION INFORMATION PER SERVING:
535 calories, 5 grams fat, 95 milligrams cholesterol, 325 milligrams sodium, 40 grams protein, 75 grams carbohydrate

Orange Mustard Chicken

Mashed Potatoes with Peas and Onions

*M*ashed potatoes with peas, of course. Every American has eaten them in some form. Maybe not with dill, but this updated version provides as much comfort as the more traditional version. Use new potatoes and you won't have to peel them, which saves one step. ❧ Shallots give a more distinctive flavor to the chicken than onions would, and with the garlic provide just the contrast you want with the sweetness of the orange. The soothing mashed potatoes are the perfect foil.

Orange Mustard Chicken

8 ounces (½ pound) skinless boneless chicken breasts
2 teaspoons olive oil
2 to 4 shallots, depending on size (⅓ cup minced)
1 clove garlic
1 orange
½ cup fresh orange juice
2 teaspoons honey mustard
Freshly ground black pepper

1. Wash and dry the chicken breasts and cut in half. Sauté in 1 teaspoon hot oil in a nonstick pan until brown on both sides. Set aside.
2. Mince the shallots and garlic.
3. Add the remaining teaspoon of oil to the pan and sauté the shallots and garlic until the shallots begin to brown.
4. Grate the orange rind and stir the orange juice, rind, mustard, and pepper to taste into the pan. Reduce the heat and return the chicken to pan. Cover and simmer about 5 to 7 minutes, until the chicken is cooked through. Serve topped with sauce.

Yield: 2 servings

Mashed Potatoes with Peas and Onions

16 ounces (1 pound) new
   potatoes
6 ounces whole onion or
   5 ounces chopped
   ready-cut onion (1⅓ cups)
1 teaspoon olive oil
1 cup defrosted frozen peas
½ cup nonfat plain yogurt
3 to 4 sprigs dill, to yield
   2 tablespoons chopped
¼ teaspoon salt (optional)
Freshly ground black pepper

1. Cut up the potatoes and cook in water to cover in a covered pot, about 10 minutes.
2. Chop whole onion and sauté in hot oil in a nonstick skillet until it softens and begins to brown. Stir in the peas and cook a few minutes longer, until peas are heated through.
3. When the potatoes are cooked, drain and place in the food processor with the yogurt. Process to mash.
4. Chop the dill; add the potatoes to the onion and peas in the skillet and season with dill, salt, if desired, and pepper. Mix gently and heat through.

Yield: 2 servings

G A M E P L A N

Sauté chicken breasts.

Mince shallots and garlic.

Prepare and cook potatoes.

Sauté shallots and garlic.

Chop and sauté onion.

Add peas to onion.

Finish chicken.

Finish potatoes.

APPROXIMATE NUTRITION INFORMATION PER SERVING, NOT INCLUDING SALT: 600 calories, 10 grams fat, 65 milligrams cholesterol, 510 milligrams sodium, 40 grams protein, 90 grams carbohydrate

Chicken Hunter-Style

Spaghetti

Greens with Creamy Vinaigrette

*T*he chicken cacciatore, or chicken hunter-style, of my youth had a far different flavor from the recipe below. I remember large pieces of chicken on the bone in a sauce made with whole tomatoes, lots of garlic, and lots of oil. This version calls for a good red wine, far less sauce, and boned chicken breasts without skin. It takes less time to cook and has far fewer calories due to reduced oil and the leaner chicken. This dish probably would be even better if cooked a day in advance of serving, but most of us are in too much of a hurry to think like that.

Chicken Hunter-Style

8 ounces (½ pound) whole
   onion or 7 ounces
   chopped ready-cut onion
   (1⅔ cups)
1 tablespoon olive oil
1 clove garlic
12 ounces (¾ pound)
   skinless, boneless chicken
   breasts
½ teaspoon dried oregano
Freshly ground black pepper
½ cup dry red wine
1½ tablespoons balsamic
   vinegar
3 tablespoons no-salt-added
   tomato paste
1 cup no-salt-added chicken
   stock or broth

1. Chop whole onion. Heat the oil in a nonstick skillet, and add the onion. Mince the garlic and add; cook until the onion begins to brown.
2. Add the chicken pieces and brown on both sides; remove and set chicken aside.
3. Add the oregano, black pepper, wine, vinegar, and tomato paste. Cook over high heat, stirring, until the liquid is reduced by a third.
4. Stir in the chicken stock; return the chicken pieces, reduce heat, and simmer, covered, until the chicken is cooked through, 7 to 10 minutes. Serve over spaghetti.

Yield: 2 servings

Spaghetti

8 ounces spaghetti

1. Bring 6 quarts of water to boil in a covered pot.
2. Add the spaghetti to the boiling water and cook according to the package directions. Drain and serve with sauce from chicken.

Yield: 2 servings

Greens with Creamy Vinaigrette

6 or 8 large soft lettuce
   leaves
1 small clove garlic
¼ cup nonfat plain yogurt
1 teaspoon Dijon mustard
1 teaspoon balsamic vinegar
Freshly ground black pepper

1. Wash and dry the lettuce.
2. Mince the garlic or put it through a garlic press.
3. In a bowl large enough to hold the salad, whisk together all the ingredients but the greens until smooth.
4. Tear the lettuce into small pieces, add to the dressing, and toss to coat.

Yield: 2 servings

G A M E   P L A N

Bring water to boil for pasta.

Chop whole onion and sauté with garlic.

Cut up chicken and brown.

Wash and dry salad greens.

Add seasonings, wine, vinegar, and tomato paste to chicken sauce; reduce.

Begin salad dressing.

Cook spaghetti.

Add stock and chicken to sauce; cover and simmer.

Finish salad.

Drain spaghetti and add sauce.

APPROXIMATE NUTRITION INFORMATION PER SERVING:
785 calories, 15 grams fat, 100 milligrams cholesterol,
305 milligrams sodium, 60 grams protein, 105 grams
carbohydrate

Curried Chicken with Sweet Potatoes and Vegetables

Rice

*T*he colors in this curried dish are very handsome. Adjust the level of curry powder to your personal taste; likewise the amount of lemon juice—wait until the dish is almost completed, then taste and decide how much to use.

Curried Chicken with Sweet Potatoes and Vegetables

16 ounces (1 pound) sweet
   potatoes
8 ounces (½ pound) whole
   onion or 7 ounces sliced
   ready-cut onion (1⅔ cups)
1 tablespoon canola oil
8 ounces whole red pepper or
   7 ounces sliced ready-cut
   red pepper (1½ cups)
12 ounces (¾ pound)
   boneless, skinless chicken
   breasts or thighs
1 large Granny Smith apple
10 ounces brussels sprouts
2 teaspoons cornstarch
2 to 3 teaspoons curry
   powder
1 tablespoon brown sugar
1 cup fresh orange juice
1 to 2 tablespoons fresh
   lemon juice
Freshly ground black pepper

1. Peel and cut sweet potatoes into eighths; peel and quarter whole onion. Process the potato and onion on the regular slicing blade of food processor.
2. Heat oil in a large nonstick skillet; sauté the potato and onion, stirring occasionally.
3. Wash, trim, and seed whole red pepper and cut into eighths; slice in food processor and add to skillet.
4. Cut the chicken into 1-inch squares. Push vegetables to the side of the pan and sauté chicken on both sides until brown.
5. Wash and core but do not peel the apple, and cut it into eighths; slice in the food processor. Wash and trim the brussels sprouts and cut them in half; add to the skillet.
6. Combine the cornstarch with the curry and brown sugar and stir in a little of the orange juice to make a paste. Add to the rest of orange juice; add some of the lemon juice and stir well. Stir the juice into skillet, mix ingredients well, season with pepper to taste, reduce heat, cover, and cook over low heat until the brussels sprouts are just cooked through. Taste to adjust lemon juice. Serve over rice.

Yield: 3 servings

Rice

¾ cup long-grain rice

1. Bring 1½ cups water and the rice to boil in heavy-bottomed pot.
2. Cover, reduce heat, and simmer, cooking for a total of 17 minutes, until liquid has been absorbed and rice is tender.

Yield: 3 servings

G A M E   P L A N

Cook rice.
Prepare curried chicken dish.

APPROXIMATE NUTRITION INFORMATION PER SERVING:
630 calories, 10 grams fat, 65 milligrams cholesterol, 120 milligrams sodium, 35 grams protein, 105 grams carbohydrate

Curried Chicken with Apples and Dried Cherries

Mixed Greens

*C*urries should vary, and it hardly takes a minute longer to put in your own assortment of spices to make each curry different from the last. ❧ To add a little richness to this dish of curried chicken and apples, a small amount of light sour cream is stirred into it after it has been removed from the heat. When light sour cream is combined with other pungent flavors, you cannot tell the difference between it and its full-fat counterpart.

Food Note ❧ Surprisingly, curry powder, a mix of many spices, is not native to India: the British created it from the spices they found when they ruled that subcontinent.

Curried Chicken with Apples and Dried Cherries

8 ounces skinless, boneless
   chicken breast

2 teaspoons olive oil

8 ounces whole onion or
   7 ounces chopped
   ready-cut onion
   (1⅔ cups)

4 ounces peeled carrots or
   4 ounces sliced ready-cut
   carrots

1. Wash, dry, and cut the chicken into 1-inch cubes.
2. Heat the oil very hot in a nonstick skillet and sauté the chicken over medium-high heat until it is brown on all sides; remove from the pan and set aside.
3. Chop whole onion and slice carrots; mince the garlic; sauté together in the pan used for the chicken until the onion begins to soften.
4. Wash, core, and dice the apples. Add them to the onion mixture and stir; cook for about a minute.
5. Return the chicken to the pan; add the cumin, turmeric, ginger, and coriander and stir well for a few seconds.

CONTINUED

1 clove garlic
12 ounces apples (2 to
    3 apples)
1 teaspoon cumin
½ teaspoon turmeric
½ teaspoon ground ginger
½ teaspoon ground coriander
3 tablespoons dried cherries
½ cup no-salt-added chicken
    stock or broth
1 tablespoon white wine
    vinegar
2 tablespoons light sour
    cream
⅛ teaspoon salt
Freshly ground black pepper

6. Add the cherries, stock, and vinegar and mix well; bring to a boil, then reduce heat.
7. When ready to serve, remove from heat and stir in the sour cream. Season with salt and pepper to taste.

Yield: 2 servings

Mixed Greens

4 ounces mixed green and
    red lettuce (about 4 cups
    packed)
1 teaspoon olive oil
1 teaspoon balsamic vinegar
1 teaspoon Worcestershire
    sauce

1. Wash and dry greens.
2. Whisk oil, vinegar, and Worcestershire together in a serving bowl; add lettuce and toss to combine with dressing.

Yield: 2 servings

G A M E   P L A N

Prepare chicken through Step 3.

Wash and dry lettuces.

Make salad dressing and dress salad.

Finish chicken.

APPROXIMATE NUTRITION INFORMATION PER SERVING:
435 calories, 10 grams fat, 70 milligrams cholesterol, 300 milligrams sodium, 30 grams protein, 60 grams carbohydrate

Jamaican Chicken | Raita Rice

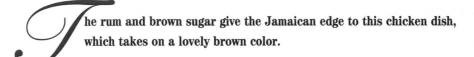

*T*he rum and brown sugar give the Jamaican edge to this chicken dish, which takes on a lovely brown color.

Food Note ❧ In Indian cooking, *raita* refers to cucumbers and yogurt with seasonings. In the side dish here, I've added many more ingredients and combined them with rice—though raita rice does not exist in India—and the dish is served at room temperature.

Jamaican Chicken

½ to 1 bunch chives, to yield
    ¼ cup chopped

1 clove garlic

1 teaspoon Worcestershire
    sauce

2 teaspoons reduced-sodium
    soy sauce

3 tablespoons golden or dark
    rum

16 ounces (1 pound)
    skinless, boneless chicken
    breasts

1 tablespoon corn or canola
    oil

2 tablespoons brown sugar

6 ounces whole onion or
    5 ounces chopped
    ready-cut onion (1⅓ cups)

1. Wash, dry, and chop the chives; mince the garlic. Combine the Worcestershire, soy, rum, chives, and garlic in a bowl.
2. Wash and dry the chicken and place in the bowl with the marinade, turning to coat both sides.
3. Heat the oil in a nonstick skillet. Add the brown sugar and cook until it is almost completely melted. Remove the chicken from the marinade, add, and brown on both sides.
4. Chop whole onion.
5. When the chicken is brown, add the marinade and onion and cook about 10 minutes longer, until the chicken is cooked through and the onions are soft.

Yield: 3 servings

Raita Rice

1 cup long-grain rice
3 Kirby cucumbers (about
    9 ounces)
5 ounces whole red bell
    pepper or 4 ounces finely
    chopped ready-cut pepper
    (1 cup)
1 slice onion, to yield
    1 tablespoon minced
10 sprigs cilantro, to yield
    2 tablespoons chopped
2 cups nonfat plain yogurt
1 tablespoon Dijon mustard
1 teaspoon ground cumin
½ cup raisins

1. Bring the rice and 2 cups water to boil in a heavy-bottomed pot. Reduce heat, cover, and simmer a total of 17 minutes.
2. Wash and trim the cucumbers, but do not peel; coarsely cube them.
3. Finely chop whole bell pepper.
4. Place the cucumbers and bell pepper in a serving bowl.
5. Mince the onion and wash, dry, and chop the cilantro; add to the serving bowl along with yogurt, mustard, cumin, and raisins.
6. When the rice is cooked, add it to the serving bowl and combine with the vegetables.

Yield: 3 servings

G A M E   P L A N

Cook rice.

Prepare and marinate chicken.

Prepare cucumbers.

Brown chicken.

Chop onion for chicken.

Prepare bell pepper for rice.

Add marinade and onion to chicken and finish cooking.

Chop onion and cilantro for rice and finish dressing.

Add rice to dressing.

APPROXIMATE NUTRITION INFORMATION PER SERVING:
710 calories, 10 grams fat, 90 milligrams cholesterol, 490 milligrams sodium, 50 grams protein, 100 grams carbohydrate

Chinese Chicken and Rotini

Broccoli di Rape

*I*s this what they mean by cross-cultural cooking? Chinese dried mushrooms, sesame oil, and soy sauce seasoning a sauce to go over Italian pasta? And to further blur the lines, the Italian vegetable known as broccoli di rape and choy sum in Chinese markets, sweetened with a bit of balsamic vinegar.

Chinese Chicken and Rotini

4 ounces (¼ pound) peeled baby carrots or 4 ounces thinly sliced ready-cut carrots (¾ to 1 cup)

8 dried Chinese mushrooms

6 ounces skinless, boneless chicken breast

2 teaspoons Asian sesame oil

¾ cup chopped scallions (1 small bunch)

8 ounces (½ pound) fresh yolkless rotini or other small pasta

2 teaspoons reduced-sodium soy sauce

3 tablespoons dry sherry

⅛ teaspoon salt

1. Bring a small amount of water to a boil in a small pot for mushrooms.
2. Thinly slice carrots.
3. Remove boiling water from heat and add mushrooms.
4. Bring water to boil for the pasta.
5. Wash, dry, and cut chicken into strips about ¼ inch thick and about 3 inches long.
6. Heat 1 teaspoon of the sesame oil in a large nonstick skillet until it is very hot.
7. Wash and trim the scallions and chop.
8. Sauté the chicken and scallions in the hot skillet until the chicken browns on both sides.
9. Cook the pasta and carrots together in boiling water according to the package directions for pasta.
10. Drain the mushrooms.
11. When the pasta is cooked, drain it and the carrots and stir into the chicken mixture along with the mushrooms. Reduce heat and add the soy, sherry, remaining teaspoon of sesame oil, and salt. Stir well to heat through and meld flavors, and serve.

Yield: 2 servings

Broccoli di Rape

16 ounces (1 pound) broccoli di rape
2 teaspoons balsamic vinegar
1 teaspoon olive oil
⅛ teaspoon hot pepper flakes

1. Wash and trim the tough stems from the broccoli di rape. Cut the remaining stems into bite-size pieces and steam over simmering water until tender, about 3 minutes.
2. In a serving bowl combine the vinegar, oil, and hot pepper flakes; when broccoli is cooked, drain and stir into serving bowl, mixing well.

Yield: 2 servings

GAME PLAN

Prepare chicken through Step 7.
Prepare broccoli di rape and cook.
Sauté chicken and scallions.
Cook pasta.
Make dressing for broccoli di rape and dress.
Finish pasta and chicken dish.

APPROXIMATE NUTRITION INFORMATION PER SERVING:
745 calories, 10 grams fat, 50 milligrams cholesterol, 695 milligrams sodium, 45 grams protein, 115 grams carbohydrate

Chicken Fajitas with Tomato Salsa and Mango

*T*he popularity of fajitas has not diminished, though it is doubtful that those who made them first would recognize their incredible modern permutations. I'm not certain you can even call this version a fajita. The store had no flour tortillas, no avocado, and no cilantro, so perhaps this recipe is simply for grilled chicken and salsa wrapped in flat bread. ❧ For the tortillas I substituted Afghan bread; for the cilantro, a bit of mint; and for the avocado, slices of mango. ❧ The result was an enticing combination of sweet, tart, tangy, and spicy wrapped in a warm, puffy bread about the thickness of a tortilla. But I much prefer cilantro to mint and recommend that as the first choice for this recipe.

Chicken Fajitas with Tomato Salsa and Mango

Juice of 2 small limes
1 teaspoon ground cumin
Freshly ground black pepper
12 ounces (¾ pound) skinless, boneless chicken breasts
½ to 1 whole jalapeño or serrano chile
1 small clove garlic
1 medium bunch fresh cilantro, to yield ½ cup chopped
8 ounces (½ pound) whole red pepper or 7 ounces chopped ready-cut pepper (1½ cups)
12 ounces (¾ pound) ripe tomatoes
1 piece Afghan bread
1 mango

1. Preheat the broiler if using. Cover the broiler pan with aluminum foil.
2. In a bowl, combine the juice from 1 lime with the cumin and black pepper.
3. Cut the chicken into ¼-inch-wide strips and combine with the lime mixture.
4. Turn on oven to 350 degrees.
5. Wash, trim, and seed the jalapeño. With the food processor running, drop the jalapeño and the garlic clove into the feed tube.
6. Wash, dry, and coarsely chop the cilantro; put through the feed tube and process briefly.
7. Wash, seed, and cut whole red pepper into chunks and put into the processor through the feed tube, processing just long enough to chop medium-coarse. Remove contents from processor bowl, squeeze to eliminate excess moisture, and spoon into a serving bowl.
8. Wash, trim, and cut the tomatoes into large chunks and process to chop coarsely; add to the red pepper mixture with the remaining lime juice. Stir to blend.
9. Prepare stove-top grill, if using. Grill or broil the chicken, turning

once; cook about 5 minutes altogether, just until the chicken is no longer pink inside.

10. Cut the bread into 5 pieces as square as possible. Wrap them in aluminum foil and warm in the oven, about 5 minutes.

11. Slice mango.

12. To serve, arrange a few pieces of chicken on a piece of bread; top with salsa and a couple of slices of mango and roll up.

Yield: 5 pieces, serves 2

G A M E   P L A N

Follow recipe.

APPROXIMATE NUTRITION INFORMATION PER SERVING:
500 calories, 5 grams fat, 100 milligrams cholesterol, 610 milligrams sodium, 50 grams protein, 70 grams carbohydrate

Middle East Chicken with Bulgur

Greens and Goat Cheese Dressing

*T*his chicken-and-bulgur dish was originally designed for entertaining. But with a few nips and tucks, it is simple enough to put together for a meal to make quickly after work. ❧ The easy, creamy salad dressing is equally good with tomatoes.

Middle East Chicken with Bulgur

4 ounces (¼ pound) whole onion or 3 ounces chopped ready-cut onion (1 cup)

1 rib celery or 2 ounces chopped ready-cut celery

2 teaspoons canola oil

8 ounces (½ pound) skinless, boneless chicken breast

1 cup bulgur

1½ cups no-salt-added chicken stock or broth

Freshly ground black pepper

2 tablespoons fresh lemon juice

6 tablespoons fresh orange juice

2 tablespoons honey

2 to 3 dashes cayenne pepper

8 small pitted prunes

1. Chop whole onion and whole celery coarsely in the food processor.
2. Heat 1 teaspoon oil until it is very hot in a nonstick pot large enough to hold the bulgur; reduce heat and add the onion and celery and sauté until the onion begins to turn golden.
3. Wash and dry the chicken breast and cut it into quarters.
4. Heat the remaining teaspoon of oil in another nonstick skillet and brown the chicken pieces on both sides.
5. When the onion is golden, stir in the bulgur and toss to coat well. Add the stock and bring to a boil. Season with pepper. Reduce heat, cover, and cook bulgur until liquid has been absorbed and bulgur is cooked, about 10 minutes.
6. Mix the lemon juice, orange juice, honey, and cayenne together. Stir into the chicken along with the prunes. Season with pepper. Cook until the chicken is done and the liquid begins to thicken slightly, 12 to 15 minutes total.
7. Spoon the bulgur into a shallow serving dish and arrange chicken and sauce over bulgur.

Yield: 2 servings

Greens and Goat Cheese Dressing

6 to 8 large, soft lettuce
    leaves
2 tablespoons fresh goat
    cheese
2 to 3 tablespoons skim milk
2 to 4 sprigs thyme,
    marjoram, or oregano,
    to yield 1 tablespoon
    chopped leaves

1. Wash and dry the lettuce and arrange on two salad plates.
2. In a small bowl mash the cheese with the milk until smooth.
3. Wash, dry, and chop the herbs and stir into the cheese mixture; drizzle over lettuce.

Yield: 2 servings

GAME PLAN

Follow directions for chicken through Step 5.

Make salad.

Finish chicken.

APPROXIMATE NUTRITION INFORMATION:
645 calories, 10 grams fat, 80 milligrams cholesterol,
245 milligrams sodium, 45 grams protein, 95 grams
carbohydrate

Chicken, Peppers, Tomatoes, and Bulgur

Sweet and Sour Cucumber Salad

*T*here are so many ways to prepare and enjoy bulgur beyond tabbouleh, the cracked wheat (bulgur) salad that makes a refreshing light summer supper or side dish. But cracked wheat is as good in hot dishes as it is in cold, and it only takes about 10 minutes to cook. ❧ Bulgur makes a happy marriage with cinnamon and cumin and as much hot pepper as you like. The simple sweet and sour cucumber salad provides a refreshing counterpoint.

Chicken, Peppers, Tomatoes, and Bulgur

10 ounces skinless, boneless
   chicken breast
1 teaspoon olive oil
8 ounces whole onion or
   7 ounces chopped
   ready-cut onion (1⅔ cups)
8 ounces long pale-green
   peppers (Italian) or red
   bell peppers
½ to 1 jalapeño pepper
1 large clove garlic
1 teaspoon ground cumin
½ teaspoon ground cinnamon
12 ounces plum tomatoes
3 tablespoons no-salt-added
   tomato paste
½ cup bulgur
1½ cups no-salt-added
   chicken stock or broth
Freshly ground black pepper

1. Wash, dry, and cut the chicken into large chunks. Heat the oil in a large nonstick skillet, add the chicken, and sauté.
2. Coarsely chop whole onion. Wash, trim, and seed the peppers and cut them into thin strips. Wash, trim, seed, and mince the jalapeño.
3. When the chicken is brown on one side, turn and brown on second side and add the onions and peppers.
4. Mince the garlic and add it with the cumin and cinnamon. When chicken is browned on the second side, remove it and set aside. Continue sautéing the vegetables about 5 minutes longer.
5. Wash, trim, and cut the tomatoes into small chunks. Add the tomatoes, tomato paste, bulgur, chicken stock, pepper, and chicken pieces. Cover and cook over medium-high heat 10 minutes, or until the liquid is absorbed and the bulgur is tender.

Yield: 2 servings

Sweet and Sour Cucumber Salad

1 teaspoon sugar
1 tablespoon apple cider
  vinegar
2 medium Kirby cucumbers,
  about 6 ounces

1. Stir the sugar into the vinegar in a serving bowl.
2. Scrub, trim, and thinly slice the cucumbers. Add to the bowl and stir well to coat.

Yield: 2 servings

G A M E   P L A N

Prepare chicken and bulgur recipe.
While bulgur cooks, prepare cucumber salad.

APPROXIMATE NUTRITION INFORMATION PER SERVING:
475 calories, 10 grams fat, 85 milligrams cholesterol,
350 milligrams sodium, 45 grams protein, 60 grams
carbohydrate

Pacific Rim Chicken Pizza

For a long time, I thought store-bought unbaked pizza crusts had no place in quick meals because of the time required to preheat an oven and then bake the crust. But I tried one more time, and found that by putting the unbaked crust directly into the oven after the oven was turned on, it would be just right after 10 minutes and that it took just a few minutes more, after the filling was added, to finish the whole process. ❧ The unusual combination of ingredients for this topping is presented with a tip of the hat to Fisher & Levy, the New York City catering company that makes a Thai chicken pizza. Their recipe inspired this version.

Pacific Rim Chicken Pizza

12-inch unbaked pizza round
4 ounces whole peeled
  carrots or 4 ounces
  ready-cut finely julienned
  carrots (1 cup)
5 ounces whole green pepper
  or 4 ounces ready-cut
  julienned green pepper
  (1 cup)
2 scallions
6 ounces skinless, boneless
  chicken breast
Fresh or frozen ginger to yield
  1 tablespoon coarsely grated
2 tablespoons mango chutney
1 tablespoon water
3 tablespoons unsalted,
  natural peanut butter
2 tablespoons dry sherry
2 tablespoons rice vinegar
¼ teaspoon hot chili oil
10 sprigs cilantro, to yield
  2 tablespoons chopped
  leaves

1. Turn on the oven to 550 degrees. Place pizza dough directly on oven rack as soon as the oven is turned on. (Do not preheat.) Bake for 10 minutes.
2. When the pizza is cooked, turn oven to broil, if using the broiler. (Cover the broiler pan with aluminum foil.)
3. Wash, trim, and finely julienne whole carrots; wash, trim, seed, and julienne whole green pepper; trim and cut the scallions into ¼-inch pieces. Steam carrots, green pepper, and scallions together for 2 minutes; drain and set aside.
4. If using stove-top grill, prepare. Grill or broil chicken, turning once, just until cooked through, about 10 minutes.
5. Coarsely grate ginger and finely chop chutney. Combine ginger and chutney with water, peanut butter, sherry, vinegar, and chili oil in a large bowl; mix well.
6. When the chicken is cooked, return oven to 550 degrees, cut chicken into fine julienne strips, and mix with the peanut dressing, carrots, green pepper, and scallions. Turn onto partially baked pizza dough, spreading evenly and close to the edges. Return to the oven, directly on a rack, and broil 4 or 5 minutes, until edges of the pizza are browning.
7. Wash, dry, and chop cilantro.
8. Remove pizza from oven; sprinkle with cilantro.

Yield: 2 servings

Follow recipe.

APPROXIMATE NUTRITION INFORMATION PER SERVING:
720 calories, 20 grams fat, 50 milligrams cholesterol,
800 milligrams sodium, 40 grams protein, 90 grams
carbohydrate

Grilled Chicken Sandwich with Orange Honey Mustard

Warm Potato and Scallion Salad

*G*rilled chicken, grilled pineapple, and grilled peaches on grilled country bread spread with honey mustard—this dish is an excuse to buy a large stove-top grill, one with enough space to cook for four or to make a dish like this chicken sandwich that has four grilled components. ❧ Without a grill? Broil ingredients instead.

Grilled Chicken Sandwich with Orange Honey Mustard

2 medium peaches
½ a small pineapple or
    4 large spears fresh
    pineapple
4 large slices country bread
1 tablespoon canola oil
8 ounces skinless, boneless
    chicken breasts
1 orange
1½ tablespoons honey
    mustard

1. Turn on the broiler, if using. Cover broiler pan with aluminum foil.
2. Wash, dry, and slice the peaches; slice the pineapple into thin spears; slice the bread. Brush the peaches, pineapple, and bread on both sides lightly with the oil.
3. Wash and dry the chicken and brush it lightly on both sides with oil.
4. Prepare stove-top grill, if using.
5. Broil or grill the chicken, turning once, just until it is cooked through, about 10 minutes total.
6. Grill or broil pineapple about 8 minutes, turning once; grill or broil the peaches and bread about 4 minutes, turning once.
7. Grate the orange rind to yield ½ teaspoon and mix it with the mustard.
8. To serve, brush the slices of bread with honey mustard; top each of 2 slices with half the chicken, pineapple, and peaches. Cover with the remaining slices, cut in half, and serve.

Yield: 2 servings

Warm Potato and Scallion Salad

16 ounces (1 pound) tiny
   new potatoes
2 teaspoons olive oil
1 tablespoon rice vinegar
1 tablespoon dry white wine
1 tablespoon mustard
2 scallions
1 or 2 sprigs fresh oregano,
   to yield 2 teaspoons
   chopped
Freshly ground black pepper

1. Scrub but do not peel the potatoes. Cook in water to cover in a covered pot 10 to 20 minutes, depending on size.
2. Whisk oil, vinegar, wine, and mustard together.
3. Wash, trim, and thinly slice the scallions. Wash, dry, and chop oregano; stir the scallions and oregano into the dressing.
4. When the potatoes are cooked, drain them, cut into halves or quarters, and mix well with the dressing. Season with pepper.

Yield: 2 servings

GAME PLAN

Turn on broiler, if using.

Cook potatoes.

Prepare fruit, bread, and chicken.

Prepare grill and grill chicken.

Begin preparation of dressing for potato salad.

Grill pineapple.

Finish potato salad dressing.

Grill peaches and bread.

Drain potatoes and add to dressing.

Grate and mix orange rind with mustard for chicken.

Finish potato salad.

APPROXIMATE NUTRITION INFORMATION PER SERVING:
850 calories, 15 grams fat, 65 milligrams cholesterol, 790 milligrams sodium, 40 grams protein, 135 grams carbohydrate

Spiced Chicken and Potatoes | Arugula and Soft Lettuce Salad

*B*orrowing a little of this and that from many different culinary cultures makes it hard to categorize this spiced chicken dish, but there is a decided Indian slant, because of all the spices. Toast flat bread (lavosh) to make it cracker-crisp to complete the meal.

Spiced Chicken and Potatoes

8 ounces (½ pound) whole onion or 7 ounces chopped ready-cut onion (1⅔ cups)

2 teaspoons canola oil

12 ounces (¾ pound) tiny new potatoes

1 teaspoon ground coriander

1 teaspoon ground cumin

¼ teaspoon ground cinnamon

½ teaspoon turmeric

⅛ teaspoon ground nutmeg

⅛ teaspoon ground cardamom

⅛ teaspoon ground cloves

8 ounces skinless, boneless chicken breasts

½ to 1 jalapeño pepper

1 (28-ounce) can chopped no-salt-added tomatoes in tomato purée

1 tablespoon dark molasses

10 sprigs cilantro, to yield 2 tablespoons chopped

1. Chop whole onion. Heat the oil in a large nonstick skillet; add the onion, and sauté for a minute or two.
2. Scrub and slice potatoes less than ¼ inch thick. Stir the potatoes and all the spices into the onion and push to one side.
3. Wash and dry the chicken and cut it into large chunks. Add the chicken to the skillet and brown on all sides.
4. Wash, trim, seed, and finely mince the jalapeño; add to the pan along with the tomatoes and molasses and stir all the ingredients together. Reduce the heat, cover, and simmer about 10 minutes, until the potatoes are cooked through.
5. Wash, dry, and chop the cilantro and sprinkle over.

Yield: 2 servings

Arugula and Soft Lettuce Salad

2 teaspoons olive oil
2 teaspoons balsamic vinegar
½ teaspoon Dijon mustard
2 ounces arugula (about
    1 cup packed)
2 ounces soft lettuce such as
    limestone or butter
    (about 1 cup packed)

1. Whisk the oil, vinegar, and mustard together in a serving bowl.
2. Thoroughly wash arugula and lettuce and dry. Toss with dressing.

Yield: 2 servings

G A M E   P L A N

Make chicken through Step 4.
Make salad.
Chop cilantro and finish chicken.

APPROXIMATE NUTRITION INFORMATION PER SERVING:
500 calories, 10 grams fat, 70 milligrams cholesterol,
200 milligrams sodium, 35 grams protein, 65 grams
carbohydrate

Chicken with Vegetables | Herbed Polenta

*C*hicken with vegetables is hardly the name of a recipe that inspires cooks to run to the kitchen, but don't be fooled. In some ways this dish resembles more interesting-sounding chicken cacciatore, except for the addition of orange flavoring and brandy; they add an interesting dimension to the other seasonings and take the edge off the sharp tomatoes.

Chicken with Vegetables

1 tablespoon olive oil

12 ounces (¾ pound) skinless, boneless chicken breast halves

8 ounces (½ pound) whole onion or 7 ounces thinly sliced ready-cut onion (1⅔ cups)

1 clove garlic

1 sprig fresh rosemary and 2 sprigs fresh thyme, to yield 1½ teaspoons each chopped leaves, or ½ teaspoon each, dried

8 ounces (½ pound) mushrooms

4 ounces (¼ pound) whole green pepper or 3 ounces ready-cut pepper cut in strips (¾ cup plus)

½ a 28- or 29-ounce can no-salt-added crushed tomatoes

½ cup dry red wine

Freshly ground black pepper

2 tablespoons brandy

2 teaspoons cornstarch

1 orange

1. Heat the oil in a large nonstick skillet. Add the chicken and brown well on both sides. Remove the chicken from the pan and set it aside.
2. Slice whole onion, mince the garlic and the fresh rosemary and thyme; add to the pan and sauté until the onion softens and begins to brown.
3. Wash, trim, and slice the mushrooms; slice whole green pepper; stir into the onions in the pan along with the tomatoes, wine, and freshly ground black pepper to taste; cover and cook a few minutes until the green pepper begins to soften.
4. Return the chicken to the pan; cover and cook about 5 minutes longer, until it is cooked through.
5. Make a smooth paste of the brandy and cornstarch and stir it into the pan. Cook about a minute, until the sauce thickens slightly.
6. Grate the peel of the orange and stir in.

Yield: 3 servings

Herbed Polenta

1 sprig fresh thyme, to yield
    1 tablespoon leaves, or
    1 teaspoon dried thyme
1 clove garlic
3 cups no-salt-added chicken
    stock or broth
⅛ teaspoon salt
¾ cup instant polenta
2 ounces Parmigiano-
    Reggiano (½ cup plus
    2 tablespoons coarsely
    grated)

1. Chop the fresh thyme; mince the garlic and add both to the stock with the salt; bring to a boil and reduce the heat to medium.
2. Slowly stir in the polenta; reduce the heat and continue stirring until the mixture thickens.
3. Grate the cheese and sprinkle it over the polenta.

Yield: 3 servings

G A M E   P L A N

Prepare chicken through Step 4.
Bring water and seasonings to boil for polenta.
Make paste of brandy and cornstarch and cook.
Finish polenta.
Grate orange rind and add to chicken.

APPROXIMATE NUTRITION INFORMATION PER SERVING:
545 calories, 15 grams fat, 80 milligrams cholesterol,
550 milligrams sodium, 40 grams protein, 50 grams
carbohydrate

Far Eastern Chicken

Rice and Broccoli with Raisins and Pine Nuts

*E*verything we like about Chinese food can be found in the purée that is spooned over the chicken breasts: heat from the chile, spiciness from the garlic and coriander seed, sweetness from the sugar and onion. The undercurrent that runs through all the other flavors is the toastiness of the sesame paste. ✸ Simply seasoned rice and broccoli is appropriate for the highly seasoned chicken, and cooking the broccoli with the rice means one less pot.

Far Eastern Chicken

6 ounces whole onion or
    5 ounces chopped
    ready-cut onion (1⅓ cups)
5 sprigs cilantro, to yield
    1 tablespoon coarsely
    chopped, plus additional
    leaves for garnish
¼ a small jalapeño pepper
    (or more to taste)
1 clove garlic
½ teaspoon ground coriander
    seed
¼ teaspoon brown sugar
1½ teaspoons reduced-
    sodium soy sauce
1½ teaspoons fresh lemon
    juice
2 teaspoons Asian sesame
    paste
12 ounces skinless, boneless
    chicken breasts

1. Turn on the broiler. Cover the broiler pan with aluminum foil.
2. Coarsely chop whole onion. Wash, dry, and coarsely chop the cilantro.
3. Wash, trim, and seed the jalapeño. With the food processor running, put ¼ of the jalapeño and the garlic through the feed tube. Add the onion, 1 tablespoon cilantro, coriander seed, brown sugar, soy, lemon juice, and sesame paste, and process to purée.
4. Arrange chicken breasts on the foil-lined broiler pan and spread purée over top of breasts.
5. Broil breasts 6 inches from the source of heat 12 to 15 minutes.
6. Garnish with the remaining cilantro leaves.

Yield: 2 servings

Rice and Broccoli with Raisins and Pine Nuts

½ cup long-grain rice

1 cup water

2 ounces chopped onion
(½ cup)

1 tablespoon canola oil

1 teaspoon ground cumin

Freshly ground black pepper

8 ounces (½ pound) whole
broccoli or 4 ounces
ready-cut broccoli florets
(1½ to 2 cups)

2 tablespoons raisins

2 tablespoons pine nuts

2 to 3 tablespoons balsamic
vinegar

1. Bring the rice to boil with the water in a heavy-bottomed pot. Cover and simmer for a total of 17 minutes.

2. Chop whole onion. Heat the oil in a small skillet. Add the onion and sauté with the cumin until the onion begins to brown; add to the rice along with the black pepper.

3. Trim whole broccoli and cut florets into bite-size pieces. About 7 minutes before the rice is done, stir in the broccoli florets, raisins, and pine nuts.

4. When rice and broccoli are cooked, stir in the vinegar to taste.

Yield: 2 servings

GAME PLAN

Cook rice.

Turn on broiler.

Combine and purée sauce ingredients for chicken.

Prepare and sauté onion and cumin for rice.

Broil chicken.

Finish rice and broccoli.

APPROXIMATE NUTRITION INFORMATION PER SERVING:
590 calories, 20 grams fat, 100 milligrams cholesterol, 290 milligrams sodium, 50 grams protein, 60 grams carbohydrate

Alice's Chicken

Warm Potato and Green Bean Salad

$\mathcal{T}$he Alice who inspired this recipe is Alice Brock of "Alice's Restaurant," Arlo Guthrie's wildly popular counterculture song that helped define the seventies antiwar movement. Years after becoming a cult hero, Alice was still a good cook and presided over her wonderful restaurant and inn in the Berkshire mountains. ❧ Use the tender French green beans called haricots verts if you can find them; they are delicious in the warm potato salad. But don't hesitate to use regular green beans. And if tiny potatoes are not available, use regular potatoes cut into cubes.

Alice's Chicken

1 clove garlic
2 tablespoons hoisin sauce
¼ cup dry sherry
2 tablespoons catsup
8 ounces skinless, boneless
    chicken breasts

1. Turn on the broiler if using. Cover broiler pan with aluminum foil.
2. Mince the garlic and combine with the hoisin, sherry, and catsup in a dish large enough to hold the chicken.
3. Wash and dry the chicken and add to the marinade, turning to coat well.
4. Prepare top-of-the-stove grill, if using. Grill or broil the chicken, turning once or twice and basting with marinade, until the chicken is cooked through, about 10 minutes. There should be no pink showing at the center of the chicken, but take care not to overcook.
5. Slice on the diagonal and serve.

Yield: 2 servings

Turkey Saté | Tangy Rice and Peppers

*S*omewhat neutral in flavor, turkey breast can be cooked in ways that keep diners from recognizing it for what it is. Occasionally it is mistaken for chicken, most of the time for veal. ❧ Here, a paste of soy sauce, brown sugar, onion, and peanut butter makes it difficult to tell that underneath it all is part of a turkey, not of a cow.

Turkey Saté

12 ounces (¾ pound)
    skinless, boneless turkey
    breast
1 clove garlic
2 tablespoons natural
    smooth peanut butter
2 slices onion, each about
    ¼ inch thick
1½ tablespoons fresh lemon
    juice
2 teaspoons reduced-sodium
    soy sauce
1 tablespoon brown sugar
Dash or two hot pepper
    sauce

1. Preheat broiler and cover the pan with aluminum foil.
2. Wash, dry, and cut the turkey breast into 2-inch cubes.
3. With the food processor running, put the garlic clove through feed tube to mince.
4. Turn off food processor and add peanut butter, onion, lemon juice, soy sauce, brown sugar, and hot pepper sauce. Process to a paste.
5. Dip the turkey pieces into the peanut butter mixture and coat well. Arrange the pieces on the broiler pan. Broil to brown on one side, about 8 minutes; turn, spoon the peanut butter mixture onto the second side if necessary, and broil until the turkey is cooked through, about 15 minutes altogether.

Yield: 2 servings

Warm Potato and Green Bean Salad

16 ounces (1 pound) tiny
new potatoes
8 ounces (½ pound) regular
green beans or French
green beans (haricots
verts)
2 to 3 ounces red onion
(½ cup chopped)
1 tablespoon olive oil
3 tablespoons balsamic
vinegar
1 tablespoon lemon juice
1 teaspoon Dijon mustard
1 teaspoon anchovy paste
Freshly ground black pepper
⅛ teaspoon salt

1. Scrub but do not peel the potatoes; cover with water and boil in a covered pot until tender, 10 to 20 minutes, depending on size.
2. Wash the green beans and trim the ends.
3. Chop the onion.
4. In a serving bowl large enough to hold the potatoes and green beans, whisk together the oil, vinegar, lemon juice, mustard, and anchovy paste; add the onion.
5. Five to 7 minutes—depending on the thickness of the beans—before the potatoes are cooked, add the green beans to the water. Cook until the beans are crisp-tender.
6. When the potatoes and beans are cooked, drain; cut the potatoes in quarters and the beans in half. Gently stir into the dressing. Season with pepper to taste and salt. Mix well and serve.

Yield: 2 servings

GAME PLAN

Turn on broiler, if using.

Cook potatoes.

Marinate chicken.

Prepare green beans.

Prepare stove-top grill; grill or broil chicken.

Start dressing for potatoes and green beans.

Add green beans to potatoes.

Baste chicken.

Finish dressing.

Drain green beans and potatoes; cut up; finish salad.

Finish chicken.

APPROXIMATE NUTRITION INFORMATION PER SERVING:
545 calories, 10 grams fat, 65 milligrams cholesterol,
565 milligrams sodium, 35 grams protein, 80 grams
carbohydrate

Tangy Rice and Peppers

½ cup long-grain rice
12 ounces (¾ pound) whole
    red, yellow, and/or orange
    peppers or 11 ounces
    diced ready-cut peppers
    (2½ cups)
12 ounces (¾ pound)
    whole onion or 11 ounces
    diced ready-cut onion
    (2½ cups)
1 large clove garlic
1 tablespoon olive oil
3 or 4 sprigs fresh oregano,
    to yield 2 tablespoons
    chopped
2 tablespoons sherry vinegar
1 tablespoon fresh lemon
    juice
Freshly ground black pepper
¼ teaspoon salt (optional)

1. Combine the rice with 1 cup of water in a heavy-bottomed pot and bring to a boil. Reduce heat, cover, and cook over low heat until the rice is tender, and water absorbed, 17 minutes total.
2. Wash, trim, seed, and dice whole pepper; dice whole onion, and mince the garlic.
3. Heat the oil in a large nonstick skillet and sauté the peppers, onion, and garlic until the onion and peppers begin to brown.
4. Wash, dry, and chop oregano. Add the oregano, vinegar, lemon juice, pepper, and salt if you wish to the onion and peppers. Stir well, add the cooked rice, and combine thoroughly.

Yield: 2 servings

GAME PLAN

Cook rice.
Prepare turkey and cook.
Finish preparations for rice dish.

APPROXIMATE NUTRITION INFORMATION PER SERVING, WITHOUT SALT: 655 calories, 20 grams fat, 105 milligrams cholesterol, 415 milligrams sodium, 50 grams protein, 70 grams carbohydrate

Turkey Apple Patties

Herbed Potato-Tomato Salad

*A*s the summer begins to wind down, there is always more than the usual urgency to take advantage of its many wonderful treasures: fragrant fresh herbs, crisp cucumbers, and the tomatoes that will not be better until next season. ❧ If you can easily find lemon basil, do try it. It adds a freshness to the potato salad quite different from the usual sweet basil.

Turkey Apple Patties

12 ounces (¾ pound)
    skinless, boneless turkey
    breast
1 medium apple (about
    6 ounces)
About 1 ounce onion (¼ cup
    chopped)
¼ teaspoon ground nutmeg
¼ teaspoon sweet Hungarian
    paprika
¼ teaspoon ground marjoram
Dash ground cloves
Freshly ground black pepper
Pan spray
3 whole-wheat burger buns
2 ripe, flavorful medium
    tomatoes
3 leaves leaf lettuce
3 tablespoons catsup

1. Grind the turkey in the food processor.
2. Wash, stem, core, and finely chop the apple and the onion in the food processor.
3. Combine the ground turkey, apple, onion, and all the spices, and gently shape into 3 patties.
4. Spray nonstick skillet with pan spray and sauté the patties until just cooked through, 10 minutes or less. Do not overcook or the burgers will be dry.
5. Meanwhile toast the buns and slice the tomatoes. Serve the burgers on the buns with tomatoes, lettuce, and catsup.

Yield: 3 turkey burgers

Herbed Potato-Tomato Salad

12 ounces (¾ pound) tiny new potatoes

1 tablespoon finely chopped red onion

4 sprigs fresh thyme, to yield 1 tablespoon chopped leaves

1 sprig fresh basil (lemon basil, if possible), to yield 1 tablespoon chopped

½ cup nonfat plain yogurt

1 tablespoon Dijon mustard

2 teaspoons white wine vinegar

1 medium Kirby cucumber

10 ounces ripe flavorful tomato (1 large)

Freshly ground black pepper

1. Scrub but do not peel the potatoes; cook in water to cover in a covered pot 10 to 20 minutes.
2. Chop the onion. Wash, dry, and chop the thyme and basil, and combine in a serving bowl with the yogurt, mustard, onion, and vinegar.
3. Scrub and trim the cucumber. Cut in half lengthwise, then crosswise into thin slices.
4. Wash, trim, and cut the tomato into small chunks. Add the cucumber and tomato to dressing.
5. When the potatoes are cooked, drain, cut in halves or quarters, and add to the bowl. Season with pepper.

Yield: 3 servings

G A M E   P L A N

Cook potatoes.
Make turkey burgers and cook.
Finish potato salad.

APPROXIMATE NUTRITION INFORMATION PER SERVING:
440 calories, 5 grams fat, 70 milligrams cholesterol, 710 milligrams sodium, 35 grams protein, 65 grams carbohydrate

Turkey with Shallot-Mushroom Sauce

Deviled Green Beans

*V*eal is expensive. Turkey breast is not and is a natural substitute. Turkey breast is available in slices, like scaloppine, or whole. Follow the recipe directions for whole turkey breast. If using the thinly sliced breast, brown the slices, remove from the pan, then cook the sauce. Return the slices to heat through.

Turkey with Shallot-Mushroom Sauce

4 large shallots

1 tablespoon olive oil

½ pound large fresh white mushrooms

½ cup reduced-fat ricotta

6 tablespoons nonfat plain yogurt

2 tablespoons apple brandy or apple cider

1½ teaspoons cornstarch

¼ cup frozen orange juice concentrate

1 tablespoon Dijon mustard

1 pound skinless, boneless turkey breast

⅛ teaspoon salt

3 to 4 sprigs parsley, to yield 1 tablespoon chopped

1. Peel the shallots and mince in the food processor.
2. Heat the oil in a nonstick skillet large enough to hold all the ingredients. Add the shallots and sauté about 1 minute, stirring occasionally.
3. Clean and trim the mushrooms and slice them in the food processor; add to the shallots and sauté until they soften.
4. Blend the ricotta and yogurt together in the food processor. Blend the apple brandy and cornstarch together to make a smooth paste. Add to the yogurt mixture along with the orange juice concentrate and mustard.
5. Remove the mushrooms and shallots from the pan and set aside.
6. Cut the turkey breast into 2- or 3-inch chunks. In the same pan brown the turkey thoroughly on all sides. Add the yogurt sauce and the mushroom-shallot mixture and continue cooking until the turkey is cooked through and the mixture has thickened. Season with salt.
7. Wash, dry, and chop the parsley; spoon the turkey mixture onto plates and sprinkle with the parsley.

Yield: 3 servings

Deviled Green Beans

10 ounces fresh green beans
2 tablespoons water
1 tablespoon balsamic
    vinegar
1 tablespoon grainy mustard

1. Wash and trim the green beans and steam 7 to 10 minutes, until tender but still firm.
2. In a serving bowl mix together the water, vinegar, and mustard.
3. When the beans are cooked, cut them in half and combine thoroughly with the dressing.

Yield: 3 servings

G A M E   P L A N

Prepare turkey vegetables and sauce through Step 4.

Prepare and cook green beans.

Make dressing for green beans.

Combine turkey and sauce and finish cooking.

Chop parsley.

Drain green beans and mix with dressing.

APPROXIMATE NUTRITION INFORMATION PER SERVING:
410 calories, 15 grams fat, 75 milligrams cholesterol,
425 milligrams sodium, 40 grams protein, 30 grams
carbohydrate

Turkey and Turkey Sausage Burritos | Peach Salsa

*U*se meat as an accent, not the centerpiece: That's the mantra for the nineties. But serving a naked little 4-ounce portion of steak or other meat to someone who has been eating 10 ounces at a sitting is not likely to make any friends or win any converts. ❧ If, on the other hand, you disguise this tiny portion of meat—turkey here, to be specific—inside a tortilla, mixed with lots of tomatoes and hot seasonings, even the 8-ounce-a-portion eater won't notice. ❧ Highly seasoned turkey sausage provides the flavoring without all the fat.

Turkey and Turkey Sausage Burritos

4 ounces (¼ pound) skinless, boneless turkey breast

4 ounces (¼ pound) low-fat turkey sausage

9 ounces whole onion or 8 ounces chopped ready-cut onion (1¾ cups)

1 large clove garlic

1 teaspoon canola oil

1 teaspoon ground cumin

½ teaspoon ground cinnamon

¼ teaspoon ground cloves

4 large (9-inch diameter) flour tortillas

2 cups canned crushed no-salt-added tomatoes

½ to 1 whole jalapeño pepper (according to taste)

2 tablespoons raisins

1 cup defrosted frozen corn niblets

1. Set oven or toaster oven to 400 degrees and heat while cooking filling.
2. Grind the turkey breast; slice the sausage in half lengthwise and then crosswise into ⅛-inch-thick pieces. Heat a nonstick skillet, add the sausage, and sauté along with the ground turkey until they begin to color; break up the ground turkey as it cooks.
3. Chop whole onion and mince the garlic.
4. Add the oil to the pan, add the onion, and sauté until it begins to soften.
5. Add the garlic, cumin, cinnamon, and cloves and sauté 30 seconds longer.
6. Wrap 2 tortillas in aluminum foil and heat in the oven or toaster oven 2 or 3 minutes, until softened.
7. Add the tomatoes to the filling; reduce the heat and simmer. Mince the jalapeño. Add the jalapeño, raisins, and corn to the skillet and cook 2 or 3 minutes or so, just until corn is heated through.
8. Spoon ¼ of the filling onto each of 2 tortillas; roll and serve.
9. Heat and fill remaining 2 tortillas when ready for seconds.

Yield: 2 servings

Peach Salsa

1 teaspoon brown sugar
1 tablespoon fresh lime juice
Fresh or frozen ginger to
    yield 1 tablespoon
    coarsely grated
Fresh cilantro, to yield
    2 tablespoons chopped
4 large ripe peaches

1. In a serving bowl stir together the brown sugar and lime juice.
2. Grate the ginger; wash, dry, and chop the cilantro; peel and slice the peaches. Add to the bowl and stir to mix well.

Yield: 2 servings

GAME PLAN

Prepare turkey through Step 4.
Mix sugar and lime juice for salsa.
Grate ginger for salsa and chop cilantro.
Cook garlic and spices for turkey.
Heat tortillas.
Finish filling for burritos.
Peel and slice peaches and finish salsa.
Stuff burritos and serve.

APPROXIMATE NUTRITION INFORMATION PER SERVING:
850 calories, 20 grams fat, 90 milligrams cholesterol, 385 milligrams sodium, 45 grams protein, 145 grams carbohydrate.

Turkey Piccata | Potatoes with Zucchini Purée

*I*n an old-style menu, there would be more turkey and less potato. In the newer, healthier style of eating, you get most of your calories from fruits, vegetables, and grains rather than from meat. Carbohydrates fill you up without adding a lot of fat to the diet.

Turkey Piccata

8 ounces (½ pound) turkey
   breast fillet
1 tablespoon flour
1 tablespoon olive oil
2 large shallots
⅓ cup dry sherry
2 tablespoons dry white wine
Dash Worcestershire sauce
1 tablespoon lemon juice
2 tablespoons capers
1 sprig parsley, to yield
   1 tablespoon chopped

1. Wash and dry turkey breast and dredge in flour.
2. Heat oil in nonstick skillet and brown turkey breast on both sides until almost cooked.
3. Chop shallots and add to pan; sauté a few seconds.
4. Reduce heat and stir in sherry, wine, and Worcestershire. Squeeze in lemon juice. Rinse capers and add. Stir to blend well. Place on platter.
5. Sprinkle with chopped parsley.

Yield: 2 servings

Potatoes with Zucchini Purée

16 ounces (1 pound) Yukon
  Gold potatoes or tiny new
  potatoes
8 ounces (½ pound) zucchini
1 small clove garlic
2 or 3 sprigs fresh oregano,
  to yield 1 tablespoon
  chopped
¼ teaspoon nutmeg
¼ teaspoon salt (optional)
Freshly ground black pepper

1. Scrub potatoes; do not peel. Cut large potatoes into bite-size chunks; leave tiny potatoes whole. Put in pot with water to cover, bring to a boil, and cook, about 7 minutes for the cut-up potatoes, 10 to 20 minutes for whole potatoes.
2. Wash and trim zucchini. Cut in half, then cut each half into 6 pieces. Steam about 5 minutes. Drain.
3. With food processor running, put garlic through feed tube to mince.
4. Add zucchini, oregano, nutmeg, salt if desired, and pepper and process to purée.
5. When potatoes are cooked, drain; cut the tiny whole potatoes into quarters. Spoon zucchini purée over potatoes and serve.

Yield: 2 servings

G A M E   P L A N

Prepare turkey through Step 1.
Prepare potatoes through Step 2.
Continue with turkey through Step 3.
Continue with potatoes through Step 4.
Finish turkey.
Finish potatoes.

APPROXIMATE NUTRITION INFORMATION PER SERVING, WITHOUT SALT: 520 calories, 10 grams fat, 65 milligrams cholesterol, 295 milligrams sodium, 35 grams protein, 65 grams carbohydrate

Orzo with Turkey Sausage and Tomatoes

*R*ather than turning up the culinary nose at all things frozen, it is far better to choose judiciously. Three frozen vegetables that are well worth having on hand: corn kernels, peas, and lima beans. ❧ With those frozen staples this meal requires only the purchase of some low-fat turkey or chicken sausages, which generally are available in most supermarkets and specialty stores (or see Mail Order, page 26). Those, too, are useful to have on hand, frozen, for a month at a time. Serve with a thick peasant bread.

Orzo with Turkey Sausage and Tomatoes

9 ounces spicy low-fat turkey or chicken sausages

4 ounces (¼ pound) whole onion or 3 ounces chopped ready-cut onion (1 cup)

1 large clove garlic

1 teaspoon olive oil

4 ounces (¼ pound) whole fresh mushrooms

1 (28-ounce) can no-salt-added crushed tomatoes

½ teaspoon hot pepper flakes, or to taste

Freshly ground black pepper

6 ounces orzo or other rice-shaped pasta

1 cup frozen peas

1 cup frozen corn kernels

1. Bring water to boil in a covered pot for orzo.
2. Place the sausages in another pot with water to cover; cover pot and boil sausages until cooked through, about 10 to 15 minutes, depending on size.
3. Chop whole onion and mince the garlic. Heat the oil in a nonstick skillet; add the onion and sauté until it begins to brown. Add the garlic.
4. Wash, trim, and chop the mushrooms. Add with the tomatoes, hot pepper flakes, and black pepper to the onion and cook over medium heat for about 5 minutes.
5. Cook orzo.
6. Stir the peas and corn into the skillet and cook 3 or 4 minutes longer.
7. Meanwhile, drain the sausages; slice thickly; add to the sauce and mix well.
8. Drain the orzo and toss with the sauce.

Yield: 3 servings

Follow recipe.

APPROXIMATE NUTRITION INFORMATION PER SERVING,
WITHOUT BREAD: 535 calories, 15 grams fat, 65 milligrams
cholesterol, 525 milligrams sodium, 30 grams protein,
75 grams carbohydrate

Fusilli with Tomatoes, Corn, and Turkey Sausage

*T*his one-dish meal is so simple there is plenty of time to cook the corn, scrape off the kernels, add them to the sauce, and still have dinner on the table in considerably less than half an hour. Again, low-fat turkey or chicken sausages make this a healthful dish. ❧ Add some good country bread and dinner is served.

Fusilli with Tomatoes, Corn, and Turkey Sausage

4 ears corn (to yield about
   1½ cups kernels)
6 ounces reduced-fat turkey
   or chicken sausages
16 ounces (1 pound) ripe,
   flavorful tomatoes
2 tablespoons tomato paste
½ cup dry white wine
¾ pound fresh fusilli or
   other small pasta
⅛ teaspoon salt (optional)
2 slices good country bread

1. Bring 3 quarts of water to boil in a covered pot for the pasta.
2. Shuck the corn and steam for 3 or 4 minutes.
3. Cut the sausages into bite-size pieces and brown in a nonstick pan 4 to 5 minutes.
4. Wash, trim, seed, and finely dice the tomatoes and add to the sausages; cook about 2 minutes.
5. Scrape the kernels from the corn.
6. Add the tomato paste and wine to the sausages and tomatoes and continue cooking for 2 minutes.
7. Cook the pasta.
8. Add the corn kernels to the sausage mixture and cook just to heat through. Season with salt, if desired.
9. Drain the pasta and serve topped with sauce.

Yield: 2 servings

Follow recipe.

APPROXIMATE NUTRITION INFORMATION PER SERVING,
INCLUDING 1 SLICE OF BREAD BUT NOT INCLUDING SALT:
905 calories, 15 grams fat, 185 milligrams cholesterol,
970 milligrams sodium, 40 grams protein, 145 grams
carbohydrate

Peppers, Potatoes, and Turkey Sausage

*E*ven sausages can fit into a healthful diet if they are used sparingly, for flavor, rather than as the centerpiece of the meal.

Peppers, Potatoes, and Turkey Sausage

20 ounces (1¼ pounds) new potatoes
1 tablespoon olive oil
16 ounces (1 pound) whole onions or 14 ounces chopped ready-cut onions (3¼ to 3½ cups)
2 large cloves garlic
16 ounces (1 pound) whole green and red peppers or 14 ounces sliced ready-cut peppers (4 cups)
8 ounces (½ pound) reduced-fat turkey or chicken sausages
32 ounces (2 pounds) ripe tomatoes
Freshly ground black pepper
3 slices Italian bread

1. Scrub but do not peel the potatoes. Slice them no more than ⅛ inch thick or less.
2. Heat the oil in a large nonstick skillet; add the potatoes and sauté.
3. While the potatoes cook, coarsely chop whole onion and thinly slice the garlic. When the potatoes begin to brown add the onions and garlic.
4. Wash, seed, and cut whole peppers into strips and add to vegetables as they cook.
5. Meanwhile cut the sausages into ½-inch pieces and sauté in a separate skillet.
6. Wash and trim the tomatoes and cut them into large chunks. When the vegetables in the pan begin to soften, add the tomatoes; cover and cook over medium heat until the mixture is soft and well blended, about 10 minutes longer.
7. Drain the sausages thoroughly on paper towels and mix into the vegetables; season with pepper to taste and allow to cook a minute or two to meld ingredients. Serve with some Italian bread.

Yield: 3 servings

GAME PLAN

Follow recipe directions.

APPROXIMATE NUTRITION INFORMATION PER SERVING WITH
1 SLICE OF BREAD: 620 calories, 15 grams fat, 60
milligrams cholesterol, 595 milligrams sodium, 30 grams
protein, 90 grams carbohydrate

Pork

Orange-Glazed Pork

Sweet and Sour Red Cabbage and Apples

*T*his dinner of pork and cabbage and apples accompanied by a slice of good crusty country bread is right in line with the recommendation to increase carbohydrates and reduce animal protein.

Orange-Glazed Pork

8 ounces (½ pound) pork tenderloin
½ teaspoon ground coriander
1 sprig fresh rosemary, to yield 1½ teaspoons chopped leaves, or ½ teaspoon dried
½ teaspoon ground ginger
¼ cup frozen orange juice concentrate
Freshly ground black pepper
2 slices crusty country bread

1. If using the broiler, turn it on and cover the broiler pan with aluminum foil.
2. Wash and dry the pork and cut into 4 equal pieces.
3. In a bowl just large enough to hold the pork, combine the coriander, rosemary, ginger, and orange juice concentrate and season with pepper. Add the pork and turn to coat well on all sides.
4. If using a stove-top grill, prepare.
5. Broil or grill the pork, basting with marinade, for about 10 to 12 minutes, until it is brown on all sides and just pink inside.

Yield: 2 servings

Sweet and Sour Red Cabbage and Apples

1 large clove garlic
12 ounces (¾ pound) whole
    red cabbage or shredded
    red cabbage
2 teaspoons Asian sesame oil
2 Granny Smith or other tart
    apples (about 1 pound)
¼ cup apple cider vinegar
1 tablespoon reduced-sodium
    soy sauce
1 tablespoon honey
½ teaspoon ground ginger
Freshly ground black pepper

1. Mince the garlic. If using the food processor to grate the cabbage, use it to mince the garlic; otherwise mince by hand.
2. Grate whole cabbage.
3. Heat the oil in a large nonstick pan and add the garlic and cabbage. Sauté over medium heat.
4. Meanwhile, wash, core, and cut the apples into bite-size chunks. Add to the cabbage mixture and stir well.
5. Add the remaining ingredients. Cover and cook over low heat until the apples are tender, about 7 minutes longer.

Yield: 2 servings

G A M E   P L A N

Prepare pork through Step 3.
Prepare cabbage through Step 3.
Finish pork.
Finish cabbage.

APPROXIMATE NUTRITION INFORMATION PER SERVING,
INCLUDING A SLICE OF BREAD: **540 calories, 10 grams fat,
80 milligrams cholesterol, 535 milligrams sodium,
35 grams protein, 85 grams carbohydrate**

Chinese Pork and Peppers | Rice Spinach and Raisins

A report in 1993 found some favorite Chinese restaurant dishes to be filled with fat. This menu shows that Chinese food can be not only low in fat, calories, and sodium, but also as full of flavor as those high-fat, high-calorie, high-sodium dishes that are unfairly giving Chinese food a bad name. ❧ It isn't large quantities of meat that give traditional Chinese food its appealing taste: It's the seasonings—the garlic, onions, sherry, ginger, soy sauce, and, in this case, hot pepper flakes. ❧ Spinach with garlic, ginger, and raisins may not be Chinese but it provides a nice counterpoint to the flavors in the pork and peppers. ❧ Serve it all over rice.

Chinese Pork and Peppers

12 ounces (¾ pound) whole onion or
   11 ounces chopped ready-cut onions
   (2 cups)
2 teaspoons canola oil
1 large clove garlic
8 ounces pork tenderloin
16 ounces (1 pound) whole red, yellow,
   and green peppers or 14 ounces
   ready-cut thinly sliced peppers
   (4 cups)
4 ounces (¼ pound) whole mushrooms
   (1 cup)
Fresh or frozen ginger, to yield
   1 tablespoon coarsely grated
⅛ to ¼ teaspoon hot pepper flakes
3 tablespoons dry sherry
1 tablespoon reduced-sodium soy sauce
2 tablespoons water
1 tablespoon cornstarch
½ cup no-salt-added beef stock or broth

1. Chop whole onion. Heat the oil in a large nonstick skillet, add the onion, and sauté.
2. Mince the garlic and add to the onion.
3. Trim the fat from the tenderloin and cut the pork into strips 2 or 3 inches long and ¼ inch wide. Add the pork to the pan and cook until brown on both sides.
4. Meanwhile wash, trim, seed, and slice whole peppers into thin strips about ¼ inch wide. Add the peppers to the pan and continue cooking over medium heat.
5. Wash, trim, and slice the mushrooms; grate the ginger, and add mushrooms, ginger, hot pepper flakes, sherry, and soy sauce to the pan; cook a few minutes longer, until mushrooms begin to soften.
6. Stir 1 tablespoon of water into the cornstarch to make a paste; stir the paste into the remaining water and mix with the beef stock; add to the pan and cook, stirring, over low heat until mixture thickens. Serve over rice.

Yield: 2 servings

Rice

¾ cup long-grain rice

1. Combine 1½ cups water with the rice and bring to a boil in a heavy-bottomed pot.
2. Reduce heat, cover, and cook a total of 17 minutes, until the rice is tender and the water has been absorbed.

Yield: 2 servings

Spinach and Raisins

16 ounces (1 pound) fresh loose spinach or 10 ounces trimmed packaged fresh spinach
1 small clove garlic
Fresh or frozen ginger, to yield 2 teaspoons coarsely grated
1 teaspoon olive oil
2 heaping tablespoons raisins

1. Wash and trim the tough stems from the loose spinach; wash packaged spinach.
2. Mince the garlic and grate the ginger. Heat the oil in a large nonstick pot. Add the garlic and ginger along with the spinach and raisins; cover, reduce heat, and cook about 2 minutes, until spinach is tender.

Yield: 2 servings

G A M E   P L A N

Cook rice.
Prepare pork through Step 5.
Prepare spinach; mince garlic; grate ginger.
Mix cornstarch and finish pork.
Cook spinach mixture.

APPROXIMATE NUTRITION INFORMATION PER SERVING:
450 calories, 15 grams fat, 80 milligrams cholesterol, 465 milligrams sodium, 35 grams protein, 50 grams carbohydrate

Pork and Papaya Salsa Burritos

Papaya Salsa

*T*hose who have been making and eating burritos for years will wonder at the strange-sounding combination of ingredients offered in this one-dish recipe. Certainly this is not a traditional filling, though the ingredients have a decided southwestern accent. And the dish meets the definition of a burrito—a warmed, soft tortilla filled and folded envelope-style. ❥ You will have much better results with 9- or 10-inch flour tortillas than with the 8-inch ones.

Food Note ❥ Always take care not to overheat yogurt or it will separate, unless it has been stabilized with cornstarch.

Pork and Papaya Salsa Burritos

4 or 5 (9- or 10-inch) flour
  tortillas
8 ounces (½ pound) whole
  onion or 7 ounces
  chopped ready-cut onion
  (1⅔ cups)
12 ounces (¾ pound) whole
  red pepper or 11 ounces
  chopped ready-cut
  peppers (3 cups)
¼ to ½ a jalapeño pepper
6 ounces pork tenderloin
1 tablespoon canola or corn
  oil
1 teaspoon ground cumin
⅛ teaspoon salt
Freshly ground black pepper
½ cup nonfat plain yogurt, at
  room temperature

1. Heat oven or toaster oven to 400 degrees. Wrap tortillas in foil and set aside.
2. Chop whole onion and red pepper and mince the jalapeño; grind the pork in the food processor.
3. Heat the oil in a nonstick skillet and add the pork, onion, red pepper, jalapeño, and cumin; stir to break the pork up into small pieces and cook until the onion is tender and the pork has lost its pink color.
4. Season with salt and pepper to taste.
5. Place the wrapped tortillas in the oven and heat 2 or 3 minutes, until soft and steaming.
6. Reduce the heat under the pork mixture to very low and stir in yogurt just long enough to mix thoroughly. Remove from heat.
7. Spoon ¼ to ⅕ of pork mixture down the center of each tortilla. Top with salsa; roll and serve.

Yield: 4 or 5 tortillas, enough for 2 very hungry people.

Papaya Salsa

1 large ripe papaya
¼ a jalapeño pepper
10 sprigs cilantro, to yield
    2 tablespoons chopped
1 teaspoon fresh lime juice

1. Cube the papaya; mince the jalapeño and chop the cilantro.
2. Combine all the ingredients well.

Yield: Enough for 4 or 5 servings

G A M E   P L A N

Follow burrito recipe through Step 5.
Make papaya salsa.
Finish burrito recipe.

APPROXIMATE NUTRITION INFORMATION PER SERVING:
640 calories, 15 grams fat, 60 milligrams cholesterol,
740 milligrams sodium, 35 grams protein, 90 grams
carbohydrate

Linguine with Prosciutto and Arugula

Warm Cauliflower Salad

*T*he recent popularity of various dishes of pasta with bitter greens probably began with broccoli di rape, the Italian bitter green that has become popular over the last five years. Such combinations have moved into mainstream American cooking, and other greens also have made their way into pasta dishes. Arugula is one; others are Swiss chard and mustard greens. ❧ Arugula, generally eaten raw in salads, takes very little cooking and in this case is just wilted. Many dishes including prosciutto often call for cooking it, but I prefer it just as it comes off the bone: It has a sweeter, more interesting flavor. ❧ The cauliflower dish is the kind that makes fans out of enemies. Careful cooking and the oil and vinegar and spices help avoid a cabbagy taste not everyone loves.

Linguine with Prosciutto and Arugula

8 ounces (½ pound) arugula
1 medium clove garlic
1 teaspoon olive oil
1½ cups no-salt-added chicken stock or broth
4 teaspoons flour
8 ounces (½ pound) fresh eggless linguine
3 ounces prosciutto
Freshly ground black pepper

1. Bring water for pasta to boil in a covered pot.
2. Wash the arugula; trim off stems and cut leaves coarsely.
3. Mince the garlic. Heat the oil in a skillet, add the garlic, and sauté for 30 seconds.
4. Add the arugula to the garlic and cook until wilted, no more than a minute or so.
5. Mix a little of the chicken stock with the flour to make a smooth paste. Stir into the remaining stock. Add to the skillet and cook, stirring occasionally, until the mixture thickens.
6. Cook the linguine according to the package directions.
7. Coarsely cut the prosciutto and stir into the sauce just before serving. Season with pepper.
8. Drain linguine and top with sauce.

Yield: 2 servings

Warm Cauliflower Salad

1 32-ounce (2-pound) head cauliflower or 16 ounces (1 pound) ready-cut florets (2 cups)
2 tablespoons balsamic vinegar
1 teaspoon olive oil
½ teaspoon turmeric
½ teaspoon ground coriander
5 sprigs cilantro, to yield 1 tablespoon chopped
⅛ teaspoon salt

1. Trim whole cauliflower and break into bite-size florets; steam for 7 to 10 minutes, until just tender or al dente.
2. In a bowl large enough to hold florets, whisk together the vinegar, oil, turmeric, and coriander.
3. Wash, dry, and chop the cilantro.
4. When the cauliflower is cooked, drain well and stir into the bowl, coating thoroughly with dressing. Sprinkle with cilantro and season with salt.

Yield: 2 servings

G A M E   P L A N

Boil water for pasta.
Prepare and cook cauliflower.
Prepare garlic and sauté.
Prepare arugula and sauté.
Prepare chicken stock and add to arugula.
Make dressing for cauliflower.
Cook linguine.
Prepare prosciutto.
Drain cauliflower and mix with dressing.
Prepare cilantro and add to cauliflower.
Finish pasta and sauce.

APPROXIMATE NUTRITION INFORMATION PER SERVING:
620 calories, 15 grams fat, 30 milligrams cholesterol, 615 milligrams sodium, 35 grams protein, 95 grams carbohydrate

Chinese Pork Tenderloin | Rice Papaya or Cantaloupe Salsa

*D*on't take the name of the pork dish too literally: The Chinese don't use rum in their cooking and are unlikely to use lime juice either. But the combination of ingredients is certainly Chinese in flavor. If you like very hot food, add more chili paste. ❧ To cool the heat, the salsa, despite its jalapeño pepper, is soothing as well as handsome. When peaches and nectarines are in season either or both may be substituted for the papaya or cantaloupe.

Chinese Pork Tenderloin

12 ounces (¾ pound) pork tenderloin

Fresh or frozen ginger, to yield 1 tablespoon coarsely grated

1 clove garlic

½ teaspoon hot Chinese chili paste

1 tablespoon hoisin sauce

1 teaspoon catsup

1 tablespoon rum

1 teaspoon reduced-sodium soy sauce

1 teaspoon fresh lime juice

½ cup no-salt-added chicken stock or broth

1. Wash and dry the pork and cut into ¾-inch-thick slices.
2. Grate the ginger, mince the garlic, and combine with the remaining ingredients in a bowl large enough to hold the pork. Add the pork and turn to coat.
3. Heat a nonstick skillet. Remove the pork from the marinade; reserve the marinade. Brown the pork slices in the skillet on both sides.
4. Add the marinade, reduce heat, cover, and simmer pork 5 to 7 minutes longer, until it is cooked through and only slightly pink at the center. Serve over rice.

Yield: 2 servings

Rice

½ cup long-grain rice
1 cup water

1. Combine the rice and water in a heavy-bottomed pot and bring to a boil.
2. Reduce heat, cover, and simmer rice until water is absorbed and rice is cooked, 17 minutes total.

Yield: 2 servings

Papaya or Cantaloupe Salsa

1 large papaya or ¼ to ½ cantaloupe, to yield 1 cup diced
¼ cup chopped red pepper, about 1 ounce (part of 1 small pepper)
About 12 sprigs fresh cilantro, to yield ¼ cup chopped
½ a small jalapeño pepper, or more
1 teaspoon olive oil
1 tablespoon fresh lime juice

1. Dice papaya or cantaloupe. Chop whole red pepper.
2. Wash, dry, and chop cilantro; wash, trim, seed, and mince jalapeño.
3. Mix all ingredients together and serve.

Yield: 2 servings

GAME PLAN

Cook rice.

Prepare pork; marinate.

Dice papaya or cantaloupe; chop red pepper.

Cook pork.

Finish salsa.

APPROXIMATE NUTRITION INFORMATION PER SERVING:
455 calories, 10 grams fat, 110 milligrams cholesterol, 700 milligrams sodium, 40 grams protein, 50 grams carbohydrate

Cumin Pork Orange Orzo and Corn

Tomatoes, Basil, and Goat Cheese

*T*here seems to be such urgency in the fall to make dishes with fresh local tomatoes and local corn before the frost gets them. At the same time the cooler weather of the fall beckons, and so does slightly heartier fare, such as pork. ❧ Patrick O'Connell, chef and co-owner of the Inn at Little Washington, Virginia, inspired this orange-flavored orzo dish, though his, served with lobster, was not only more elegant but more complex. This is the poor tired cook's quick version.

Cumin Pork

8 ounces (½ pound) pork
    tenderloin
¾ teaspoon ground cumin
⅛ to ¼ teaspoon cayenne

1. Preheat the broiler, if using. Cover broiler pan with aluminum foil.
2. Wash, dry, and cut the pork tenderloin into 4 to 6 pieces; rub all over with cumin and cayenne.
3. Prepare stove-top grill if using. Broil or grill the tenderloin pieces 5 to 7 minutes, turning once, until cooked through but still a little pink at the center.

Yield: 2 servings

Orange Orzo and Corn

¾ cup orzo
2 ears corn or 1 cup frozen
    corn kernels
Enough orange to yield
    ½ teaspoon grated rind
3 tablespoons frozen orange
    juice concentrate
1 teaspoon unsalted butter

1. Bring 2 quarts water to boil in a covered pot.
2. Add orzo and cook 9 to 11 minutes.
3. Scrape fresh corn from cobs. One minute before orzo is done, stir in fresh or frozen kernels.
4. Grate orange rind. Drain orzo and corn and return to pan; stir in orange juice concentrate, orange rind, and butter, and reheat, if necessary.

Yield: 2 servings

Tomatoes, Basil, and Goat Cheese

16 ounces (1 pound) ripe,
flavorful tomatoes
(2 medium)
2 tablespoons low-fat goat
cheese
4 or 5 leaves fresh basil

1. Wash, trim, and slice each tomato into 4 slices. Arrange 4 slices on each of 2 salad plates and place half the goat cheese in the center of each plate.
2. Wash, dry, and cut basil into strips; sprinkle over tomatoes.

Yield: 2 servings

G A M E   P L A N

Preheat broiler, if using.

Boil water for orzo.

Prepare pork.

Prepare fresh corn; measure frozen corn.

Cook orzo.

Prepare stove-top grill.

Broil or grill pork.

Prepare tomatoes and basil.

Add corn to orzo.

Finish tomato salad with cheese.

Finish orzo and corn.

APPROXIMATE NUTRITION INFORMATION PER SERVING:
620 calories, 10 grams fat, 90 milligrams cholesterol,
110 milligrams sodium, 40 grams protein, 90 grams
carbohydrate

Grilled Pork Tenderloin | Potatoes with Citrus and Herbs

*T*his comes with thanks to Yuca Restaurant in Miami for a fresh and sparkling way to serve pork. Some liberties have been taken with the recipe and I've changed a side dish (yuca, the vegetable) to potatoes. Certainly anyone who is familiar with yuca will find the seasonings superb with it, too.

Grilled Pork Tenderloin

5 to 10 sprigs fresh oregano, to yield ⅓ cup chopped oregano, tightly packed

15 sprigs cilantro, to yield ⅓ cup chopped cilantro, tightly packed

2 ounces onion, to yield ⅓ cup chopped

2 small eating oranges

⅓ cup fresh orange juice

Juice of 1 lime

Freshly ground black pepper

1 teaspoon olive oil

10 ounces pork tenderloin, trimmed of fat and cut crosswise into about 6 pieces

½ bunch arugula or watercress

1. If using the broiler, preheat and cover the broiler pan with aluminum foil.
2. Wash and dry oregano and cilantro. With food processor running, put oregano and cilantro through the feed tube and process until finely chopped. Measure.
3. Put the onion through the feed tube and process until chopped. Measure. Return to processor with oregano and cilantro.
4. Grate and add the rind from the oranges along with the orange and lime juices, pepper to taste, and olive oil, and process to blend well.
5. Transfer the marinade to a bowl large enough to hold the pork. Trim pork and cut crosswise into about 6 pieces; add to marinade and turn to coat well. Set aside until ready to cook.
6. If using top-of-the-stove grill, prepare it. Remove the pork from the marinade. To cook the meat, lightly oil the grill and arrange the pork on the broiler or grill. Cook until brown on one side, basting with marinade. Turn; baste again and brown on second side, cooking only until the meat is still slightly pink at the center, about 10 minutes altogether.
7. Wash and dry the arugula or watercress; trim off stems and make a bed of it on each plate. Peel the oranges and break them into sections. Arrange the orange sections and pork slices on the bed of greens, leaving room for the potatoes.

Yield: 2 servings

Potatoes with Citrus and Herbs

16 ounces (1 pound) new
    potatoes
4 ounces (¼ pound) whole
    onion or 3 ounces thinly
    sliced onion (1 cup)
1 teaspoon olive oil
1 clove garlic
Bunch parsley, to yield
    ⅓ cup chopped parsley,
    tightly packed
5 to 10 sprigs oregano, to
    yield ⅓ cup chopped
    oregano, tightly packed
¾ cup fresh orange juice
1 tablespoon lemon juice
1 tablespoon fresh lime juice
Freshly ground black pepper

1. Scrub but do not peel the potatoes; slice with the slicing blade of the food processor. In a covered pot bring the potatoes to a boil in enough water to cover and cook until they are tender, about 10 minutes.
2. Thinly slice whole onion. Heat the oil in a nonstick pan. Add the onion. Mince the garlic. When the onion begins to brown, add the garlic and cook a minute more.
3. Wash and dry the parsley and oregano. With the food processor running, put the parsley and oregano through the feed tube to chop. Measure. Add the herbs to the onion, along with the orange, lemon, and lime juices and pepper to taste. Cook over high heat until the mixture is boiling and has reduced slightly.
4. When the potatoes are cooked, drain, stir into the onion-citrus mixture, and combine well.

Yield: 2 servings

G A M E   P L A N

If using broiler, preheat.

Cook potatoes.

Make marinade for pork and marinate.

Prepare and cook onion for potatoes.

Prepare and process parsley and oregano for potatoes.

If using stove-top grill, prepare; grill pork.

Prepare arugula.

Cook parsley, oregano, and juices with onion.

Prepare oranges.

Turn pork.

Finish potatoes.

Arrange pork and oranges on dinner plates; add potatoes.

APPROXIMATE NUTRITION INFORMATION PER SERVING:
575 calories, 10 grams fat, 90 milligrams cholesterol,
120 milligrams sodium, 40 grams protein, 85 grams
carbohydrate

Barbecued Pork

Rotini and Vegetables with Tahini Sauce

*S*mall pasta shapes can be combined with bite-size pieces of vegetables to create an almost endless variety of dishes. Any number of sauces can become part of the scheme, though those that are tomato-based are most common. ❧ The vegetables in this version are familiar enough, though the sauce is not. It calls for tahini or sesame paste—ground sesame seeds. In traditional cooking, tahini is usually mixed with lemon juice, but here balsamic vinegar is used, providing a sharp and slightly sweet contrast to the richness of the tahini. Cumin reinforces the Middle Eastern accent, and completes a cross-cultural dish.

Barbecued Pork

1 teaspoon oil

Fresh or frozen ginger, to
    yield 1 tablespoon

1 tablespoon sherry vinegar

1 teaspoon reduced-sodium
    soy sauce

8 ounces (½ pound) pork
    tenderloin

1. If using the broiler, preheat. Cover the broiler pan with double thickness of aluminum foil and lightly coat with oil.
2. Grate the ginger coarsely and combine in a dish large enough to hold the meat with the vinegar and soy.
3. Wash and trim the fat from the pork; cut into 3 pieces, making the thin end longer than the middle and the other end. Coat the pieces with the marinade and allow to marinate until it is time to cook the meat.
4. If using top-of-the-stove grill, prepare it. Cook the meat, turning once, allowing about 10 minutes for the thin tail end and 15 minutes for the rest; the meat should still be slightly pink at the center when done.

Yield: 2 servings

Rotini and Vegetables with Tahini Sauce

4 ounces (¼ pound) peeled baby carrots or 4 ounces ready-cut carrot slices (¾ to 1 cup)

16 ounces (1 pound) whole broccoli or 8 ounces ready-cut broccoli florets (3½ to 4 cups)

1 clove garlic

3 tablespoons toasted sesame tahini

3 tablespoons balsamic vinegar

1 teaspoon ground cumin

6 tablespoons water

8 ounces (½ pound) fresh rotini or other small shaped pasta

3 scallions

⅛ teaspoon salt (optional)

Freshly ground black pepper

1. Bring water to boil in a covered pot for the pasta.
2. Cut whole carrots into thirds and steam about 10 minutes before adding broccoli.
3. Cut whole broccoli into bite-size florets.
4. Press the garlic through a press, or mince, and combine in a serving bowl with the tahini, vinegar, cumin, and water.
5. Add the broccoli to the carrots and steam about 5 minutes longer.
6. Cook the pasta according to package directions.
7. When the carrots and broccoli are cooked, drain and add to the tahini mixture.
8. Wash, trim, and thinly slice the scallions.
9. When the pasta is cooked, drain and stir into the vegetables. Stir in the scallions. Season with salt if desired and pepper to taste. (If the mixture is too thick, add more water by the tablespoon.)

Yield: 2 servings

GAME PLAN

Bring water to boil for pasta.

Turn on broiler, if using.

Prepare marinade and marinate pork.

Prepare carrots and steam; prepare broccoli.

Prepare stove-top grill if using: broil or grill pork.

Finish rotini, carrot, and broccoli dish.

APPROXIMATE NUTRITIONAL ANALYSIS PER SERVING, WITHOUT SALT: 735 calories, 15 grams fat, 80 milligrams cholesterol, 460 milligrams sodium, 50 grams protein, 110 grams carbohydrate

Spiced Pork Tenderloin

Sweet Potatoes and Apples in Apple Cider

*F*or the pork you will need whole coriander seeds and whole cumin. Ground spices won't do because they are too fine to make a coating for the pork tenderloin. ❧ To accompany this rather untraditional flavor for the pork, an otherwise very traditional sweet potato and apple dish that omits the fat. It will take less than 20 minutes to put this fall menu together.

Spiced Pork Tenderloin

1 tablespoon whole cumin
   seeds
1 tablespoon whole coriander
   seeds
1 medium clove garlic
1-inch piece fresh or frozen
   ginger
8 ounce (½ pound) pork
   tenderloin

1. Turn on the broiler. Cover the broiler pan with a double thickness of aluminum foil.
2. Turn on the food processor; put the cumin, coriander, garlic, and ginger through the feed tube, and process to chop the garlic and ginger fine and the spices coarsely.
3. Wash and dry the tenderloin and remove excess fat. Pat both sides with the spice mixture and arrange on the broiler pan. Place the broiler pan about 3 inches from the source of heat. Broil until the pork browns on one side; turn and continue broiling until meat is still slightly pink at the center, a total of 15 to 18 minutes.

Yield: 2 servings

Sweet Potatoes and Apples in Apple Cider

16 ounces (1 pound) sweet
   potatoes
16 ounces (1 pound) tart
   apples
½ cup apple cider
⅓ cup dried cranberries or
   dried cherries
⅛ teaspoon salt

1. Peel the sweet potatoes and cut into slices about ⅛ inch thick. Place in a pot with water to cover; cover and bring to a boil. Cook potatoes about 10 minutes, until they are soft.
2. Wash and quarter the apples; remove cores and slice the apples, using a food processor.
3. Place the apples, apple cider, and dried fruit in a pot; cover and cook until the apples soften, about 5 minutes.
4. When the potatoes are cooked, drain and stir gently into apples; continue cooking over low heat until pork is ready. Season with salt and serve.

Yield: 2 servings

GAME PLAN

Turn on broiler.

Prepare and cook sweet potatoes.

Prepare pork.

Broil pork.

Prepare and cook apples.

Finish sweet potatoes and apples.

APPROXIMATE NUTRITION INFORMATION PER SERVING:
585 calories, 5 grams fat, 80 milligrams cholesterol, 220 milligrams sodium, 30 grams protein, 110 grams carbohydrate

Vinegared Pork and Peppers over Potatoes

Arugula and Pear Salad

*T*he flavor of this pork and peppers dish is quite similar to the famous French dish of chicken cooked in vinegar. ❥ You might expect to serve the pork and peppers over noodles, but the potatoes here absorb the delicious flavors completely. ❥ For the salad, the slight bitterness of arugula is especially good with the sweetness of a fully ripe pear.

Vinegared Pork and Peppers over Potatoes

12 ounces (¾ pound) tiny
    new potatoes
8 ounces (½ pound) pork
    tenderloin
2 teaspoons olive oil
8 ounces (½ pound) whole
    onion or 7 ounces
    julienned ready-cut onion
    (1⅔ cups)
16 ounces (1 pound) whole
    green and red peppers or
    14 ounces julienned
    ready-cut peppers
    (4 cups)
2 tablespoons balsamic
    vinegar
¼ teaspoon salt

1. Scrub the potatoes but do not peel. Boil in water to cover in a covered pot 10 to 20 minutes.
2. Cut the pork crosswise into 4 equal pieces and pat dry with paper towels. Heat 1 teaspoon of the oil in a nonstick pan, add the pork, and brown on all sides, cooking until almost done, about 5 minutes.
3. Cut whole onions and peppers into eighths. Slice in the food processor. Remove the browned pork from the pan and set it aside; add the remaining 1 teaspoon oil to the pan, along with the onions and peppers, and cook over medium-high heat until they soften, about 5 minutes.
4. Stir in the vinegar, return the pork to the pan, and cook another minute or two.
5. Drain the potatoes and place in a shallow serving dish; mash coarsely and season to taste with salt; spoon the pork and vegetables over the potatoes.

Yield: 2 servings

Arugula and Pear Salad

2 teaspoons olive oil
2 teaspoons sherry wine
    vinegar
4 ounces arugula (about
    2 cups)
½ of one large ripe pear

1. Whisk the oil and vinegar in a serving bowl.
2. Wash the arugula and trim the stems; dry and add to the bowl.
3. Wash and dry the pear, cut into small cubes, and toss with the arugula and dressing.

Yield: 2 servings

GAME PLAN

Cook potatoes.

Brown pork.

Cut onion and peppers.

Set meat aside; sauté vegetables.

Prepare salad.

Add pork and vinegar to vegetables and continue cooking.

Drain potatoes; mash coarsely; top with pork and vegetables.

APPROXIMATE NUTRITION INFORMATION PER SERVING:
550 calories, 15 grams fat, 80 milligrams cholesterol,
370 milligrams sodium, 30 grams protein, 75 grams
carbohydrate

Couscous Pork and Apricots | Arugula with Raspberry Vinaigrette

*L*ess than ten years ago Americans learned that couscous could be used in something besides the eponymous Moroccan dish that took hours to prepare and cook. The reason was simple: Instant couscous—a tiny semolina grain—that is ready in 5 minutes arrived on the scene. Today, couscous is another pasta in the American culinary arsenal that can be substituted for rice, for other small pasta, for bulgur, for buckwheat groats. ❧ A few years ago another form of quick-cooking couscous made its debut in health-food stores—whole-wheat couscous, even better because it cooks just as quickly and provides the fiber missing from regular couscous. ❧ This recipe has its origins in Middle European cooking, where the combination of long-cooking dishes of meat and fruit is quite common. This version, pork with fruits, is filled with flavor despite the fact that it is ready in less than 30 minutes. ❧ For salad my favorite, arugula, is suggested, but any mix of baby greens will be just as good with the raspberry vinaigrette.

Couscous Pork and Apricots

8 ounces (½ pound) whole onion or 7 ounces ready-cut chopped onion (1⅔ cups)

2 teaspoons olive oil

8 ounces (½ pound) mushrooms, white, wild, or assorted

8 ounces (½ pound) pork tenderloin

1 lemon

1 orange

10 dried apricots

1. Chop whole onion. Heat the olive oil in a nonstick pan over high heat until it is very hot. Reduce heat to medium-high; add the onions and sauté until they begin to brown.

2. Meanwhile, clean, trim, and slice the mushrooms; add them to the onion as it cooks.

3. Wash, dry, and cut the pork into small cubes; add to onion and mushrooms as they cook, and stir to brown on all sides.

4. Following the package directions, bring water to boil for the couscous.

5. Finely grate the lemon and orange rinds; cut up the apricots.

6. Add the couscous to the boiling water along with the lemon and orange rinds; turn off heat, cover the pot, and allow the couscous to sit until the water has been absorbed, about 5 minutes.

CONTINUED

1 cup whole-wheat couscous
1 teaspoon ground cumin
¼ teaspoon hot red pepper
    flakes
2 tablespoons no-salt-added
    tomato paste
¾ cup fresh orange juice
1 sprig parsley, to yield
    1 tablespoon chopped
¼ teaspoon salt

7. Add the cumin and red pepper flakes to the pork mixture and stir well. Stir in the apricots, tomato paste, and orange juice; reduce heat to low and continue cooking.
8. Wash, dry, and mince parsley.
9. Stir the cooked couscous into the pork mixture; season with salt and sprinkle with parsley.

Yield: 2 servings

Arugula with Raspberry Vinaigrette

1 bunch arugula, about
    4 ounces (about 2 cups)
2 teaspoons raspberry
    vinegar
2 teaspoons walnut oil

1. Wash, trim, and dry arugula.
2. Whisk together the vinegar and oil in a salad bowl; toss with the arugula.

Yield: 2 servings

GAME PLAN

Prepare pork through Step 3.

Prepare arugula.

Continue pork preparation through Step 7.

Finish salad.

Finish pork.

APPROXIMATE NUTRITION INFORMATION PER SERVING:
805 calories, 15 grams fat, 80 milligrams cholesterol, 390 milligrams sodium, 45 grams protein, 120 grams carbohydrate

Lamb

Grilled Lamb
and Potato
Salad

*T*his meal in a dish derives its interest from the sharp flavors of the mustard and cornichons. But cornichons—French pickled gherkins—may not be available on every block. Try a smaller amount of capers instead if you cannot find the cornichons. ❧ If you are serious about lean lamb, use meat from a boneless leg and trim off the fat. ❧ The meal is complete with some good, dense bread with a substantial crust.

Grilled Lamb and Potato Salad

20 ounces (1¼ pounds) very
    small new potatoes
12 ounces (¾ pound)
    boneless lean lamb
1 sprig rosemary, to yield
    1 tablespoon leaves
¼ cup cornichons
1 sprig parsley, to yield
    2 tablespoons minced
4 ounces (¼ pound) whole
    red onion or 3 ounces
    chopped ready-cut onion
    (1 cup)
1 tablespoon olive oil
¼ cup balsamic vinegar
1 tablespoon Dijon mustard
Freshly ground black pepper
12 to 16 cherry tomatoes
½ head Boston lettuce or
    1 head Bibb lettuce

1. Preheat the broiler if using. Cover the broiler pan with aluminum foil.
2. Scrub but do not peel the potatoes and cook in water to cover in a covered pot 10 to 20 minutes, depending on size.
3. Trim the fat from the lamb. If using a stove-top grill, prepare. Grill or broil lamb, turning once, for 7 to 10 minutes altogether, depending on its thickness and the desired degree of doneness.
4. Remove rosemary leaves, finely cut the cornichons, mince the parsley, and finely chop onion.
5. In a serving bowl beat the oil with the vinegar and mustard. Stir in the rosemary, cornichons, parsley, and onion.
6. When the potatoes are cooked, drain, cut in halves or quarters, and add to the dressing; cut the grilled lamb into bite-size pieces and add. Season with pepper. Mound in the center of a large plate or platter.
7. Wash and dry the tomatoes and lettuce. Tuck the lettuce around the edges of the salad and arrange the tomatoes around the perimeter. Serve warm.

Yield: 3 servings

Follow recipe.

APPROXIMATE NUTRITION INFORMATION PER SERVING, WITHOUT BREAD: 465 calories, 15 grams fat, 80 milligrams cholesterol, 380 milligrams sodium, 30 grams protein, 55 grams carbohydrate

Grilled Lamb with Peppers and Onions

Cook some onions and peppers together and you have the beginnings of an Italian meal. But add black beans, jalapeño, and cilantro, and the dish becomes Southwestern. Served with strips of grilled lamb and a piece of crusty bread, the meal is complete.

Grilled Lamb with Peppers and Onions

8 ounces (½ pound) whole
onion or 7 ounces
julienned ready-cut onion
(1⅔ cups)

2 teaspoons olive oil

1 clove garlic

14 ounces whole red and
yellow bell peppers or
12 ounces (¾ pound)
julienned ready-cut
peppers (3 cups)

½ to 1 jalapeño pepper

8 ounces (½ pound) boneless
leg of lamb

1 cup canned no-salt-added
black beans

¼ teaspoon salt

Freshly ground black pepper

2 tablespoons chopped
cilantro

2 slices dense crusty bread

1. Heat the broiler, if using. Cover the broiler pan with aluminum foil.
2. Cut whole onion into julienne strips and sauté in the hot oil in a nonstick pan.
3. Mince the garlic and add to the onion.
4. Wash, trim, seed, and julienne whole bell peppers, and add to the onion.
5. Wash, trim, seed, and mince the jalapeño, and add to the vegetables.
6. Wash, dry, and trim the lamb and cut into inch-wide slices about ¼ inch thick. Prepare stove-top grill if using. Grill or broil lamb just until pink, about 5 minutes.
7. Drain and rinse the black beans. Stir into the vegetables with salt and pepper to taste, and cook a couple of minutes.
8. Wash, dry, and chop the cilantro. Arrange the vegetables on plates and top with strips of lamb. Sprinkle with cilantro, and serve with bread.

Yield: 2 servings

Follow recipe.

APPROXIMATE NUTRITION INFORMATION PER SERVING,
INCLUDING BREAD: 415 calories, 10 grams fat,
60 milligrams cholesterol, 655 milligrams sodium,
30 grams protein, 50 grams carbohydrate

Pitas Stuffed with Lamb Salad

Lemon Broccoli

"A little lamb goes a long way" should be the subtitle of the lamb recipe here. ❧ If you make this dish when tomatoes are not in season, you will have to substitute red cherry tomatoes or the tiny pear-shaped yellows. ❧ If your produce market, like most, rarely has ready-ripe avocados available, plan this menu in advance and get the avocado a few days ahead of time.

Pitas Stuffed with Lamb Salad

8 ounces (½ pound) lean boneless leg of lamb
2 teaspoons olive oil
2 teaspoons balsamic vinegar
2 ounces red pepper (½ cup sliced)
½ small avocado
10 cherry tomatoes or tiny pear-shaped tomatoes
8 medium Greek, Italian, or French olives
2 scallions
4 medium-size pitas

1. If using the broiler, turn it on and line the pan with aluminum foil.
2. Remove all excess fat from the lamb and cut it into 4 pieces.
3. If using top-of-the-stove grill, prepare.
4. Broil or grill the lamb until it is medium-rare.
5. Meanwhile beat the oil and vinegar in a bowl large enough to hold all the ingredients except the pitas.
6. Wash, core, seed, and thinly slice the red pepper. Peel and cut the avocado into small slices; wash and halve the tomatoes. Rinse, pit, and halve olives. Wash, trim, and thinly slice the scallions. Add the vegetables to the oil and vinegar.
7. Toast the pitas.
8. When the lamb is cooked, cut it into strips and mix with the ingredients in the bowl. Serve the filling in the pitas.

Yield: 2 servings

Lemon Broccoli

16 ounces (1 pound) whole
   broccoli or 8 ounces
   florets (3½ to 4 cups)
1 medium lemon

1. Remove the tough stems from whole broccoli; cut the tops into florets. Place broccoli florets in a steamer. Grate the lemon rind directly onto the broccoli.
2. Steam the broccoli over simmering water 5 to 7 minutes, until tender but still bright green.

Yield: 2 servings

GAME PLAN

Prepare lamb filling through Step 6.
Prepare broccoli and lemon and steam.
Finish lamb and pita recipe.

APPROXIMATE NUTRITION INFORMATION PER SERVING:
610 calories, 20 grams fat, 55 milligrams cholesterol,
885 milligrams sodium, 35 grams protein, 75 grams
carbohydrate

Lamb Chili | Greens and Vinaigrette

*L*amb chili probably sounds like a dish for deepest winter, but in the nineties it's not nearly as heavy as traditional chili recipes of the past. The amount of meat is greatly reduced: The emphasis is on the tomatoes, beans, and other vegetables. Today's chili is, in fact, more like poor people's chili of long ago, when meat was an expensive treat for the affluent. ❧ A salad with a sharp vinaigrette will stand up to the spiciness of the chili.

Lamb Chili

16 ounces (1 pound) whole onion or 14 ounces chopped ready-cut onion (3 to 3½ cups onion)
2 teaspoons olive oil
8 ounces (½ pound) lean lamb cut from the leg
1 jalapeño pepper
1 large clove garlic
4 ounces whole green pepper or 3 ounces chopped ready-cut green pepper (¾ cup)
1 teaspoon ground cumin
½ teaspoon ground coriander
½ teaspoon ground ginger
16 ounces (1 pound) ripe plum tomatoes
1 cup no-salt-added beef stock or bouillon
15- or 16-ounce can no-salt-added kidney beans
⅛ teaspoon salt
Freshly ground black pepper

1. Chop the whole onion in a food processor; squeeze out excess liquid. Heat the oil in a large nonstick pan, add the onion, and sauté until it begins to soften but not brown.
2. Trim the lamb of all fat and grind coarsely in the food processor. Add to the onion and cook until the meat browns.
3. Cut the jalapeño in half and seed. With the food processor running, put the jalapeño half and the garlic through the feed tube to mince.
4. Wash, trim, seed, and cut up whole green pepper and process by pulsing. (If the pepper throws off much liquid, squeeze it before adding to meat.) Add processor contents to the meat.
5. Stir in the cumin, coriander, and ginger; reduce heat to a simmer.
6. Wash the tomatoes, trim and halve; coarsely chop in the food processor and add to the meat along with the beef stock; cook over medium-high heat.
7. Rinse the beans thoroughly, drain and add to the meat; stir well and cook to heat through.
8. Season with salt and pepper to taste.

Yield: 2 servings

Greens and Vinaigrette

4 ounces assorted salad
    greens (about 4 cups
    packed)
2 teaspoons olive oil
1 tablespoon balsamic
    vinegar
1 teaspoon Dijon mustard

1. Wash and dry the greens.
2. Whisk together the oil, vinegar, and mustard in a salad bowl; toss in the greens.

Yield: 2 servings

G A M E   P L A N

Prepare chili through Step 6.

Begin salad.

Finish chili.

Finish salad.

APPROXIMATE NUTRITION INFORMATION PER SERVING:
580 calories, 15 grams fat, 60 milligrams cholesterol,
590 milligrams sodium, 40 grams protein, 70 grams
carbohydrate

Grilled Lamb | Potatoes, Pepper, and Tomato Salad

A Chinese-style marinade is good not only for lamb but for pork and beef as well; it penetrates small cuts of any meat quickly. ❧ Potato salad always goes well with grilled meats, and the version offered here is filled with brightly colored vegetables that take advantage of the middle of summer. If local tomatoes at their peak are not available, use cherry or pear tomatoes instead.

Grilled Lamb

8 ounces (½ pound) boneless leg of lamb

Fresh or frozen ginger, to yield 1 tablespoon coarsely grated

1 clove garlic

1 teaspoon brown sugar

1 tablespoon reduced-sodium soy sauce

1 teaspoon ground coriander

1. If using the broiler, turn it on. Cover the broiler pan with aluminum foil.
2. Wash and trim lamb.
3. Grate the ginger and mince the garlic. Mix with brown sugar, soy sauce, and coriander in a dish deep and large enough to hold the lamb. Add the lamb and set aside to marinate.
4. If using top-of-the-stove grill, prepare it. Grill or broil lamb about 10 minutes, basting with marinade occasionally.

Yield: 2 servings

Potatoes, Pepper, and Tomato Salad

16 ounces (1 pound) tiny
new potatoes
8 ounces (½ pound) whole
red peppers or 7 ounces
chopped ready-cut
peppers (1½ cups)
8 ounces (½ pound) ripe
tomatoes
8 oil-cured black olives
1 or 2 sprigs oregano, to
yield 1 tablespoon
chopped
1 tablespoon olive oil
2 tablespoons balsamic
vinegar
⅛ teaspoon salt (optional)
Freshly ground black pepper

1. Scrub but do not peel the potatoes; cover with water and cook in a covered pot until tender, 10 to 20 minutes, depending on their size.
2. Wash, trim, seed, and cut whole peppers into julienne strips and then cut strips into quarters; place in a serving bowl.
3. Wash, trim, and dice the tomatoes and add to peppers.
4. Pit and cut up the olives; add to the bowl.
5. Wash, dry, and chop oregano and add to bowl.
6. Stir in oil and vinegar.
7. When potatoes are cooked, drain and cut into small dice; stir into the bowl and mix well to coat with dressing. Season with salt, if desired, and pepper.

Yield: 2 servings

G A M E   P L A N

Turn on broiler, if using.

Cook potatoes.

Marinate lamb.

Make potato salad through Step 3.

If using top-of-the-stove grill, prepare; broil or grill lamb.

Finish potato salad.

APPROXIMATE NUTRITION INFORMATION PER SERVING,
WITHOUT SALT: 515 calories, 15 grams fat, 55 milligrams
cholesterol, 430 milligrams sodium, 25 grams protein,
70 grams carbohydrate

Lamb with Orange and Prunes

Couscous Lemony Brussels Sprouts

*T*his recipe was tested on someone who, like many Americans, has never been fond of meat and fruit in combination, but it made him a convert. The sauce is all-purpose and will taste as good with chicken or duck or pork as it does with lamb. ❧ If your butcher won't sell you a small quantity of lamb, buy a whole boneless leg; cut it into suitable portions and freeze what you are not using. The North African accent of this dish makes couscous the appropriate grain, but rice would be fine, too. ❧ Finish the dinner off with some steamed Brussels sprouts that have been seasoned with plenty of lemon juice.

Lamb with Orange and Prunes

8 ounces (½ pound) boneless leg of lamb

1 teaspoon olive oil

12 ounces (¾ pound) whole onion or 11 ounces sliced ready-cut onion (2¼ to 2½ cups)

1 large clove garlic

⅓ cup pitted prunes

Fresh or frozen ginger, to yield 1 tablespoon coarsely grated

Orange, to yield 1 teaspoon finely grated orange peel

¼ teaspoon cinnamon

⅛ teaspoon ground allspice

1 cup fresh orange juice

Freshly ground black pepper

1. Trim all fat from the lamb and cut into ¼-inch-thick strips. Heat the oil in a nonstick skillet. Place the lamb strips in the hot oil to brown on one side.
2. Slice whole onion; chop the garlic.
3. Turn meat and brown on second side; add the onion and garlic. Sauté until the onion begins to brown and soften.
4. Chop the prunes coarsely; grate ginger coarsely; finely grate orange peel, and add with cinnamon, allspice, orange juice, and black pepper to the meat. Continue cooking over low heat until the mixture has thickened slightly; this will take just a few minutes. Serve over couscous.

Yield: 2 servings

Couscous

½ cup quick-cooking
   whole-wheat couscous

1. Following package directions, bring water to boil.
2. Stir in couscous; cover and immediately remove from heat. Allow to sit 5 minutes or until water is completely absorbed.

Yield: 2 servings

Lemony Brussels Sprouts

10 ounces Brussels sprouts
Juice of ½ lemon or more

1. Trim the Brussels sprouts and steam about 7 to 10 minutes over boiling water in a steamer.
2. Drain and spoon into a serving bowl; sprinkle with lemon juice.

Yield: 2 servings

G A M E   P L A N

Cook lamb, onions, and garlic.
Prepare brussels sprouts.
Boil water for couscous.
Prepare prunes and ginger.
Cook brussels sprouts.
Cook couscous.
Finish lamb.

APPROXIMATE NUTRITION INFORMATION PER SERVING:
575 calories, 10 grams fat, 55 milligrams cholesterol, 90 milligrams sodium, 30 grams protein, 95 grams carbohydrate

Lamb, Lima, and Potato Stew | Tangy Cauliflower

*S*tews always conjure up hearty, steaming dishes with lots of inexpensive meat that has to be cooked for a long time. In the lighter, late-twentieth-century version, the meat is neither stringy and tough nor cheap and fat. ❧ The emphasis in the lamb, lima, and potato stew here is on the vegetables. There is enough lamb to add texture and flavor but it is more accent than star. For this quick dish it is ground, but you will have to grind it yourself, choosing the leanest cut you can find, like leg, and trimming it very well. ❧ The accompanying dish of cauliflower finds its verve in the quick sauce made of anchovy paste, lime juice, and a touch of balsamic vinegar. The touch of olive oil softens the edge.

Lamb, Lima, and Potato Stew

12 ounces (¾ pound) whole onion or 11 ounces chopped ready-cut onion (2¼ to 2¾ cups)
2 teaspoons canola oil
1 large clove garlic
8 ounces (½ pound) lean lamb
9 ounces small new potatoes
⅛ to ¼ teaspoon hot pepper flakes
2 cups canned no-salt-added crushed tomatoes
1½ cups frozen baby lima beans
1 cup dry red wine
⅛ teaspoon salt
Freshly ground black pepper

1. Chop whole onion and sauté in very hot oil in a nonstick skillet.
2. Mince the garlic and add to the onion.
3. Trim and grind the lamb.
4. Scrub but do not peel the potatoes; slice in the food processor. If they are not small, the potatoes should be quartered before slicing.
5. When the onions begin to take on color, add the lamb, breaking it up to keep it from clumping, and the potatoes. Stir well and cook over medium heat until the lamb is browned.
6. Stir in the hot pepper flakes, tomatoes, lima beans, and wine; cover and continue to cook until the potatoes are done, 5 to 7 minutes longer. Season with salt and pepper to taste.

Yield: 3 servings

Tangy Cauliflower

48 ounces (3 pounds) whole
  cauliflower or 24 ounces
  (1½ pounds) ready-cut
  cauliflorets (7 to 8 cups)
2 teaspoons balsamic vinegar
2 teaspoons anchovy paste
2 teaspoons fresh lime juice
2 teaspoons olive oil

1. Trim whole cauliflower and steam florets over simmering water for 5 to 7 minutes.
2. In a serving bowl mix together the vinegar, anchovy paste, lime juice, and oil.
3. When the cauliflower is cooked, drain and stir into dressing, mixing well but carefully to coat.

Yield: 3 servings

G A M E   P L A N

Prepare lamb dish through Step 5.

Prepare cauliflower and steam.

Add remaining ingredients to lamb dish and continue cooking.

Make dressing for cauliflower.

Drain cauliflower and dress.

APPROXIMATE NUTRITION INFORMATION PER SERVING:
505 calories, 10 grams fat, 40 milligrams cholesterol,
245 milligrams sodium, 30 grams protein, 65 grams
carbohydrate

Lamb with Red Wine and Dried Cherries

Mushroom Caponata

*T*his recipe for lamb with red wine and cherries calls only for a small part of a leg of lamb. So it is bound to prompt the question, What can I do with the rest of the leg? ❧ You can try to find a butcher who will sell you a half pound of leg of lamb, but often that isn't possible. If you have to buy a whole or a half leg, ask the butcher to cut it into 8-ounce portions and freeze what you don't use for other lamb dishes. ❧ To freeze, wrap each portion separately in plastic wrap or wax paper and then in aluminum foil to keep the meat from getting freezer burn. That small a portion will defrost overnight in the refrigerator. In some places, lamb steaks, which are thick, cross-cut slices from the leg, can be found in the meat case—they are just about the right weight for this and other recipes. ❧ It isn't always easy to find dried cherries. So when you do, lay in a supply; they keep as well as raisins, and their tart-sweetness adds a nice dimension to the grilled lamb. ❧ The idea for the caponata made with mushrooms instead of eggplant comes from Le Relais du Parc, Joel Robuchon's bistro in Paris. There, the mushrooms were small enough to be cooked whole. If you can find such small ones, they provide the most appealing texture for the dish. Otherwise, cut up larger ones.

Lamb with Red Wine and Dried Cherries

8 ounces (½ pound) boneless
  leg of lamb
1 large clove garlic
½ cup dry red wine
3 tablespoons dried cherries
Freshly ground black pepper

1. If using a broiler, turn it on. Cover the broiler pan with aluminum foil.
2. Wash, dry, and remove the excess fat from the lamb. Cut the meat into ¼-inch-thick slices.
3. Mash the garlic and combine with the wine in a bowl large enough to hold the lamb. Add the lamb and turn it to coat it. Allow the lamb to marinate until time to cook, or at least 10 minutes.
4. If using a stove-top grill, prepare it. Remove the lamb from the marinade, reserving the marinade; broil or grill until the lamb is brown on both sides and pink inside, 7 to 10 minutes total.
5. Pour the marinade into a small pan, add the cherries, and boil until the liquid is reduced by half. When the lamb is cooked, combine it with the cherry mixture, season with pepper, and serve.

Yield: 2 servings

Mushroom Caponata

9 ounces whole onion or
  8 ounces chopped ready-
  cut onion (1¾ cups)
1 tablespoon olive oil
8 ounces (½ pound) whole
  green pepper or 7 ounces
  chopped ready-cut pepper
  (1½ cups)
1 pound (16 ounces)
  mushrooms
6 large Greek olives
1 teaspoon dried oregano
1 teaspoon sugar
3 tablespoons tomato paste
2 tablespoons water
1 tablespoon balsamic
  vinegar
⅛ teaspoon salt (optional)
Freshly ground black pepper

1. Chop the whole onion.
2. Heat the oil in a nonstick skillet and sauté the onion.
3. Meanwhile, wash, trim, and seed whole green pepper; chop, and add to the onion.
4. Wash, trim, and chop the mushrooms and add to the skillet. Cover and simmer over medium-high heat about 2 minutes.
5. Pit and chop the olives and add to the vegetables along with the oregano, sugar, tomato paste, water, vinegar, salt (if you wish), and pepper to taste. Reduce the heat to a simmer, cover, and continue cooking another few minutes, until flavors are blended.

Yield: 2 servings

GAME PLAN

Turn on broiler, if using.

Marinate lamb.

Make caponata through Step 3.

Prepare stove-top grill, if using; grill or broil lamb.

Prepare and cook mushrooms.

Add cherries to lamb marinade and reduce.

Finish caponata.

Finish lamb.

APPROXIMATE NUTRITION INFORMATION PER SERVING, WITHOUT SALT: 460 calories, 20 grams fat, 80 milligrams cholesterol, 205 milligrams sodium, 35 grams protein, 45 grams carbohydrate

Beef

Spaghetti and Meat Sauce | Arugula and Radicchio Salad

*T*he difference between this spaghetti and meat sauce recipe and my mother's is that it has half the meat and twice the garlic. And it doesn't cook as long, 15 minutes instead of an hour. There's no question that it would be even better if it were simmered for an hour, but it is certainly a reasonable facsimile. The recipe yields enough for four servings, so a family of two will have an opportunity to taste it when it is even better—the second night. And, of course, it can be doubled and kept frozen. ❧ For extra-lean ground beef buy flank steak and grind it yourself. ❧ To accompany this old-fashioned dish there is a new-fashioned salad with arugula and radicchio. Double it if you are serving four at one time.

Spaghetti and Meat Sauce

8 ounces (½ pound)
   extra-lean ground beef
12 ounces (¾ pound) whole
   onion or 11 ounces
   chopped ready-cut onion
   (2½ cups)
2 cloves garlic
1 (28-ounce) can chopped
   no-salt-added tomatoes
2 (6-ounce) cans
   no-salt-added tomato
   paste
1 teaspoon dried basil
1 teaspoon dried oregano
1 teaspoon sugar
16 ounces (1 pound)
   spaghetti

1. Bring water to boil in a covered pot for the spaghetti.
2. Brown the beef in a nonstick skillet.
3. Chop whole onion, mince the garlic, and add both to the pan with the beef; continue to brown beef and cook onion until onion softens.
4. Stir in the tomatoes, breaking them up between your fingers while adding; add the tomato paste, basil, oregano, and sugar to the skillet. Cook over medium heat at a simmer; adjust the heat accordingly.
5. When the water boils, add the spaghetti and cook according to package directions. When the spaghetti is ready, the sauce will be also. Drain the spaghetti and serve with sauce.

Yield: 4 servings

Arugula and Radicchio Salad

4 leaves radicchio

3 ounces arugula (about
   1½ cups)

2 teaspoons olive oil

2 teaspoons balsamic vinegar

1. Wash and dry the radicchio and arugula; trim stems off arugula.
2. In a salad bowl, whisk oil and vinegar together, and toss with the salad greens to coat them well.

Yield: 2 servings

G A M E P L A N

Prepare spaghetti and sauce.

While spaghetti cooks, prepare salad.

APPROXIMATE NUTRITION INFORMATION PER SERVING:
735 calories, 15 grams fat, 35 milligrams cholesterol,
140 milligrams sodium, 35 grams protein, 120 grams
carbohydrate

Singapore Noodles | Gingery Cucumbers

*T*his dish is a low-fat version of a recipe Germaine Swanson, who owns Germaine's in Washington, D.C., gave me years ago. Her Singapore noodles called for copious quantities of oil. For this version, the oil has been reduced considerably. Intense flavor is provided by ginger, garlic, coriander, cumin, and hot pepper flakes. If you cannot find Vietnamese or Thai rice noodles, use fresh eggless fettuccine. A cucumber salad offers a cooling contrast.

Singapore Noodles

Fresh or frozen ginger, to
    yield 1 tablespoon
    coarsely grated
1 large clove garlic
8 ounces (½ pound) whole
    peeled carrots or 8 ounces
    chopped ready-cut carrots
    (about 1½ cups)
3 large leeks
8 ounces (½ pound) flank
    steak
1 teaspoon canola oil
½ teaspoon ground coriander
¼ to ½ teaspoon hot pepper
    flakes
1 teaspoon ground cumin
8 ounces (½ pound) rice
    noodles
1 tablespoon cornstarch
1 cup no-salt-added beef
    stock or broth

1. Bring water to boil in a covered pot for the noodles.
2. With the food processor on, put the ginger and garlic through the feed tube to mince; remove and set aside.
3. Cut whole carrots in quarters. Trim the green part from leeks. Thoroughly wash the white part of leeks, and put the carrots and leeks in the food processor. Chop fine by pulsing.
4. Cut the beef against the grain into thin slices.
5. Heat the oil in a nonstick skillet; sauté ginger and garlic for a few seconds. Add coriander, hot pepper flakes, and cumin, and stir-fry a few seconds. Remove and set aside.
6. Add the beef to the skillet and brown on both sides; add the carrots and leeks and sauté a minute or two.
7. Cook the noodles.
8. Mix the cornstarch with a little beef stock and then combine with the remainder of the stock to make a smooth mixture. Add to the skillet with reserved seasonings. Cook over medium heat until the mixture thickens.
9. Drain noodles and stir in.

Yield: 2 servings

Gingery Cucumbers

2 medium-size Kirby
    cucumbers
Fresh or frozen ginger, to
    yield 1 teaspoon coarsely
    grated
2 teaspoons apple cider
    vinegar
½ teaspoon sugar
¼ teaspoon sesame oil

1. Scrub and trim the cucumbers, but do not peel. Slice thinly.
2. Chop or grate the ginger and place in a serving bowl with the vinegar, sugar, and sesame oil. Stir in the cucumbers.

Yield: 2 servings

GAME PLAN

Prepare noodle sauce through Step 4.

Begin salad.

Continue with noodles and sauce through Step 8.

Finish salad.

Finish noodles.

APPROXIMATE NUTRITION INFORMATION PER SERVING:
965 calories, 15 grams fat, 65 milligrams cholesterol,
195 milligrams sodium, 30 grams protein, 150 grams
carbohydrate

Uncovered Empanadas | Orange and Fennel Salad

*T*he strange name for this main dish comes from its origins. Since quick meals preclude dough-making or empanada-baking, this dish includes a filling similar to what is found in some empanadas, but omits the wrapping. ❧ If you want very lean ground beef, buy a very lean beef cut like flank steak and grind it yourself.

Uncovered Empanadas

6 ounces very lean ground beef

12 ounces (¾ pound) new potatoes

8 ounces (½ pound) whole onion or 7 ounces chopped ready-cut onion (1⅔ cups)

1 clove garlic

6 large Greek, Italian, or French olives

1 cup dry red wine

2 tablespoons balsamic vinegar

¼ cup raisins

1 cup frozen corn kernels

⅛ to ¼ teaspoon hot pepper flakes

½ teaspoon ground cumin

Freshly ground black pepper

¼ teaspoon salt (optional)

1. Brown the beef in a nonstick skillet and stir to break up. Push the beef to one side and drain off any excess fat.
2. Scrub but do not peel the potatoes and cut into ¼-inch cubes. Cook potatoes in water to cover in a covered pot just until tender, 5 to 7 minutes.
3. Chop whole onion; mince the garlic and add the onion and garlic to the skillet with the beef; cook until the onion begins to soften and take on some color.
4. Rinse, pit, and cut up the olives. Stir them into beef mixture with the wine, vinegar, raisins, corn, hot pepper flakes, cumin, pepper, and optional salt. Bring to a boil and cook at a high simmer.
5. When the potatoes are cooked, drain and stir into the beef mixture. Cook until all but a tablespoon or two of the liquid has evaporated.

Yield: 2 servings

Orange and Fennel Salad

1 large eating orange
4 ounces (¼ pound) fennel
   (about 1 cup thinly
   sliced)
1 tablespoon fresh orange
   juice
1 teaspoon balsamic vinegar

1. Using a sharp knife, peel the orange and remove the pith. Cut the orange into small chunks and place in a serving bowl.
2. Wash, dry, and trim the fennel. Slice the bulb very thinly and combine with the orange.
3. Toss with the orange juice and vinegar and serve.

Yield: 2 servings

GAME PLAN

Prepare empanada filling through Step 4.

Begin preparation of salad.

When potatoes are cooked, stir into empanada mixture.

Finish salad.

APPROXIMATE NUTRITION INFORMATION PER SERVING, WITHOUT SALT: 595 calories, 10 grams fat, 55 milligrams cholesterol, 550 milligrams sodium, 25 grams protein, 100 grams carbohydrate

Bulgur and Beef | Spinach and Apple Salad

*T*o cut down on fat, ground turkey breast is combined with lean ground beef in this dish. To make certain that it has plenty of zip, use imported olives. Most California black olives are big but lack flavor. ❧ A salad of spinach and apples is served with the bulgur and beef. The apples add a pleasing sweet accent to the slight bitterness of the spinach.

Bulgur and Beef

12 ounces (¾ pound) whole onion or 11 ounces chopped ready-cut onion (2 to 2¼ cups)

1 teaspoon olive oil

1 large clove garlic

8 mushrooms

4 ounces (¼ pound) lean beef

4 ounces (¼ pound) turkey breast meat

6 large Italian, Greek, or French olives

2 cups canned no-salt-added tomatoes

½ cup bulgur (cracked wheat)

¼ cup dry sherry

½ teaspoon dried oregano

⅛ teaspoon salt (optional)

Freshly ground black pepper

1. Chop whole onion, and sauté it in a nonstick skillet in hot oil until it begins to soften.
2. Meanwhile, mince the garlic and add it to the onion.
3. Wash, dry, trim, and dice the mushrooms.
4. Trim the beef and grind it and the turkey in the food processor. When the onion has begun to soften, stir in the meat, and keep stirring to break up; cook until the meat loses its color.
5. Rinse the olives, pit, and cut up. Crush the tomatoes, and add olives, tomatoes, mushrooms, bulgur, sherry, and oregano to the skillet. Reduce the heat; cover and simmer about 10 minutes, until the bulgur is cooked.
6. When the bulgur is cooked, season with salt, if desired, and pepper to taste.

Yield: 2 servings

Spinach and Apple Salad

4 ounces fresh spinach
   (about 4 cups)
1 small tart apple
1 tablespoon olive oil
1 teaspoon fresh lemon juice
2 teaspoons white wine
   vinegar
Freshly ground black pepper

1. Wash the spinach and remove the tough stems; break into bite-size pieces.
2. Wash but do not peel the apple, and cut it into thin strips.
3. In a serving bowl, whisk together the oil, lemon juice, and vinegar; add the spinach and apple and toss thoroughly to coat well. Season with pepper to taste.

Yield: 2 servings

GAME PLAN

Prepare beef through Step 5.
Prepare salad.
Finish beef.

APPROXIMATE NUTRITION INFORMATION PER SERVING, WITHOUT ADDED SALT: 580 calories, 20 grams fat, 80 milligrams cholesterol, 255 milligrams sodium, 35 grams protein, 65 grams carbohydrate

Bulgur, Bow Ties with Mushrooms, and Beef

Sherried Brussels Sprouts

The origins of a recipe calling for bulgur and bow tie pasta are found in a well-known Jewish side dish called kasha varnishkes that calls for buckwheat groats, or kasha, and the bow ties. It is traditionally served with brisket, with the gravy from the meat poured liberally over the starches. ❥ While bulgur does not have the same nutty flavor as buckwheat groats, it has a similar texture and marries well with the bow tie egg noodles. By adding a number of other ingredients, one can produce a main dish instead of a side; the only thing lacking from the menu would be a green vegetable. ❥ Hearty food like this calls for a wintery vegetable such as Brussels sprouts. Instead of just steaming them, I have mixed them with a little oil and with sherry vinegar, which moderates the cabbagy quality of the Brussels sprouts and may well turn haters into lovers. Other vinegars can be used, but the sherry vinegar works particularly well. ❥ To save a pot, steam the Brussels sprouts in the same pot as the bow ties are cooking.

Bulgur, Bow Ties with Mushrooms, and Beef

8 ounces (½ pound) whole onion or 7 ounces chopped ready-cut onion (1⅔ cups)

2 teaspoons Asian sesame oil

1 clove garlic

½ cup bulgur

8 ounces (½ pound) extra-lean beef

6 ounces white mushrooms or assorted wild mushrooms

1. Bring water to a boil for the bow tie noodles in a covered pot.
2. Chop whole onion; sauté in very hot oil in a nonstick pan until it begins to brown.
3. Mince the garlic and add to the onion.
4. In a saucepan, combine the bulgur with 1 cup water and cook over high heat until the water boils; cover and cook until the water has been absorbed and the bulgur is tender, about 15 minutes.
5. Grind the beef and stir it into the onion, breaking the beef up and cooking until brown.
6. Meanwhile, wash, trim, dry, and slice the mushrooms; add to the beef and onions.

CONTINUED

2 cups bow tie noodles

2 tablespoons no-salt-added tomato paste

½ cup no-salt-added chicken stock or broth

¼ cup dry red wine

¼ teaspoon salt

Freshly ground black pepper

7. Cook bow tie noodles according to package directions.
8. Add tomato paste, chicken stock, and wine to the beef mixture. Cook over very low heat.
9. Drain bow ties; drain any liquid left in bulgur. Stir bulgur and bow ties into beef mixture; season with salt and pepper to taste and serve.

Yield: 3 servings

Sherried Brussels Sprouts

15 ounces Brussels sprouts

2 teaspoons olive oil

2 teaspoons sherry vinegar

1. Wash and trim Brussels sprouts.
2. Place in a steamer basket and place the basket in the pot in which the bow ties are cooking. Cook Brussels sprouts about 7 minutes, until they are tender but firm. Remove and drain.
3. Whisk together the oil and vinegar in a serving dish; add the sprouts and stir gently to coat.

Yield: 3 servings

G A M E   P L A N

Prepare beef and bow ties through Step 7.

Prepare brussels sprouts and steam.

Do Step 8 in beef recipe.

Make dressing for sprouts.

Finish beef recipe.

Drain sprouts and mix with dressing.

APPROXIMATE NUTRITION INFORMATION PER SERVING:
675 calories, 20 grams fat, 50 milligrams cholesterol, 295 milligrams sodium, 35 grams protein, 95 grams carbohydrate

New-Fangled Beef and Vegetables

Rice Steamed Asparagus

*N*ew-fangled beef and vegetables illustrates the concept of meat as an accent rather than the center of the meal. In this Chinese-style menu, each serving has just 3 ounces of beef, a far cry from the 1-pound sirloin that some steak houses still serve. This dish is so filled with flavor you will never miss more meat.

New-Fangled Beef and Vegetables

2 teaspoons cornstarch

1 tablespoon reduced-sodium soy sauce

1 tablespoon dry sherry

6 ounces flank steak

13 ounces whole green and red peppers or 12 ounces (¾ pound) ready-cut peppers, cut in strips (2¼ to 2½ cups)

2 teaspoons canola oil

6 ounces mushrooms

6 ounces whole zucchini or 6 ounces sliced ready-cut zucchini (1⅓ cups)

Fresh or frozen ginger, to yield 1 tablespoon coarsely grated

1 large clove garlic

¼ teaspoon hot red pepper flakes

1 tablespoon red wine vinegar

1 tablespoon water

1 tablespoon sugar

1. Combine 1 teaspoon cornstarch with ½ tablespoon soy sauce in a bowl large enough to hold the beef, and stir to blend. Stir in ½ tablespoon sherry.
2. Thinly slice the beef across the grain into strips. Combine the meat with the cornstarch mixture to coat; set aside.
3. Wash, core, and seed whole peppers and cut into strips.
4. Heat the oil in a large nonstick skillet; add the pepper strips and cook about 2 minutes.
5. Wash, trim, dry, and thinly slice the mushrooms. Wash, trim, and slice whole zucchini.
6. Add the mushrooms and zucchini to the peppers and continue cooking another minute or two.
7. Grate the ginger, mince the garlic, and add them with the hot pepper flakes to the vegetables. Cover and cook 2 more minutes, just until the vegetables begin to soften.
8. Mix the remaining 1 teaspoon of cornstarch with the remaining ½ tablespoon soy and stir to blend. Stir in the remaining ½ tablespoon sherry, the vinegar, water, and sugar and set aside.
9. Push the vegetables to one side of the pan, and then add the beef, cooking until it is brown on both sides. Stir in the reserved sauce mixture, combine the vegetables with the beef, cover, and continue cooking a few minutes longer, until the beef is done—do not overcook. Serve over rice.

Yield: 2 servings

Rice

½ cup long-grain rice

1. Combine 1 cup water with rice and bring to boil in a heavy-bottomed pot.
2. Reduce heat; cover, and simmer, cooking a total of 17 minutes, until rice is cooked and liquid has been absorbed.

Yield: 2 servings

Steamed Asparagus

16 asparagus spears

1. Wash and trim asparagus by breaking at the point where the tough stems meet the tender upper part; discard tough stems.
2. Steam over hot water 5 to 7 minutes, depending on the thickness of the stems.

Yield: 2 servings

GAME PLAN

Cook rice.

Make cornstarch mixture; slice beef and add.

Prepare peppers and cook.

Prepare and cook asparagus.

Prepare mushrooms and zucchini and cook.

Grate ginger and add to vegetables with garlic and pepper flakes.

Make beef sauce.

Add beef to vegetables; stir in sauce and finish cooking.

APPROXIMATE NUTRITION INFORMATION PER SERVING:
500 calories, 15 grams fat, 40 milligrams cholesterol,
380 milligrams sodium, 30 grams protein, 70 grams
carbohydrate

Steak and Potatoes Our Way, with Salad

*T*t's a dinner from the past: 1 pound of sirloin, baked potato wrapped in aluminum foil and topped with sour cream, and a lettuce and tomato salad with blue cheese dressing. If you still long for such a meal, this menu may not be quite what you had in mind, but you may still like the results. ❧ Here we have a little flank steak, a lot of potatoes, and a salad of arugula, the dressing for which comes right from a jar—two jars, actually, of marinated artichoke hearts. The menu reflects today's emphasis on the parts of the meal that once were known as "side dishes." ❧ Add your favorite kind of bread and sit down to nouveau steak and potatoes.

Steak and Potatoes Our Way, with Salad

16 ounces (1 pound) tiny new potatoes

8 ounces (½ pound) flank steak

2 (6-ounce) jars marinated artichoke hearts

1 medium clove garlic

2 tablespoons white wine vinegar

¼ cup white wine

1 teaspoon dried thyme

Freshly ground black pepper

6 ounces arugula (or other bitter greens) (about 2 bunches) (3 or 4 cups packed)

12 cherry or 18 pear tomatoes, red or yellow or mixed

1. If using the broiler, preheat. Cover the broiler pan with aluminum foil.
2. Scrub but do not peel the potatoes. Bring to a boil in a covered pot with water to cover and cook for 10 to 20 minutes.
3. Trim any fat from the flank steak and score the meat on the diagonal. If using a stove-top grill, prepare it. Grill or broil the steak until well browned on both sides and medium-rare in the center, 7 to 10 minutes altogether.
4. Drain the artichokes, reserving 2 tablespoons of the marinade. Place the artichokes in a strainer and run hot tap water over them; drain.
5. Turn on a food processor and put the garlic through the feed tube to mince. Add the artichokes, reserved marinade, vinegar, wine, and thyme and process until the artichokes are smooth. Season with pepper.
6. Wash and dry the arugula and trim the stems; wash and dry the tomatoes.
7. When the flank steak is cooked, cut on the diagonal against the grain into julienne strips and then cut each strip into 3 or 4 pieces.

CONTINUED

8. When the potatoes are cooked, drain and cut them into small pieces; combine well with the steak and the artichoke purée.
9. Arrange the arugula on three plates; divide the salad among them, and decorate with tomatoes.

Yield: 3 servings

G A M E P L A N

Follow recipe directions.

APPROXIMATE NUTRITION INFORMATION PER SERVING, WITHOUT BREAD: 380 calories, 10 grams fat, 40 milligrams cholesterol, 220 milligrams sodium, 20 grams protein, 50 grams carbohydrate

Chinese Beef and Vegetables | Rice

*L*ooking back at recipes in the first Chinese cookbook I ever owned, I discovered a startling fact: The proportion of meat to the other ingredients in a dish was quite small. That is the way the Chinese traditionally eat. But after Chinese cooking crossed the Pacific, the proportions began to change: The meat became central, vegetables secondary. ❧ Now health professionals are telling us that the Chinese got it right the first time. ❧ This recipe for beef and vegetables combines the best of at least three different classic Chinese dishes, and for good measure, adds Western Brussels sprouts.

Chinese Beef and Vegetables

8 ounces (½ pound) flank steak

2 teaspoons cornstarch

1 tablespoon canola oil

1 clove garlic

12 ounces (¾ pound) whole onion or 11 ounces sliced ready-cut onion (2¼ to 2¾ cups)

16 ounces (1 pound) green and red or yellow peppers or 14 ounces sliced ready-cut peppers (4 cups)

8 Brussels sprouts

Fresh or frozen ginger, to yield 1 tablespoon coarsely grated

¼ teaspoon five-spice powder

1 tablespoon reduced-sodium soy sauce

2 tablespoons dry sherry

¼ teaspoon hot pepper flakes

1. Wash, dry, and cut beef against the grain into ¼-inch strips; then cut each strip in 1-inch pieces.
2. Sprinkle the meat with cornstarch.
3. Heat the oil in a wok, add the beef, and sauté until it browns on both sides.
4. Meanwhile, with food processor running, put the garlic through the feed tube to mince. Turn off the processor and, using the slicing attachment, slice whole onion. Add the garlic and onion to the wok and stir.
5. Wash, trim, and seed whole peppers; cut into quarters and slice in food processor. Add the peppers to the wok and stir.
6. Wash, trim, and slice Brussels sprouts in the food processor and stir into the wok.
7. Coarsely grate the ginger and add to the wok along with the five-spice powder, soy sauce, sherry, and hot pepper flakes.
8. Continue to cook until the vegetables are tender but not overcooked; serve over rice.

Yield: 2 servings

Rice

¾ cup long-grain rice

1. Combine the rice and 1½ cups of water in a heavy-bottomed pot and bring to boil.
2. Reduce the heat to a simmer, cover, and cook a total of 17 minutes.

Yield: 2 servings

G A M E   P L A N

Cook rice.

Prepare beef and vegetables.

APPROXIMATE NUTRITION INFORMATION PER SERVING:
675 calories, 20 grams fat, 60 milligrams cholesterol,
350 milligrams sodium, 35 grams protein, 85 grams
carbohydrate

Desserts

*S*o many of the menus in this book can easily be turned into dinner for company with a little wine and a dessert.

In keeping with the philosophy of the book—good taste, good health—the desserts have small amounts of fat, sometimes none. And the small amount of fat does not mean tiny portion size: These portions are normal to generous.

Tapioca Pudding with Dried Fruit Compote

*T*apioca pudding is still a comfort food. Here it has been slimmed by using skim milk and jazzed up with a dried fruit compote. ❧ This is not a fancy dessert, but it's very homey and good.

Tapioca Pudding with Dried Fruit Compote

1 cup mixed dried fruit—
    apples, cherries, pears,
    peaches
1½ cups apple cider
7½ tablespoons sugar
1 egg, separated
3 tablespoons quick-cooking
    tapioca
2 cups skim milk
½ teaspoon ground cinnamon
¼ teaspoon ground nutmeg
1 teaspoon vanilla

1. Cut up large pieces of fruit and combine in a pot with the cider and 1½ tablespoons of the sugar; bring to simmer and cook at a simmer for ½ hour. Drain.
2. Beat the egg white until foamy. Gradually beat in 3 tablespoons of the sugar, beating until soft peaks form.
3. Mix the tapioca with the remaining sugar and the milk, cinnamon, nutmeg, and egg yolk in a saucepan and let stand for 5 minutes.
4. Cook and stir the tapioca mixture over medium heat until it comes to a full boil. Gradually add the egg white mixture, stirring just enough to blend; stir in vanilla.
5. Stir in stewed fruit; cool 20 minutes and serve warm, or refrigerate and serve chilled.

Yield: 6 servings

APPROXIMATE NUTRITION INFORMATION PER SERVING:
210 calories, 1 gram fat, 35 milligrams cholesterol, 60 milligrams sodium, 5 grams protein, 45 grams carbohydrate

Strawberry Soufflé

espite its lack of fat, this is a rather spectacular-looking creation, all puffed up with lots of egg whites but still filled with strawberry flavor.

Strawberry Soufflé

32 large strawberries
½ cup sugar
8 egg whites
Pinch cream of tartar
3 tablespoons orange liqueur

1. Preheat the oven to 350 degrees.

2. Wash the strawberries and trim. Slice.

3. Combine the berries with 5 tablespoons of sugar and cook over medium heat until the berries are soft, 8 to 10 minutes.

4. Purée the berry mixture in the food processor and measure out 2 cups.

5. Beat the egg whites until foamy. Add the cream of tartar and slowly beat in the remaining 3 tablespoons of sugar until the whites are stiff and shiny.

6. Mix the 2 cups of berries with a little of the whites and the orange liqueur and then fold the remaining whites into the berries. Spoon into a 3-quart soufflé dish and bake in the lower third of the pre-heated oven for 30 to 35 minutes. Do not open the oven door for the first 30 minutes or the soufflé might fall. Serve immediately.

Yield: 6 servings

APPROXIMATE NUTRITION INFORMATION PER SERVING:
135 calories, 0 grams fat, 0 milligrams cholesterol,
75 milligrams sodium, 5 grams protein, 25 grams
carbohydrate

Pumpkin Custard

A reader deserves credit for this dessert. I've made a few changes, but otherwise this is pretty much what you would find in a pumpkin pie, minus the crust.

Pumpkin Custard

2 cups skim milk

½ cup nonfat dry milk powder

1 (29-ounce) can pumpkin purée

1 cup firmly packed brown sugar

2 tablespoons minced crystallized ginger

2 teaspoons ground cinnamon

¼ teaspoon ground cloves

2 whole eggs

2 egg whites

1 teaspoon vanilla

1. Preheat the oven to 375 degrees.

2. In a large bowl mix the skim milk with the nonfat dry milk.

3. Add the remaining ingredients and mix well.

4. Spoon into a 6-cup baking dish and bake for about 1 hour and 10 minutes, until the center of the custard is cooked. Insert a toothpick into the center of the custard; if it comes out clean, the custard is cooked. Cool and serve warm or chilled.

Yield: 10 servings

APPROXIMATE NUTRITION INFORMATION PER SERVING:
170 calories, 1 gram fat, 45 milligrams cholesterol, 80 milligrams sodium, 5 grams protein, 35 grams carbohydrate

Fresh Apple
Yogurt Coffee Cake

*P*at Henry, who has been a finalist at the Pillsbury Bake-Off so many times she is not allowed to enter anymore, created this dessert for the staff at the Golden Door, the spa in Escondido, California. When I first published it in the *New York Times,* one person wrote in wanting to know what was wrong with it because it was only an inch high. ❥ Well, that's as high as it is supposed to be, but I thought it would be interesting to try baking it in a 9- by 9-inch brownie pan, producing a much higher cake, which also is extremely moist. If you do not want quite such a moist cake you have two choices: Bake it the way Pat does in a 9- by 13-inch pan or bake it in the 9- by 9-inch pan but at a lower temperature—325 degrees—for a longer time: about 40 minutes.

Fresh Apple Yogurt Coffee Cake

1½ cups all-purpose flour

1 cup sugar

1 teaspoon baking soda

1 teaspoon cinnamon

½ teaspoon mace or nutmeg

¼ teaspoon salt

½ teaspoon grated orange rind

1½ cups nonfat plain yogurt

1 tablespoon cornstarch dissolved in ¼ cup nonfat milk

1 large apple, peeled and coarsely chopped

1 tablespoon vanilla

Pan spray

1. Preheat the oven to 350 degrees.

2. Sift the first 6 ingredients into a large bowl; add the remaining ingredients except pan spray and blend by hand until well mixed.

3. Spoon the mixture into a 9- by 9-inch baking pan that has been lightly sprayed with pan spray. Bake for 25 to 30 minutes, until a knife inserted in center comes out clean.

4. Remove from oven and place on rack to cool. Serve warm or cool.

Yield: 9 servings

APPROXIMATE NUTRITION INFORMATION PER SERVING:
155 calories, 0 grams fat, 0 milligrams cholesterol, 245 milligrams sodium, 5 grams protein, 35 grams carbohydrate

New Age Plum Torte

*T*he most requested recipe I ever printed in the *New York Times* was for a plum torte. Its popularity, of course, has to do with its incredibly delicious old-fashioned flavor, but it doesn't hurt that it is so easy to make. Once, I decided to experiment with the torte to see if some of the fat could be removed without destroying its integrity. It took four tries and a final willingness to use an egg substitute in place of the eggs. Half of the butter was replaced by puréed bananas. ❧ The result: The fat was cut in half and the calories reduced by 40 per serving. ❧ This is a dessert for late summer and early fall, when Italian plums, also known as prune plums or purple plums, are in season. But you can make the same recipe using one pint of blueberries in place of the plums, if you like. Equally delicious. ❧ These tortes freeze beautifully. If you are ever in the mood, make a bunch and put them away until the winter. What a treat on a miserable January day.

New Age Plum Torte

¼ cup (½ stick) unsalted
    butter
¾ cup plus 2 teaspoons
    sugar
1½ ripe medium bananas,
    cut into large chunks
1 cup unbleached flour,
    sifted
1 teaspoon baking powder
½ cup egg substitute
24 halves ripe pitted prune
    plums
½ lemon
1 teaspoon cinnamon, or to
    taste

1. Preheat the oven to 350 degrees.
2. Beat the butter, ¾ cup of the sugar, and the bananas in an electric mixer until well blended. Beat in the flour, baking powder, and egg substitute until well blended.
3. Spoon the batter into an 8-, 9-, or 10-inch ungreased springform pan. Arrange the plum halves, skin side down, on top; sprinkle with the remaining 2 teaspoons of sugar, or more if plums are very tart, a few squeezes of lemon juice, and about 1 teaspoon of cinnamon —more if you like cinnamon.
4. Bake 1 hour, approximately, until center tests done with toothpick. Remove and cool; refrigerate or freeze, if desired. Or cool to luke-warm and serve.
5. To serve torte that has been frozen, defrost and reheat briefly at 300 degrees.

Yield: 8 servings

APPROXIMATE NUTRITION INFORMATION PER SERVING:
235 calories, 6 grams fat, 15 milligrams cholesterol,
60 milligrams sodium, 5 grams protein, 50 grams
carbohydrate

Banana Date Loaf

*B*anana date loaf from Michel Stroot at the Golden Door in Escondido, California, keeps moist despite the tiny amount of oil. Be sure the bananas are good and ripe because they will add sweetness, too. This is an amazingly good, very low-fat fruit loaf.

Banana Date Loaf

1½ cups unbleached white flour

1¼ cups whole-wheat flour

1 teaspoon baking powder

1 teaspoon baking soda

1 teaspoon allspice

2 teaspoons cinnamon

½ teaspoon salt

1 whole egg and 1 egg white, lightly beaten

1 tablespoon canola oil

1 cup chopped dates

½ cup firmly packed brown sugar

2 large, very ripe bananas

1½ cups nonfat buttermilk

1 teaspoon vanilla

1. Preheat the oven to 350 degrees.
2. Sift together into a large bowl the white and whole-wheat flours, baking powder, baking soda, allspice, cinnamon, and salt.
3. Make a well in the center of the dry ingredients and add the egg and egg white, oil, dates, and brown sugar. Stir to mix well.
4. Mash the bananas in the food processor; add the buttermilk and vanilla and process to blend. Pour into the batter and mix thoroughly.
5. Pour the batter into a nonstick 8½- by 4-inch loaf pan and bake for 40 to 55 minutes in the bottom third of the oven, or until a toothpick inserted in the center comes out clean.
6. Cool the cake for 10 minutes on a rack; remove from pan and continue to cool on the rack.

Yield: 14 slices

APPROXIMATE NUTRITION INFORMATION PER SERVING:
205 calories, 2 grams fat, 15 milligrams cholesterol, 195 milligrams sodium, 5 grams protein, 45 grams carbohydrate

Nectarine-Raspberry Crisp

*S*crumptious is the only word to describe the results when you combine nectarines, brown sugar, raspberries, and ginger. When nectarines are at their peak, no one would suspect that this recipe had been altered to reduce the fat significantly.

Nectarine-Raspberry Crisp

3 to 4 pounds ripe nectarines
8 tablespoons dark brown
    sugar
1½ tablespoons flour
½ teaspoon cinnamon
¼ cup tightly packed
    chopped crystallized
    ginger
1 pint raspberries
1 cup old-fashioned oats
4 tablespoons (½ stick)
    unsalted butter, melted
2 tablespoons defrosted
    frozen orange juice
    concentrate

1. Preheat the oven to 450 degrees and adjust a shelf to top third of oven.
2. Wash, pit, and slice the nectarines about ¼ inch thick. Add 6 tablespoons of the brown sugar to the nectarines, along with the flour, cinnamon, and ginger; toss. Gently stir in raspberries.
3. Place the fruit mixture in a 6-cup gratin dish or large pie plate.
4. Process the oats in the food processor until the mixture is like fine grain. Add the butter, the remaining 2 tablespoons of brown sugar, and the orange juice concentrate; process to mix.
5. Spoon the oat mixture over the fruit and bake 25 to 35 minutes. If the topping begins to burn, cover the dish loosely with aluminum foil. Serve warm.

Yield: 10 servings

APPROXIMATE NUTRITION INFORMATION PER SERVING:
260 calories, 5 grams fat, 10 milligrams cholesterol,
55 milligrams sodium, 5 grams protein, 50 grams
carbohydrate

Plum Buttermilk Sherbet

*S*ome people think that sorbet is just a fancy French way of saying sherbet, but sorbet and sherbet are different. Sorbet has no dairy products in it, while sherbet has milk. In this superb version of a sherbet, the milk is buttermilk, which adds a creamy tartness to the plums.

Plum Buttermilk Sherbet

7 or 8 large ripe plums
1 cup water
1 stick cinnamon
1 cup sugar
1 tablespoon fresh lemon juice
1 tablespoon grated lemon rind
1 quart nonfat or low-fat buttermilk

1. Wash the plums and combine in a pot with the water and the cinnamon stick. Cover and cook at a simmer until the plums are soft, 10 to 15 minutes.
2. Remove the plums from the liquid; discard the liquid and reserve the cinnamon stick. Remove the plum pits and purée the flesh in the food processor. There should be about 2 cups of purée.
3. Return purée to the pot with the cinnamon stick, sugar, lemon juice, and rind, and cook about 3 minutes, until the sugar dissolves. Remove the pot from the heat and set aside to cool to room temperature.
4. When the mixture is cool, stir in the buttermilk and process the mixture in an ice cream maker according to directions, or pour into a shallow metal pan and freeze until almost firm. Spoon into the processor and process until smooth. Return the sherbet to the pan and freeze again.

Yield: 5 servings, about 1 cup each

APPROXIMATE NUTRITION INFORMATION PER SERVING:
295 calories, 1 gram fat, 0 milligrams cholesterol, 200 milligrams sodium, 5 grams protein, 65 grams carbohydrate

Layered Summer Fruit, Brown Sugar, and Yogurt

*W*hat goes into this dessert depends on what is ripe and what is local. Try peaches, blueberries, strawberries, raspberries, nectarines, seedless red grapes. It's a "real" dessert and a really simple one. In the winter, kiwi, mangoes, papaya, and bananas also are good.

Layered Summer Fruit, Brown Sugar, and Yogurt

6 cups assorted fresh fruit
2 cups nonfat plain yogurt
6 tablespoons brown sugar

1. Wash, dry, and slice the fruits and place a layer of them in a glass bowl. Top with ⅓ of the yogurt, evenly spread. Sprinkle with ⅓ of the sugar.
2. Repeat the layering twice, topping each layer with the yogurt and brown sugar. Cover and chill at least 1 hour to overnight, so that the sugar can blend with the yogurt.

Yield: 6 servings

APPROXIMATE NUTRITION INFORMATION PER SERVING:
155 calories, 1 gram fat, 1 milligram cholesterol,
65 milligrams sodium, 5 grams protein, 35 grams
carbohydrate

Rhubarb and Apple Compote with Orange Meringue

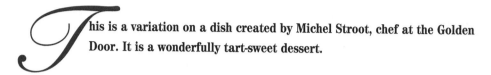

his is a variation on a dish created by Michel Stroot, chef at the Golden Door. It is a wonderfully tart-sweet dessert.

Rhubarb and Apple Compote with Orange Meringue

4 cups fresh rhubarb cut in 1-inch lengths

1 large apple, peeled, cored, and coarsely chopped

2 tablespoons water

1 cup brown sugar

Orange Meringue (recipe follows)

1. Preheat the oven to 350 degrees.
2. Combine the rhubarb, apple, water, and brown sugar in a pot; cover and cook the ingredients until the rhubarb softens, about 10 minutes; remove the lid and stir. Cook until most of the juice has evaporated, about 10 more minutes.
3. Spoon the rhubarb mixture into four 10-ounce ramekins. Set aside while making the meringue.

ORANGE MERINGUE

2 egg whites

3 tablespoons sugar

¼ cup defrosted frozen orange juice concentrate

1. Whip the egg whites with an electric mixer until soft peaks form.
2. Slowly beat in the sugar until stiff peaks form.
3. Slowly beat in the orange juice concentrate.
4. Spoon meringue evenly over each ramekin. Bake at 350 degrees for 8 to 10 minutes, until the meringue just begins to brown. Cool and serve warm or chilled.

Yield: 4 servings

APPROXIMATE NUTRITION INFORMATION PER SERVING:
335 calories, 0 grams fat, 0 milligrams cholesterol, 55 milligrams sodium, 5 grams protein, 80 grams carbohydrate

Orange
Meringues

After tasting the orange meringue topping that is spooned over the Rhubarb and Apple Compote (page 316), I decided to make orange meringues. ❧ These are very soft, so they must cool completely before they can be peeled from the wax paper, and even then it isn't easy. But they taste so wonderful that you won't care if they are a little crooked.

Orange Meringues

2 egg whites
3 tablespoons sugar
3 tablespoons orange juice
    concentrate

1. Preheat the oven to 250 degrees.
2. Beat the egg whites with an electric mixer until soft peaks form.
3. Slowly beat in the sugar to form stiff peaks.
4. Beat in the orange juice concentrate.
5. Spoon heaping tablespoons of the meringue onto a wax-paper-lined cookie sheet and bake for about 30 minutes, until the meringues are firm. Cool completely and remove from the wax paper using a sharp knife.

Yield: 1 dozen meringues

APPROXIMATE NUTRITION INFORMATION PER MERINGUE:
20 calories, 0 grams fat, 0 milligrams cholesterol,
10 milligrams sodium, 1 gram protein, 5 grams
carbohydrate

Apple-Cranberry Tart in Phyllo

he Middle Eastern dough called phyllo, or sometimes filo, is usually associated with melted butter, lots and lots of it between the paper-thin layers of the dough. But there are other ways to take advantage of these layers that turn crisp and flaky when baked. This is one of them. ❧ This recipe can be prepared a day or two in advance and refrigerated. To serve, return to room temperature and reheat at 350 degrees to warm through, about 15 or 20 minutes. ❧ If phyllo is purchased frozen, allow the package to defrost in the refrigerator overnight, or for several hours at room temperature.

Apple-Cranberry Tart in Phyllo

5 apples (3½ to 4 pounds), peeled, cored, quartered, and thinly sliced

½ pound dried cranberries and/or dried cherries

1 cup coarsely chopped pecans

2 teaspoons cinnamon

2 tablespoons fresh lemon juice

6 tablespoons sugar

4 teaspoons grated lemon rind

½ cup finely cut candied ginger

2 tablespoons flour

16 sheets phyllo

3 tablespoons unsalted butter

2 tablespoons canola oil

Pan spray

1. Preheat the oven to 400 degrees.
2. Combine the apples, dried fruits, pecans, cinnamon, lemon juice, sugar, lemon rind, candied ginger, and flour in a bowl and mix well.
3. Unwrap the phyllo and cover with wax paper and a damp towel. Keep covered to prevent drying out.
4. Heat the butter; add the oil.
5. Spray with pan spray a baking pan that is approximately the same size or a little larger than the sheets of phyllo. (They come in different sizes. If the sheets are too large for the pan, trim them.)
6. Arrange 1 sheet of phyllo on the bottom of the pan and brush the sheet lightly with the butter mixture. Repeat, buttering between sheets, using 8 sheets in all.
7. Spread the apple filling evenly over the phyllo and top with another sheet, brushing lightly with butter. Repeat. Butter each sheet, using 8 sheets in all, brushing the top sheet with butter. Cut the phyllo all the way through into 20 rectangles.
8. Bake in the lower third of the oven about 30 minutes, until the top is brown. Cool and serve at room temperature.

Yield: 20 servings

APPROXIMATE NUTRITION INFORMATION PER SERVING:
225 calories, 5 grams fat, 5 milligrams cholesterol, 5 milligrams sodium, 5 grams protein, 40 grams carbohydrate

Menus for Entertaining

Sometimes the only thing missing to turn a speedy family dinner into one for company is the dessert and, perhaps, a good loaf of bread.

The dozen desserts in the book, though not necessarily in the category of speedy, do meet the other two criteria for the book: good taste and healthfulness.

Perhaps you will have one or more of these desserts stashed in the freezer, or perhaps you can select one of the speedy ones for a company dinner.

Early Winter
Chinese Pork and Peppers (page 248)
Rice (page 249)
Spinach and Raisins (page 249)
Apple-Cranberry Tart in Phyllo (page 318)

Winter
Lamb with Red Wine and Dried Cherries
(page 285)
Mushroom Caponata (page 285)
Banana Date Loaf (page 312)

Early Spring
Risotto with Asparagus and Porcini (page 74)
Mesclun and Tart-Sweet Dressing (page 75)
Rhubarb and Apple Compote with
Orange Meringue (page 316)

Spring
Salmon with Grainy Mustard and Lime Topping
(page 118)
Broccoli, Sautéed Onion, and
Potato Purée (page 119)
Plum Buttermilk Sherbet (page 314)

Summer
Scallops and Peppers with Black Bean Sauce
(page 166)
Orange Rice (page 167)
Layered Summer Fruit, Brown Sugar,
and Yogurt (page 315)

Mid-Summer
Rotini with Fresh Tomato Sauce (page 66)
Corn on the Cob (page 67)
Plum Buttermilk Sherbet (page 314)

Hungarian Chicken with Peppers, Tomatoes,
and Yogurt (page 190)
Polenta (page 191)
Strawberry Soufflé (page 308)

Singapore Noodles (page 290)
Gingery Cucumbers (page 291)
Nectarine-Raspberry Crisp (page 313)

Late Summer
Linguine with Wild Mushrooms in
Buttermilk Sauce (page 64)
Yellow Tomatoes, Black Olives, and
Red Onion (page 65)
New Age Plum Torte (page 311)

Early Fall
Alice's Chicken (page 226)
Warm Potato and Green Bean Salad
(page 227)
Tapioca Pudding with Dried Fruit Compote
(page 307)

Grilled Tuna (page 130)
Eggplant, Tomatoes, and Onion Pasta
(page 131)
Orange Meringues (page 317)

Late Fall
Chicken Hunter-Style (page 200)
Spaghetti (page 201)
Greens with Creamy Vinaigrette (page 201)
Pumpkin Custard (page 309)

Your Government
and Your Food:
The Politics of Food

✦ ✦

*W*hat's political about food? my friends often ask.

Listen up.

Almost everything about food is political. What we eat and what we know about what we should eat is determined by the United States Department of Agriculture and the Food and Drug Administration. The kind of pesticides allowed on our food falls under the jurisdiction of the Environmental Protection Agency. What advertisers are allowed to claim about the virtues—real and imagined—of the food we eat is the responsibility of the Federal Trade Commission.

Ultimately, what these agencies do is determined by the party in power. Depending on the administration, ordinary citizens and consumer groups have more or less influence on the government.

The people who run these agencies are political appointees, and they take their cues from the administration that hires them. When the executive branch is anticonsumer and probusiness, the only recourse citizens have is through Congress.

What we haven't seen before is a proconsumer executive branch and a probusiness Congress, and that's what the 1994 election has brought, according to the political experts. The administration can propose all the laws it wants, but Congress has to pass them. Congress may have different ideas about regulatory practices and can pass all the laws it likes. The president can veto some of those that are contrary to his philosophy, but it is unlikely he will veto all of them.

As I write this at the end of November 1994, the experts are not certain how the Republican-dominated House and Senate will respond to some of the concerns that are addressed by the regulatory agencies. There are a couple of signals that indicate much less regulation in the future.

The Republicans said they wanted to slash government spending by 25 percent. Leaving out programs like defense and social security, much of that 25 percent would come from the budgets of regulatory agencies.

In addition, a section of the Republicans' Contract with America is specifically devoted to government regulations. One can only hope that in efforts to reduce costs and get rid of meaningless regulations—of which the federal government has quite a few—the important regulations that protect consumers will not get caught in the crossfire.

But can Congress really slash the budget 25 percent? Certainly in the first hundred days, when most legislation is likely to pass, few in Congress will be discussing whether the new food labels should be modified; if microbial testing of meat should be permitted; how to modify the laws regulating pesticides.

But industry lobbyists will certainly find a Congress much friendlier than it was under the Democrats.

Stay tuned.

Whether a particular pesticide is left on the market, a company is allowed to make a certain health claim for a particular food, or a new ingredient is given government approval has something to do with science and a lot to do with politics. The controversy over dietary supplements is only the most recent example.

Interest groups with their high-powered lobbyists spend a lot of time and money in their efforts to get what they want. They lobby the White House; they lobby on Capitol Hill; they go to see the agencies involved.

Besides the food-industry lobbyists, the fellows in the tasseled loafers, there are groups that act as lobbyists for consumers and environmentalists: The Center for Science in the Public Interest, Public Voice for Food and Health Policy, the Natural Resources Defense Council, the Environmental Defense Fund, Public Citizen Health Research Group. With a fraction of their opponents' resources, they still manage to compete with the lawyer-lobbyists for the food industry. And they do make a dent in the process because they bring to public attention the most egregious errors the federal government makes in regulating health, food safety, and nutrition.

Nowhere has the struggle between consumer interests and industry interests been more evident than at the United States Department of Agriculture.

❧ The United States Department of Agriculture (USDA)

The Agriculture Department has a dual mission: to act as an advocate for farmers and what they raise and as a lead agency in nutrition information for consumers. It doesn't take a doctorate to see the result: a two-headed hydra.

For example, the Clinton administration has suggested the removal of the inspection of meat and poultry from the Agriculture Department because it is doing such a poor job and the transfer of this responsibility to the Food and Drug Administration. There is a lot of opposition in Congress to such a change, particularly from members of Congress whose constituents raise meat and poultry. For now the matter remains unresolved.

Despite the best efforts of the Reagan and Bush Agriculture Departments to favor farmers over consumers, in one area they failed miserably to subvert healthful eating principles. The issue was the Food Guide Pyramid, which was designed make sense out of what used to be known as the Four Food Groups.

The pyramid story (it was then called the Eating Right Pyramid) begins in the "Eating Well" column in the *New York Times* on May 8, 1991:

On April 24, after three years of study, research consultations, and discussions with consumers the Agriculture Department sent its Eating Right Pyramid to the printer. This new chart was to have replaced the food wheel used since the 1950s to provide information about a healthy diet.

The next day Agriculture Secretary Edward R. Madigan announced that he was indefinitely delaying the chart's publication. Through a spokeswoman, Kelly Shipp, Mr. Madigan said many groups had complained that it was confusing and that it had not been tested on children.

But other federal officials and health professionals, outraged by the secretary's decision, said the pyramid was withdrawn because meat and dairy producers objected to what they felt was the pyramid's negative depiction of their products.

A GUIDE TO DAILY FOOD CHOICES

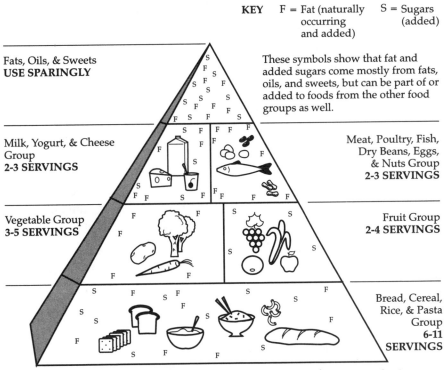

SOURCE: U.S. Department of Agriculture / U.S. Department of Health and Human Services

Further on in the column there is a quote from Marion Nestle, chairwoman of the nutrition department at New York University: "There's a long history, going way back, of U.S.D.A. changing dietary policy because of the food industry. I saw this all the time during the preparation of the surgeon general's report on nutrition and health." Dr. Nestle was the editor of the report.

Despite protests inside and outside the Agriculture Department Mr. Madigan sent the pyramid out to be tested again.

Fast forward to 1992.

After the passage of a year and the expenditure of almost $1 million, the Agriculture Department adopted the pyramid in April 1992. It was essentially the same design the department had rejected a year earlier.

The political staff had wanted a bowl, not a pyramid, because it was preferred by the meat and dairy industries, which felt it did not rank the food groups.

But the professional staff and the outside consultants could not agree with the conclusions of the political staff. "The internal people and the outside consultants were extremely consistent in their conclusions," according to an Agriculture Department staff member who requested anonymity in a story that ran in April 1992.

"The nutrition community stood up and said enough is enough. The political people wanted to drop it and said it would be a one-day story, but it just didn't die. The research would never have been done if it hadn't been for the pressure."

By 1993 Food Guide Pyramids were turning up all over and health professionals began to talk in terms of eating according to the pyramid.

With the arrival of the Clinton administration there was a new attitude at the political level in the Agriculture Department. Agriculture Secretary Mike Espy appeared to be more consumer-friendly. He appointed Ellen Haas, founder and executive director of Public Voice for Food and Health Policy, a Washington-based consumer advocacy group, Assistant Secretary for Food and Consumer Services.

Espy also more or less agreed to go along with the Food and Drug Administration on uniform nutrition labeling, something the previous administration refused to do. And in the summer of 1993 the Agriculture Department joined the FDA and the Environmental Protection Agency in calling for a reduction in the use of pesticides in food. It was the first time the three government agencies had agreed about anything.

But after agreeing to coordinate labeling with the FDA, the Agriculture Department sought to undermine the parallel labeling efforts.

In the summer of 1994 it issued a proposal to continue to permit ground beef to be labeled with expressions like "70 percent lean, 30 percent fat," or "80 percent lean, 20 percent fat." Under regulations that went into effect that summer, ground beef can be called lean only if certain criteria are met: A 3.5-ounce serving must contain less than 10 grams of fat, less than 4.5 grams of saturated fat, and less than 95 milligrams of cholesterol. Ground beef seldom meets those criteria, and some members of the beef industry were looking for an exemption. The Agriculture Department obliged.

By the time you read this, a final decision will have been made on whether such an exemption is useful to consumers.

In December 1994, Mr. Taylor said, "The basic principle of the Nutrition Labeling and Education Act was to avoid varying and confusing definitions. My inclination is to not create a second completely different meaning for the term lean."

After Espy had been on the job for two years, critics charged that he had done nothing to improve the safety of meat and poultry through better and tougher inspection methods. Actually he had done something very important: He had appointed a former deputy commissioner of the Food and Drug Administration, Michael Taylor, to head meat and poultry inspection. Mr. Taylor has been hard at work since he arrived in August 1994.

But Mr. Espy was accused of accepting favors from Arkansas-based Tyson Industries, the largest poultry producer in the United States, with close ties to the Clintons. Mr. Espy was forced to resign.

Historically the Agriculture Department has been responsible for the safety of the meat and poultry supply, but until now the agency has done a terrible job. Chickens are contaminated with salmonella; hamburgers are tainted with a bacteria so virulent that it killed four children in the Northwest in 1993 and has made dozens more ill. Meat inspection needs a drastic overhaul to bring it into the late twentieth century. It must move to microbial testing for bacterial contamination. The industry is fighting many of the changes that need to be made.

In September 1994, Taylor announced that the Department of Agriculture would test ground beef in retail stores and at processing plants for *E. coli* 0157:H7, the bacteria that had killed the four children. In November, the meat industry sued the Department of Agriculture to prevent them from testing for the bacteria. They claimed that the USDA lacked the authority to regulate bacteria in meat. In addition they said the program was unfair because the sampling size was too small—5,000 samples per year. Such a small sample, they said, would not guarantee that the meat was safe, nor would it reflect the meat's safety. And they said people might be lulled into thinking that ground beef is safe because of the testing.

In a November 3 story for the *New York Times*, I quoted Taylor on his rationale for the testing program. "We know the sampling is on a limited basis and we've made clear it will not, by itself, protect consumers. But it will provide an incentive for the industry to institute preventive measures. The whole point is for the industry to take responsibility all the way up the line. The solution to the problem is not government spending more money to do more testing. It is for industry to put in place more preventive measures."

Carol Tucker Foreman, Assistant Secretary of Agriculture for Food and Consumer Services in the Carter administration, called the move a "genius plan." She said it was "a perfect example of a small Government action having a ripple effect, making people more careful."

In December the court ruled for the Agriculture Department, and testing continues.

In addition, under Mr. Taylor, the Agriculture Department has proposed legislation that would set limits for the amount of hazardous bacteria in meat and poultry.

But keep in mind that Congress can always pass another law overruling the agency.

✦ The Food and Drug Administration (FDA)

The contest between consumers and producers is more evenly matched at the Food and Drug Administration; there, consumers have a fighting chance. The current commissioner, Dr. David A. Kessler, was appointed by George Bush, who did not realize what a powerhouse he had unleashed. Within weeks of Kessler's appointment he started enforcing laws that had been on the books for years but had generally been ignored by previous commissioners. The Clinton administration reappointed him in response to pressure from consumer groups as well as members of Congress.

Kessler faced an enormous job when he arrived at the FDA. The Reagan administration, determined to get government off the public's (read industry's) back, refused to appropriate the necessary funds for the FDA. In the short term this pleased the food industry, whose more honorable members had not counted on the more unscrupulous among them to take advantage of the laissez-faire attitude of the agency. Some companies, for instance, made outrageous health claims for their products, put misleading labels on them, and generally ignored regulations.

Kessler got right to work. In April 1991, he negotiated with Procter & Gamble to remove the word *fresh* from the name of its bottled orange juice, Citrus Hill Fresh Choice. The juice was not fresh: it was made from reconstituted orange juice. The negotiations were fruitless, and Kessler had the product seized. After the food industry stopped sputtering, it realized it had a formidable commissioner to deal with.

There were other, unexpected consequences to the FDA's hands-off policy. In some states agencies picked up the slack and began to prosecute food companies for false and misleading label claims. The food industry found itself fighting on a dozen different fronts at different times, depending on which state attorney general was after them.

Needless to say, food companies would rather have one federal government as an adversary than fifty states attorneys general. The industry found itself begging Congress to appropriate more funds for the FDA so that it could do its job and so that, as the industry is fond of saying, "there will be a level playing field." They got more money for the agency. They also got Kessler.

Kessler can take much of the credit for the passage of the Nutrition Labeling and Education Act. The fight to bring it out by a Congressionally imposed deadline at the end of 1992 went all the way up to President Bush in the waning days of his administration. Kessler held firm against special interests and, with a few small compromises, the NLEA became law.

Critics, however, fault Kessler for allowing milk from cows treated with a genetically engineered hormone, rBST, or rBGH, on the market without labeling.

❧ The Environmental Protection Agency (EPA)

Even though most Americans had never thought about the Environmental Protection Agency, they became keenly aware of it in 1989, when there was an uproar over the safety of Alar, a chemical used on apples. The Natural Resources Defense Council said Alar should be banned because it is a carcinogen; children, they pointed out, eat a lot of applesauce and apple juice. They brought the problem to the attention of the public in such a dramatic way—by telling the story on "60 Minutes" —that millions of jars of applesauce and millions of pounds of apples were destroyed.

Was such a dramatic response necessary? After all, there are any number of chemicals in the food supply and in the environment that are equally harmful. There was certainly overreaction from all quarters, but the Natural Resources Defense Council made its point.

The EPA had known for several years that Alar caused cancer in test animals and at one point had even planned to ban it. But it had backed off because in 1989 an EPA advisory board said there wasn't enough information to ban the chemical: It said additional tests were needed. So Alar stayed on the market, and apple growers—even those who had already stopped using Alar—suffered the consequences.

Today the EPA, and all the federal agencies that deal with food safety, are facing an even bigger dilemma. It's called the Delaney Clause. The clause, which is part of the Federal Food, Drug and Cosmetic Act, says that anything that causes cancer in animal or man cannot be added to food. The Delaney Clause applied only to processed food until 1992, when a federal appeals court said the government had to apply the Delaney Clause to all foods. Under that interpretation the EPA would be required to ban thirty-five chemicals used as pesticides, fungicides, and herbicides.

In 1958, when the Delaney Clause was passed, scientific techniques made it possible to find only parts per million of a carcinogen. Today we can find parts per trillion.

Many people believe Delaney should be repealed, but there are forces that will not permit that to happen until the passage of some strong law to protect consumers from cancer-causing substances added to food while it is growing or during processing.

In the summer of 1993, the EPA, the FDA, and the USDA got together and announced that there were too many pesticides in the American food supply and that the level should be reduced. This was a stunning about-face for the federal government, which had always insisted that the level of pesticides was just fine.

The joint announcement was the first time the three agencies had worked together and it endorsed, and preempted, the report from the National Academy of Sciences that was to be released a couple of days later. The report says that children are at special risk from pesticide residues in fruits and vegetables because they are more vulnerable and that alternative ways to grow fruits and vegetables must be found.

I broke the story, just before the report was to be released, writing for the *Times* on Sunday, June 27, 1993: "The federal government has decided to reduce the use of chemicals in the production of the nation's food, assigning a higher priority than in the past to protecting children's health and the environment.

"'The Agriculture Department, EPA and the Food and Drug Administration are working together in a way they have never done before to benefit the American people,' said Carol Browner, administrator of the EPA.

"Dr. Kessler called it 'a major landmark in the history of food safety.'"

The story went on to say: "If the change of policy is fully carried out, it could alter everything about the way food is grown and what Americans eat."

But before policy can be changed Congress must do something about the Delaney Clause.

If the current Congress elected in November 1994 gets to this issue, it may very well cancel the anti-pesticide initiative.

In the meantime the agency must deal with other hot issues, such as genetically engineered food, a concept that many people see as no better than and just as scary as science fiction.

At the beginning of 1994 Dr. Kessler predicted that safety will be the food fight of the nineties. He appears to be on target.

❧ The Federal Trade Commission (FTC)

The Federal Trade Commission went into its Rip Van Winkle mode during the Reagan administration and barely stirred under Bush. The result was an increase in the number of food ads that were false and misleading. As of this writing the Federal Trade Commission may be waking from its long sleep. It's too soon to tell, but Clinton has appointed a well-respected former FTC commissioner from the Carter administration, Robert Pitofsky. Congress may give the Clinton administration a hard time over this appointment.

During the Reagan-Bush years the same thing that happened to false and misleading food labeling happened to advertising as well—the states took over prosecution.

Here are a few choice examples:

In 1991 Texas settled a suit it filed in 1989 against the Quaker Oats Company over its advertising and labeling claims for oatmeal. The company contended that Quaker Oats could help reduce cholesterol. Texas said that the company was exaggerating the effect of oats on cholesterol levels and that there was insufficient evidence to make the claim.

Texas sued Quaker Oats because it could not negotiate a settlement; Quaker Oats sued Texas, contending the state did not have jurisdiction and was interfering with its right to free speech.

Both sides eventually dropped their suits, but the offending advertising and labeling were discontinued and Quaker contributed at least $75,000 worth of food products to Texas food banks.

In March 1990 Nabisco Brands settled a case with ten states over its advertising of Fleischmann's margarine. The settlement included a payment of $135,000 and the company agreed not to imply that the use of any Fleischmann's product would cure or mitigate the risk of heart disease or reduce cholesterol.

Consumer advocates believe the FTC should base its advertising standards for health claims on the new FDA regulations for food labels. The Nutrition Labeling and Education Act governing food labels and health claims has been in effect since May 1994. The NLEA allows just seven health claims on labels.

The FTC has put out new regulations that are more in line with the FDA labeling regulations, but there are so many loopholes that advertisers should have no trouble saying whatever they want. They'll just have to find new ways to do it.

WE THE PEOPLE

It is very difficult for consumers to sort out the truth in the mad, mad world of food regulation. One helpful clue: If one of the consumer advocacy groups starts bugging the government about some problem, chances are it is a problem you might be interested in, too. From time to time the public says enough is enough and lets the government know.

NEW FOOD LABELING REGULATIONS

The federal government is trying to make food shopping a little easier with numerous and sweeping new regulations for labeling food.

Prodded by Congress through the Nutrition Labeling and Education Act of 1990 and also on its own, the Food and Drug Administration churned out more food labeling regulations between 1991 and 1993 than at any time since the 1970s, when nutrition labeling was first introduced. It wasn't easy and it looked, for a while, in the waning days of the Bush administration, as if the months and months of hard work would amount to nothing because the Agriculture Department would not go along with some regulations the Food and Drug Administration was insisting on. The dispute was so acrimonious that President Bush was required to make the final decision, which didn't happen until December 2, 1992, after he had lost the election and six weeks before he left office. The fight was generally about parts of the regulation that have to do with fat and, in the end, the FDA won, partly because the food industry decided to give in and get it over with.

The effective date for the new nutrition labels was May 1994.

Here is what the new label looks like:

```
Nutrition  Facts
Serving Size 3 TBSP. (24g)
Servings Per Carton About 5

Amount Per Serving

Calories 100  Calories from Fat 15

                              % Daily Value*

Total Fat 1.5g                        2%
  Saturated Fat 0.5g                  3%
Cholesterol 10mg                      3%
Sodium 720mg                         30%
Total Carbohydrate 18g 6%
  Sugars 2g
Protein 4g

Iron 4%

* Not a significant source of dietary fiber,
  vitamin A, vitamin C and calcium.
* Percent Daily Values are based on a
  2,000 calorie diet. Your daily values may
  be higher or lower depending on your
  calorie needs:

                 Calories   2,000     2,500
Total Fat       Less than   65g       80g
  Sat Fat       Less than   20g       25g
Cholesterol     Less than   300mg     300mg
Sodium          Less than   2400mg    2400mg
Total Carbohydrate          300g      375g
  Dietary Fiber             25g       30g
```

And at the very bottom of the label there is an explanation of the number of calories per gram of fat, carbohydrate, and protein. (As you can see, protein and carbohydrates are the same, 4 calories, while fat contains more than twice as many calories.)

The information on the new nutrition label is based on a daily caloric intake of 2,000 calories. When using the information, keep in mind that it is based on a diet with 30 percent of the calories from fat. If you want to eat less fat you will have to make adjustments. And if you need fewer than 2,000 calories you will have to adjust for that, too.

The macronutrients—fat, cholesterol, and the like—are given in grams and milligrams as well as the percentage of daily intake (called Daily Value) they represent. In this example, a serving contains 13 grams of fat, which is 20 percent of the daily intake, based on consuming 2,000 calories a day. Look at the bottom of the label to see the recommended daily levels for each of these macronutrients.

The percentage of the daily intake for vitamins A and C as well as calcium and iron are also included.

SERVING SIZES

In the past, serving sizes were not uniform. One company could say a serving of cake was 1 ounce while another company might say it was 3 ounces. Now the serving size for a given class of food must be the same, more or less. That makes it somewhat easier to compare products, but there are still loopholes.

HEALTH CLAIMS

The only health claims that are permitted now are for the relationship between calcium and osteoporosis; sodium and hypertension; fat and cholesterol and coronary heart disease; dietary fat and cancer; fiber found in fruits, vegetables, and grains and cancer; and antioxidants found in fruits and vegetables and cancer. Another claim—the relationship between folic acid and the prevention of neural tube defects—has been added for dietary supplements, but not, as of this writing, for food.

-FREE

As in fat-free or sugar-free. This designation applies per serving: less than 5 milligrams sodium; less than 5 calories; less than 0.5 gram fat; less than 0.5 gram saturated fat; less than 0.5 gram sugar; less than 2 milligrams cholesterol.

Cholesterol-free claims may be made only if a food contains 2 grams or less of saturated fat.

LOW

As in low-fat or low sodium. The food in question can contain, per serving, not more than 140 milligrams of sodium; not more than 40 calories; not more than 3 grams fat; not more than 1 gram saturated fat. In addition, to use the term *low-fat* a 50-gram portion (in other words about 2 ounces) of the food must contain less than 3 grams of fat. This is to prevent foods in which the serving size is naturally very small, like nondairy creamer, from calling itself low-fat; 50 grams of the creamer has more than 3 grams of fat.

LESS, REDUCED, OR FEWER

To use the term a food must contain at least 25 percent less of the nutrient than is normally found in the particular food. The actual percentage of the reduction would have to be included. For example, 25 percent less fat.

MORE

To use the word *more,* a food must contain at least 10 percent more than is normally found.

LIGHT OR LITE

This generally means either ⅓ fewer calories or a 50-percent reduction in whatever the nutrient is that is being reduced.

If *light* refers to the way the food looks, as in color, then the label must say "light in color," not just light.

LEAN AND EXTRA LEAN

The same terms are being used by the Department of Agriculture, which has jurisdiction over meat and poultry, but see page 324. The FDA is using the terms for seafood and game.

Lean means the food contains less than 10 grams of fat, 4 grams of saturated fat, and 95 milligrams of cholesterol per serving or per 100 grams. One hundred grams is 3.5 ounces.

Extra lean may be used for products that contain less than 5 grams of fat, 2 grams of saturated fat, and 95 milligrams of cholesterol.

HEALTHY—THE ''JELLY BEAN'' RULE

Strict limits have been imposed on the word *healthy.*

To use the word, or any variation of it, like *healthful,* either in a brand name or as a descriptive term on a package, the food must be low in fat and saturated fat and have limited amounts of sodium and cholesterol. The food must also contain at least 10 percent of the recommended daily value of one of the following: vitamin A, vitamin C, iron, calcium, protein, or fiber. In most cases, those nutrients would have to occur naturally in the food; they could not be added.

The decision to require that any product using the term *healthy* have at least a small percentage of some nutrient is being referred to as the "jelly bean rule." When definitions of the term *healthy* were proposed by the Food and Drug Administration in January 1993, there was no such provision, leading to the possibility that jelly beans, which contain no fat or sodium, could be labeled as healthy. Soft drinks would have been able to use the term as well.

It tickles me that the rule is named in "my" honor. When the "healthy" rule was announced at a news conference, I asked Commissioner David Kessler if that meant jelly beans could be called healthy.

It was back to the drawing board, and the current rule is the result.

INGREDIENTS

The Nutrition Labeling and Education Act also changes the ingredient statement on food labels.

Ingredients will continue to be listed in order of predominance.

In addition:

- Artificial colors are listed by specific name instead of under the general category "artificial colors."
- Nondairy products that contain sodium caseinate must say that the casein is derived from milk.
- Fruit juices carry the percentage of fruit juice used in a blend.

◆ Hydrolized protein must state the source of the protein, because some people are allergic to some sources.
◆ All standardized foods, such as pasta, must carry ingredient labeling.
◆ In addition all fresh fruits and vegetables must be labeled if they have been waxed, but you may be hard-pressed to see those labels. They are not necessarily near the fruits and vegetables.

Is It Safe Yet?

There are two kinds of hazards in food: those you can see—mold, dirt, insects—and those you can't—bacteria, pesticides, heavy metals.

For obvious reasons the second set of hazards is more worrisome than the first. Spoiled food is not the problem in the United States that it is where there is a lack of refrigeration and sanitary storage.

But the unseen problems are plenty big enough: Being truly cautious means no more raw eggs in holiday eggnog; hamburgers that must be cooked until the New York Rangers can use them for hockey pucks; dozens of varieties of fish that pregnant women and people with compromised immune systems are told not to eat; warnings about raw shellfish.

Whether more people were getting sick and dying from tainted food in the past decade, more stories were making it into the news, forcing all of us to learn how to pronounce salmonella, campylobacter, listeria, and *E. coli* 0157.

Pesticides We Have Known

Before World War II agriculture in America was essentially organic: The use of chemical pesticides began about 1950. As the use of chemicals has increased, yields have flattened, and pests have become more resistant to chemicals.

Organically raised food is generally described as food grown by traditional farming methods without synthetically compounded fertilizers, pesticides, herbicides, or fungicides. Organic farming relies on crop rotation, manure, and biological methods to control pests. Organic farming is a stricter form of sustainable agriculture, which seeks to reduce pesticide residues in food but not necessarily eliminate them.

Further fueling the interest in organic food was the report from the National Academy of Sciences. The June 1993 report on pesticide residues in food said they were too high for children. "Infants and children differ both quantitatively and qualitatively from adults in their exposure to pesticide residues in foods because they consume more calories per unit of body weight and tend to eat fewer types of food than adults."

The academy found that the data on what children eat and on how to set tolerance levels for pesticide residues for children were inadequate to make certain they are protected.

While acknowledging the need for pesticides to increase the amount of fruits and vegetables available, the academy recommends that the EPA put health considerations, rather than agricultural production, foremost in making decisions.

This is a significant change from current policy. In determining tolerance levels for pesticide residues, the EPA now factors in economic benefits along with risks to human health.

The report urges parents to continue feeding children fruits and vegetables whether they are organic or not, because fruits and vegetables contain anticarcinogens and because they are filled with vitamins, minerals, and fiber and have virtually no fat.

The problem is further complicated by a report from the Environmental Working Group, an environmental advocacy group, that says more than one pesticide is often found in and on fruits and vegetables. Using government data, the group's report describes the number of pesticides that may be found on several fruits and vegetables it examined. No one, the report says, has ever examined the cumulative effects of these pesticides. Are they more hazardous in combination than singly? What is the synergistic effect?

In addition, the report, which was released in the spring of 1994, says that washing and peeling fruits and vegetables has very little effect on the pesticide levels they contain. This makes the advice to wash and peel fruits and vegetables less helpful than it once seemed.

It would be wonderful if all of us could buy organic food. There isn't enough to go around, and for many people what is available is too expensive. Many farmers, however, are attempting sustainable agriculture because they know that more and more pesticides are not producing higher and higher yields. And they worry about the impact of pesticide use on themselves and their families. Every reduction in pesticide use is welcome.

These suggestions to increase the availability of organic food as well as food grown with fewer pesticides are taken from *The Way We Grow,* written by Anne Witte Garland with the organization Mothers and Others for a Livable Planet (Mothers & Others, 40 West 20th Street, New York, N.Y., 10011).

---

1. "Push grocers to stock organic foods of all kinds, not just produce, or foods tested and found to have no detectable pesticide residues; then buy them.
2. "Shop at farmers' markets. The produce generally contains fewer pesticides—fungicides, insecticides, and herbicides—because crops don't have to travel long distances and farmers don't have to meet the cosmetic standards of the conventional produce market. Farmers' markets also sell more organically grown food than conventional supermarkets.
3. "When buying fresh organic food, ask for proof of third-party certification. The store should have such a certificate available. Packaged organic food should name the certifying organization on the label. Organizations like California Certified Organic Farmers do third-party certification. Organic produce should look as fresh as conven-

tionally grown produce, though it may have some blemishes because it has not be sprayed with chemicals. Such imperfections do not affect the quality and flavor.

4. "If you buy conventionally grown produce, wash and peel it to help eliminate the pesticide residues. Use a vegetable scrub brush when appropriate. When washing, add a few drops of mild soap that does not have dyes or perfumes. When washing leafy vegetables squeeze some lemon juice in the water and leave the greens for no more than a minute. Not all pesticides can be eliminated in this fashion because some of them are taken up in the roots and others penetrate the skin or peel, but every little bit helps.

5. "Avoid imported produce from countries with less stringent pesticide regulations. The easiest way to do that is to buy foods in season—in other words, don't buy cherries or plums in winter.

6. "Let your representatives in Washington know that you don't want pesticides in your food or water."

In addition here are some suggestions from the newsletter *Environmental Nutrition:*

- For organic mail order, pick a company closest to you. The food will be fresher and shipping costs should be lower.
- Cut up foods like broccoli, cauliflower, spinach, and the like before washing.
- Discard outer leaves of greens like lettuce.
- Buy seasonal foods. They are less likely to be coated with wax and less likely to have required post-harvest pesticides.
- Produce from the West Coast is less likely to have fungicides, which thrive in moist conditions, sprayed on it because the climate is less humid than on the East Coast.
- Root vegetables tend to accumulate more pesticides than vegetables that grow above the ground; therefore, it's more important to buy organic root vegetables than other varieties.
- Worry less about conventionally grown fruit with a rind or peel—melons, oranges, grapefruit, bananas.

What would help increase organic farming is the adoption of a national organic food law. The government has been working on one for several years now. By the time you read this, there may be a federal organic food regulation in place.

A BETTER WAY

rBST SAYS MOO 10 PERCENT MORE OFTEN

rBST is the easy way to say recombinant bovine somatotropin. rBST is a genetically engineered version of a hormone that occurs naturally in cows. It is also called rBGH, or recombinant bovine growth hormone. It increases milk production by 10 to 25 percent, and the Food and Drug Administration approved its use in November 1993.

Use of the drug was approved over the objections of those who believe it has not been sufficiently tested on humans.

The critics include the General Accounting Office, the investigative arm of Congress, scientists like Dr. Michael Hansen, at the Consumers Union, and Dr. Samuel Epstein, a professor of occupational and environmental medicine at the University of Illinois at Chicago, as well as some British scientists. They also include public interest groups like Mothers and Others for a Livable Planet, an environmental and consumer group; Women's Health Network, an organization devoted to women's health issues; and the Pure Food Campaign, a project of the Foundation on Economic Trends, a group headed by Jeremy Rifkin, a critic of biotechnology.

In its decision to permit the use of the hormone, the FDA acknowledged certain risks it described as "manageable." In the warning statement included with the drug, Monsanto says there are possible detrimental health effects on cows treated with the drug. They include reduced pregnancy rates and a greater risk of disorders involving reproductive and digestive organs. There is also an increased risk of mastitis, an inflammation of the udder.

The increase in mastitis is likely to increase the use of antibiotics in the cows, residues of which turn up in milk.

But there may be another problem as well, a problem that has been suggested by both Hansen and Epstein: The use of rBST may increase the risk of certain cancers. No one has ever studied the problem. Those who approve of the use of rBST say the suggestion is ludicrous; others would like to see proof one way or another.

Whatever the outcome, many consumers think they are entitled to know whether the milk and milk products they are buying come from cows treated with rBST.

Whether or not milk from untreated cows can be labeled as free of rBST became a problem because of the way the FDA handled the question. Without getting caught up in all the messy details, it is sufficient to say that Monsanto has threatened to sue a number of milk producers who have tried to label their milk as rBST-free.

The agency has received thousands of comments on the labeling issue, and little by little, those companies that are using rBST-free milk have found ways to let their customers know.

In the spring of 1994, Mothers and Others for a Livable Planet compiled lists of companies and supermarket chains that have documents to prove they are not using rBST.

Regional lists are available free from Mothers and Others, 40 West 20th Street, New York, New York 10011.

Individual markets, like Fresh Fields in the Washington, D.C., and Chicago areas, provide lists in their stores of rBST-free products.

❧ Biotechnology Fireflies in Corn, Trout in Celery, Fish in Tomatoes

In June 1992, I wrote about the growing interest—and controversy—over biotechnology: "According to the biotechnology industry gene splicing is nothing more than an advanced form of crossbreeding, a century-old practice responsible for such familiar foods as tangelos, a hybrid of tangerines and grapefruits."

Because hybridized crops have never required premarket testing or labeling, the industry does not see why food created from gene splicing should be treated differently.

But consumers do. And consumer and environmental groups believe that because genetically engineered food is so new, it should be subject to testing before it appears on the market. At the very least, they said, the foods should be labeled so that consumers can decide for themselves whether they want to eat the results of gene splicing.

Many scientists don't believe that gene splicing is an extension of the kind of breeding that has gone on for the last century.

"There is no form of crossbreeding that allows the placing of human genes into a tomato," said Dr. Margaret Mellon, the director of the biotechnology center of the National Wildlife Federation in Washington. "This is radically new. To say that it is a minor extension of older technology flies in the face of scientific truth."

Dr. Mellon was referring to the implanting of animal and human genes into plants and vice versa. For example, a firefly gene can be planted in corn, and a trout gene in celery. A new designer tomato, FlavrSavr, made by Calgene Inc. in Davis, California, contains a flounder gene that extends the tomato's shelf life.

Some critics worry whether such a gene might cause people to build up a resistance to antibiotics; others wonder what happens to the nutritional value of food if it has an unnaturally long shelf life. Critics also worry about unknown hazards and the potential for allergic reactions to genetically engineered food.

There is also a potential problem for vegetarians, Orthodox Jews, Muslims, and Buddhists when animal genes are spliced into vegetables and the vegetables are not labeled.

What everyone wanted to know is: How does the Food and Drug Administration plan to regulate gene-spliced foods and will the agency require labeling?

In December 1993, the Union of Concerned Scientists asked the government to delay commercial approval of genetically engineered crops until there is better understanding of the potential risks such plants may pose to the environment.

The concern was twofold: the unknown effects of using genetic material from plant viruses and the possibility of creating plants that could become pests themselves.

But FlavrSavr tomatoes now are available everywhere, and a biotech squash has been approved. Unlike the labeling problems with rBST, the Food and Drug Administration said it had no problem with tomato growers who wanted to make clear their tomatoes are not genetically engineered. The squash is not labeled.

❧ Foods That Glow in the Dark

An August 26, 1992, "Eating Well" column in the *Times* discussed food irradiation. "The story of food irradiation bears a striking resemblance to the story of silicone breast implants: Proponents are ignoring the risks while promoting the benefits.

"The crucial difference is that many scientists are trying to prevent approval of the irradiation process until its safety has been tested to everyone's satisfaction, instead of letting it go on the market first."

Irradiation is the process of bombing food with gamma rays to preserve the food and to kill insects and certain bacteria.

But certain questions have never been answered.

"No one knows whether the process creates new chemicals at levels that may be harmful, or whether the loss of nutrients from irradiation is unacceptably high, or to what extent adding more processing plants that use nuclear components increases the risk of nuclear accidents."

A certain amount of toxic chemicals, like benzene, are formed when the food is irradiated.

In *Food Irradiation: Who Wants It?* (Thorson Publishers Inc., 1987) Tony Webb, Tim Lang, and Kathleen Tucker write: "It is safest to assume that there is no safe level of exposure to such chemicals; any dose can cause initial damage that develops into a cancer.

"The fact that a chemical change is small does not eliminate the risk.

"There is still another safety question: The usual dose of radiation does not kill the bacteria that cause botulism, a particularly virulent form of food poisoning. The bacteria that cause off-odors and flavors are killed, so in those cases where an odor might warn of spoilage, that safety mechanism would be gone."

The May 1992 issue of the University of California *Wellness Letter* said there are no projections of actual economic benefits and though it's claimed that irradiation will make insecticides and fungicides obsolete, there's some evidence that certain foods may be more vulnerable to the ravages of fungi and insects *after* irradiation."

And then there is the question of nutrient loss. Studies have shown a loss of vitamin C, thiamin, and vitamin E in foods that have been irradiated.

Selling irradiated food as fresh is deceptive because all fruits and vegetables—irradiated or not—lose nutrients after picking. A six-week-old irradiated strawberry may look as fresh as a nonirradiated berry just a few days old, but would have fewer nutrients.

And finally, according to Dr. Shelden Margen, professor emeritus of public health nutrition at Berkeley: "There are potentially serious concerns about the issues of waste disposal, engineering safety, transport of radioactive material, production of new isotopes, handling by poorly trained personnel, and others we haven't even thought of yet."

On October 19, 1993, Marcia van Gemert, a toxicologist who was the Food and Drug Administration chairperson of the committee that investigated the studies on irradiated foods in 1982, wrote to a New Jersey assemblyman. She said the studies on the safety of irradiated foods "were not adequate by 1982 standards, and are even less adequate by 1993 standards to evaluate the safety of any product, especially a food product such as irradiated foods."

In a newspaper interview Dr. van Gemert said she had decided to speak out because approval of food irradiation had become politicized. It no longer had anything to do with science.

AVOIDING THE UNSEEN

Why this is desirable:

Salmonella and *Campylobacter jejuni* are bacteria that contaminate poultry. If ingested in large amounts, the bacteria can cause abdominal cramps, fever, or diarrhea. In the very young, the elderly, or those with weakened immune systems, they can cause death.

HANDLING POULTRY SAFELY

Don't leave a fresh bird unrefrigerated more than 30 minutes; keep it iced.

Do not defrost a bird at room temperature. Defrost it in the refrigerator, in a microwave oven, under cold running water, or in a cold water bath. If you use a cold water bath, the water must be changed every 30 minutes.

After the bird has thawed, rinse it well inside and out under cold water.

Surfaces or utensils that come in contact with a raw bird or raw eggs should be washed with hot soapy water.

Do not stuff a bird ahead of time. It is all right to make the stuffing in advance, as long as it is refrigerated until just before roasting time.

Never roast a bird partly one day and finish it the next. This is a perfect medium for growing bacteria.

When the bird is taken from the oven, the stuffing should be removed immediately to prevent the growth of bacteria.

As soon as the meal is over, put the leftover stuffing in the refrigerator.

The bird can stay out longer if people want to pick from it, but they should use knives and forks, not their fingers.

❧ Labeling Meat and Poultry

On May 5, 1993, the Department of Agriculture announced that it would require all meat and poultry to have labels with cooking and handling instructions.

Such labeling has been considered for several years, but the issue came to a head early in 1993 after four people died and more than 350 others were made ill by tainted hamburgers from a fast-food chain in Washington State.

The regulations were announced in response to a lawsuit brought by a consumer group and the parents of a child who died in the outbreak of the bacteria called *E. coli* 0157:H7. The *E. coli* came from hamburgers that had not been cooked until they were well done.

In August of 1993, the Agriculture Department issued the care-and-handling regulations and said they must be on the labels by the middle of October.

The labels say that meats may contain bacteria and explain the need for keeping meat refrigerated or frozen. The labels also emphasize the importance of keeping raw meat separate from other foods and the need to cook it thoroughly.

Not everyone was overjoyed by the new labeling regulations: Some thought they needed some refining and others said there wasn't enough time to get new labels done.

In October, three grocery associations sued the Agriculture Department to prevent the regulations from going into effect, saying the department hadn't followed proper procedure and that, since the federal court agreed with the grocers' groups, compliance wasn't required. By then, millions of labels had been printed.

Is it significant that John R. Block, a secretary of agriculture under Ronald Reagan, is head of one of those associations? When he was at the Agriculture Department, as little as possible was done to help consumers. Once a hog farmer, he told a congressional committee that dietary guidelines were not necessary: "Hogs are like people. You can provide protein and grain to a hog and he will balance his ration. People are surely as smart as hogs. I am not sure this government needs to get so deeply involved into telling people what they should or should not eat."

In 1994 the USDA started over again, following proper procedures. All packages of raw meat and poultry now carry handling instructions.

But there is something askew when we must eat overcooked hamburgers for safety. See page 325 about efforts to control bacteria in ground beef.

EGGS

Salmonella is present not only in poultry; it is found in uncracked Grade A eggs. To eliminate the risk of salmonellosis from eggs, the following practices are helpful:

HANDLING EGGS SAFELY

Do not buy unrefrigerated eggs. Eggs should be treated like other perishables and stored at 40 degrees or below. Do not leave eggs at room temperature for more than 2 hours.

Store the eggs in their cartons, not directly in egg trays. Use older eggs first.

To be especially prudent, cook eggs until well done.

When working with raw eggs, always wash your hands and use only clean utensils and equipment.

The rules that apply to raw poultry apply to raw eggs: Even when cooked eggs are being kept warm at 140 degrees or higher, they should not be left out longer than 30 minutes.

Avoid eating dishes like eggnog that are made with raw eggs and dishes made with slightly cooked eggs, like Caesar salad and hollandaise sauce. Commercially prepared mayonnaise, eggnog, and ice cream are safe because they are made with pasteurized raw eggs and pasteurization kills the salmonella.

Lightly cooked eggs, such as those in soft custard, meringues, and French toast may be risky for those with weakened immune systems: the elderly, cancer patients, and people with AIDS.

Eggs on a steam table should not be combined with a fresh batch (this occurs commonly at buffet brunches). Fresh pans should be used.

Use raw eggs within 5 weeks and hard-cooked eggs in 1 week; leftover whites and yolks should be used within 4 days, or freeze for later use.

FISH AND SHELLFISH

There are no useful regulations governing the inspection of fish and shellfish. One might ask what difference it would make since there are regulations governing the inspection of meat and poultry, and they don't seem to be working too well. The Food and Drug Administration wants to regulate fish products according to more modern techniques than those used for meat and poultry, and experts believe the Department of Agriculture should scrap its outmoded system of inspection and use the same modern method the FDA is advocating for seafood. Among other things, it relies on scientific testing for contamination. In contrast, there is no scientific testing of meat and poultry; an inspector simply looks at a carcass as it whizzes down the line.

In the meantime, consumption of raw clams and oysters has been tied to hundreds of cases of hepatitis A, a viral infection that inflames the liver, and gastroenteritis, a mild, flulike illness.

States have long warned against eating raw oysters and clams, and health officials are careful to make a sharp distinction between the hazards of fin fish and those of shellfish.

But some ocean fish are contaminated with parasites that can cause infections in humans. Thorough cooking to 140 degrees or freezing for 7 days at 10 degrees below zero is required to kill these parasites. Unless fish used to prepare sushi has been frozen, sushi is considered a hazard, as is fish that is seared on the outside but left raw or rare inside.

Some freshwater fish are contaminated with toxic substances and should generally be avoided. Each state has its own set of problems, and local health departments should be consulted before consuming the catch from sport fishing.

In January 1994, I reported in the *Times:* "Women who expect to become pregnant within a few years, and children under six years old, should avoid these fish: East Coast salmon, swordfish, shark, and lake whitefish. They may contain PCB's, which accumulate in the human body and may be harmful to a fetus or a growing child. Swordfish and tuna may have harmful levels of mercury. Other people can eat fish exposed to PCB's and mercury, but no more than once a week."

HANDLING FISH SAFELY

When buying fish look for bright, clear, bulging eyes. Fresh fish has vivid skin color. Fresh ocean fish smells briny; freshwater fish sometimes smells like cucumbers. At any rate, fresh fish does not have a strong "fishy" odor.

Do not buy fish unless it has been kept well chilled in the store. Check to see that raw fish and cooked fish are not displayed side by side. Bacteria from the raw fish can infect the cooked fish.

Bring fish home from the store as soon as possible, store it in the coldest part of the refrigerator, and use it within a day.

Always wash your hands after handling raw fish. Wash all surfaces and utensils that the raw fish touch or cross-contamination can take place.

HANDLING SHELLFISH SAFELY

Before shellfish is cooked, the shells should be scrubbed well in several changes of water to prevent the meat from being contaminated when the shells are opened.

Any bivalve with an open shell—clam, oyster, mussel, scallop—should be discarded; there is no way to know how long it has been dead. Any bivalve that fails to open after cooking should be discarded.

When eating raw shellfish you either have to trust to luck or believe, as do many people who have eaten raw shellfish from polluted waters for years without apparent ill effects, that it is possible to build up immunity to certain disease-causing microorganisms.

You go first.

Solutions?

Improving the safety of the food supply requires a change in the way many of the raw products, particularly meat, poultry, and seafood, are inspected. The system that should be initiated is called HACCP (pronounced hass-ip), which stands for Hazard Analysis Critical Control Point.

The system is used extensively in the processed-food industry and this is how it works.

HACCP identifies critical control points that occur in the processing and handling of food that require preventive measures to make sure nothing goes wrong.

These critical control points are monitored, which is quite different from the current inspection method for meat and poultry. Under the current system the product is inspected after it has gone through the process. It is also quite different for seafood inspection, for which there is very little oversight.

In January 1994, the Food and Drug Administration announced HACCP for seafood and expects that eventually the Agriculture Department will use it for meat and poultry. Whether you will see any of these changes by the time you are reading this is an unanswerable question.

❧ Zapping Dinner

Because microwave ovens cook unevenly, there is always the risk of contracting salmonellosis from poultry, parasites from fish, trichinosis from pork. The United States Agriculture Department offers this advice:

Cook both beef and pork to an internal temperature of at least 160 degrees so that it is slightly pink. The fleshy parts of poultry should reach 180 degrees. Freezing pork at 5 degrees or lower for 20 days will kill the trichinae.

The department also recommends against cooking stuffed chicken or turkey in a microwave oven because the moist conditions of the stuffing are excellent for salmonella growth.

Because microwave ovens cook so fast, microbes can also survive on the surface of the food.

To counteract the problem, cover the cooking dish with another glass or ceramic dish, not plastic; the steam that accumulates will heat the surface.

Foods cooked in a microwave should stand covered after cooking. That way, the heat concentrated in the interior radiates out, cooking the exterior and equalizing the temperature. It is important to follow the standing time in recipes.

Foods should be defrosted before cooking.

Plastic wrap should not be allowed to touch the food because some of the plasticizer in the wrap, which may contain toxic chemicals, can migrate to the food, especially foods high in fat.

✷ Grilling

There is increasing evidence that grilling meats over a hot charcoal fire produces substances that may cause cancer in humans.

Grilling, frying, or broiling beef, pork, lamb, chicken, and fish produces substances called heterocyclic aromatic amines, or HAAs, some of which have caused cancer not only in laboratory mice and rats but also in nonhuman primates. The longer the cooking time the greater the amount of HAA produced. With few exceptions substances that cause cancer in test animals are carcinogenic in humans.

That doesn't mean you have to put your grill out for the trash collection. But there are some changes you might want to make.

Since these compounds form only on the outside of the meat, the food would still be perfectly safe to eat if the outside layer were removed. This doesn't seem to be practical for beef, pork, or lamb, but fish and chicken could be cooked with the skin on and then it could be removed after cooking.

Here are preventive cooking suggestions.

1. One of the most effective ways to prevent the formation of the HAAs is to precook meat that will be barbecued: Poach, boil, or cook it in a microwave oven, then pour off the juice, which contains substances that help form cancer-causing agents. Precooking just 2 or 3 minutes destroys 80 to 90 percent of the carcinogens.
2. Choose lean rather than fat meats.
3. Eat meat that has been cooked medium or medium-rare rather than well-done.
4. Do not char or overcook meat.
5. Do not allow meat drippings to dry out before making gravy.
6. Cover the grill with aluminum foil and punch holes in the foil to let the fat drip out.
7. Trim excess fat from the meat before grilling.
8. Baste frequently but not with a fatty mixture.
9. Whenever possible use a drip pan to catch the fat so it cannot flare up. Keep a squirt bottle of water handy to dampen coals that flare up.
10. If smoke from dripping fat becomes too heavy, move the meat to another part of the grill.
11. Some foods, like fish, can be cooked in foil to protect them.
12. If you barbecue with wood, use hardwoods such as maple or hickory.

❧ Get the Lead Out

Lead is a highly toxic material that builds up in the body over a lifetime and can cause chronic illnesses of the nervous system, the reproductive and cardiovascular systems, and the kidneys. Children and fetuses are at particular risk.

We used to worry about lead in canned food. Mostly that worry is gone because lead solders no longer can be used on tins for food.

Then researchers found that there is lead in the paint used on dishes we eat from, in the water we drink, and the crystal we drink from.

Some of these problems are easier to deal with than others.

LEAD IN CRYSTAL

Let's start with the easy one first, lead in crystal.

The advice from the Food and Drug Administration is as follows:

1. Do not use lead crystal every day. Occasional use is all right, but if you have a daily glass of wine, don't drink from a crystal goblet.
2. Don't store foods or beverages for long periods in crystal. This is particularly true for acidic juices, vinegar, and alcoholic beverages. *Long* means a week or two, according to the FDA, but others say overnight is the maximum.
3. Women of child-bearing age should not use crystal ware.
4. Don't feed children from crystal bottles or tumblers.

LEAD IN DISHWARE

Lead in ceramicware is a far more complicated problem than once believed. It isn't just cheap imports or ceramicware made before 1971 that is a problem. Even some expensive new ceramicware contains some lead. And there is no way to know what is what or which is which. The fact that there may be some lead in newly made dishes is not a cause for panic, but it would be a good idea to call the manufacturer before purchasing a set of dishes, or send a self-addressed stamped envelope to: China Brochure, EDF, Box 96969, Washington, DC 20090.

And here are other useful rules to follow to reduce exposure to lead, especially for children and pregnant women.

1. Use china that has been handed down from previous generations for special occasions.
2. Be careful of all handcrafted china and of highly decorated, multicolored surfaces that touch food.
3. China with a corroded glaze or dusty chalky gray residue on the glaze after the washing should not be used at all.
4. Don't store food or beverages in china pitchers, bowls, or other containers unless you know they are lead-free. The longer food is in contact with a surface containing lead, the greater the amount of lead that can leach into it, especially if the food is highly acid.
5. Don't serve highly acidic foods, especially to children, on questionable china. Acidic foods and beverages like orange juice, apple juice, tomatoes, cola-type soft drinks, salad dressings, coffee, or tea, leach lead much faster than neutral foods like water, milk, rice, or mashed potatoes.
6. Don't use questionable ceramicware in conventional or microwave ovens. Heat can speed up the leaching process.
7. Don't store foods or beverages in ceramicware intended for decorative purposes.
8. Don't use questionable pieces of china on a daily basis.
9. If you have a bowl about which you are not certain, line it with another bowl you know is safe.
10. If you are serving cool food with very little liquid, you can line the bowl with a sheet of plastic wrap to protect the food.

LEAD IN WATER

In February 1993, *Consumer Reports,* the monthly magazine of Consumers Union, published its findings about lead in tap water. It was not very encouraging. The magazine concluded that no household can assume its water is free of lead and that the only way to be sure is by testing. Testing is particularly important for high-risk households—those where women are either pregnant or thinking of becoming pregnant or where infants are fed formulas made with tap water or where there are children under six.

The article recommended three mail-order laboratories that will test water: The Clean Water Fund in Asheville, N.C., 704-251-0518; Suburban Water Testing Labs in Reading, Pennsylvania, 800-433-6595; National Testing Laboratories, Cleveland, Ohio, 800-458-3330.

Publications of Interest

Nutrition Action is a publication of the Center for Science in the Public Interest, a public advocacy group. The monthly newsletter is provocative, accurate, and up to the minute.

Nutrition Action, Suite 300, 1875 Connecticut Avenue, N.W., Washington, D.C. 20009–5728. One-year subscription is $20.

Environmental Nutrition is written for professionals but can be understood by anyone with more than a passing interest in nutrition and health. It frequently discusses new research. It evaluates many products: cereals, frozen breakfasts, TV dinners, and others.

Environmental Nutrition, 52 Riverside Drive, New York, New York 10024. One-year subscription is $30.

Tufts University Diet & Nutrition Letter is pretty straightforward but has little new information. It is useful, however, on the matters of diet and exercise.

Tufts University Diet & Nutrition Letter, 53 Park Place, New York, New York 10007. One-year subscription is $20.

The University of California Wellness Letter is not just about food: it's about nutrition, fitness, and stress management, and it offers sound information in all categories.

University of California at Berkeley Wellness Letter, P.O. Box 420148, Palm Coast, Florida 32142. One-year subscription is $24.

Consumer Reports newsletter closely resembles *Consumer Reports.* Like the University of California newsletter, its focus is exercise and health as well as diet and nutrition.

Consumer Reports on Health, Subscription Department, P.O. Box 52148, Boulder, Colorado 80321–2148. One-year subscription is $24.

Eating Well, a magazine of healthful eating, has flavorful low-fat recipes and interesting articles, though some tend to go on a bit.

Despite the fact that the magazine "borrowed" the name of its publication from the name of my column in the *New York Times,* it is the best of the health-oriented magazines for people who want both information and good recipes.

Eating Well, Ferry Road, P.O. Box 1001, Charlotte, Vermont 05445–9977. One-year subscription is $12.97.

General Index

Advertising, 321, 328–29
Agriculture Department, U.S., 31, 321, 322–26, 344–45
    cooking and handling instructions and, 341
    dual mission of, 322
    Food Guide Pyramid and, 322–24
    food labeling and, 324–25, 329, 332
    inspection of meat and poultry and, 322, 325–26, 342, 344
    pesticides and, 324, 327–28
Alar, 327
Alcohol, 32
Almond oil, 37
Antibiotics, 21, 337, 338
Antioxidants, 41, 42, 331
Apples, Alar and, 327
Arborio rice, 19
Arrowroot, 30
Artificial colors, 332
Asian ingredients, 23
Atwater, W. O., 31
Avocado oil, 37, 38

Bacteria, 334, 340–45
    in eggs, 341–42
    in fish and shellfish, 342–43, 344
    food irradiation and, 339–40
    in meat, 325, 340–41, 344
    microbial testing and, 322, 325
    microwave cooking and, 344–45
    in poultry, 325, 326, 340–41, 344
Bananas, 336
    mail-order source for, 26
Beans, 25, 39, 40
    canned, 22
    mail-order source for, 27
    recommended consumption of, 32, 33, 35
    serving size for, 34
Beef, 21
    cooking in microwave, 345
    grilling, 345–46
    ground, labeling of, 324–25
    see also Meat
Beta carotene, 41–42

Biotechnology, 336–39
    genetically engineered food and, 328, 338–339
    rBST and, 327, 336–37
Block, Gladys, 41
Block, John R., 341
Blueberries, dried, 19
Botulism, 339
Breads, 19–20
    recommended consumption of, 32, 33, 35
    serving size for, 34
Broccoli, 336
Broiling, 345
Broths, 22
Browner, Carol, 328
Brown rice, 19
Bulgur, 188
Bush administration, 322, 326, 328, 329
Butter, 36
Buttermilk, 30

Calcium, 32
    food labeling and, 330, 331, 332
Calories, 13, 31
    in carbohydrates, 39, 40
    in fats, 38, 40
    food labeling and, 330, 331
    percent of, from fat, 31, 35–36
Campylobacter jejuni, 340
Cancer, 33, 39, 331, 337
    carcinogens and, 327, 345–46
    dietary supplements and, 41–42
    fat consumption and, 31, 32
    grilling and, 345
Canned food, 22–23, 346
Canola oil, 37, 38
Capers, mail-order source for, 27
Carbohydrates, 39–40, 41
Carcinogens, 327, 345–46
Cardiovascular disease, 32, 33
Castelli, William, 38
Cauliflower, 336
Ceramicware, lead in, 347

Cereal:
    recommended consumption of, 32, 33, 35
    serving size for, 34
Chaparral, 43
Cheese, 20, 40
    mail-order sources for, 26–27
    recommended consumption of, 33, 35
Cherries, dried, 19
    mail-order source for, 27
Chicken, 21
    bacterial contamination of, 325, 326, 340–41,
        344
    grilling, 345–46
    mail-order source for, 26
    see also Poultry
Children:
    lead and, 346, 347, 348
    pesticide residues and, 328, 334
Chiles, 18
Cholesterol (dietary), 32, 35, 38
    food labeling and, 330, 331, 332
Cholesterol level, 35, 37
    and health claims for certain foods, 328–29
Choose to Lose Diet, The (N. Goor and R. Goor),
    40
Chutney, mail-order source for, 28
Citrus Hill Fresh Choice, 326
Clinton administration, 322, 324, 326, 328
Coconut oil, 36
Coffee, mail-order source for, 28
Comfrey, 43
Complex carbohydrates, 39–40, 41
    recommended consumption of, 32, 33, 35
Condiments, 24, 30
    mail-order sources for, 27
Congress, U.S., 43, 321–22, 326, 328, 329, 337
Connor, Sonya, 31, 34–35
Connor, William E., 31, 34–35
Consumer Reports, 347
"Consumer Reports," 349
Contract with America, 321
Corn, 40
Cornmeal, mail-order source for, 27
Corn oil, 36, 37, 38
Cornstarch, thickening sauces with, 30
Cranberries, dried, 19
    mail-order source for, 27
Cream, substitute for, 30
Crystal, lead in, 346
Curry powders, 83, 204

Dairy products, 20, 40
    mail-order sources for, 26–27
    recommended consumption of, 33, 35
    serving size for, 34
Delaney Clause, 327, 328
Diabetes, 31
Dietary supplements, 32, 41–43, 322
Dishware, lead in, 347
Dry measurement equivalents, 11

Eating Well, 349
E. coli, 325, 341
Eggs, 38
    bacterial contamination of, 341–42
    recommended consumption of, 33
    reducing fat in, 30
    serving size for, 34
    tips for safe handling of, 342
"Environmental Nutrition," 336, 349
Environmental Protection Agency (EPA), 321, 324, 327–
    328, 335
Environmental Working Group, 335
Epstein, Samuel, 337
Equipment, 28–29
Espy, Mike, 324, 325
"Extra lean," labeling regulations and, 332

Faberware's Millennium Plus pans, 28
Farmers' markets, 335
Fat (dietary), 13, 14, 31–38
    cheese and, 20
    counting grams of, 35–36
    food labeling and, 324–25, 330, 331, 332
    oils and, 36–38
    percent of calories from, 31, 35–36
    reduced-fat or fat-free products and, 17, 20, 39
    reducing in cooking, 30
    30-percent plan and, 32–34
    20-percent plan and, 34–35
    see also Saturated fat
Federal Food, Drug and Cosmetic Act, 327
Federal Trade Commission (FTC), 321, 328–29
Fertilizers, 334
"Fewer," labeling regulations and, 331
Fiber, 32–33, 43–44
    food labeling and, 331, 332
Fish and shellfish, 22
    contamination of, 342–43, 344
    grilling, 345–46
    inspection of, 342, 344

Nondairy products, 332
Nonstick surfaces, 30
Nutrition, 30–44
    carbohydrates and, 39–40
    cholesterol consumption and, 38
    constantly changing information on, 14
    dietary supplements and, 41–43
    fat consumption and, 31–38
    fiber and, 43–44
    information included with recipes on, 44
    protein and, 32, 40
    sodium consumption and, 32, 38–39
    trans fatty acids and, 36–37
    vitamins and minerals and, 40–42
"Nutrition Action," 349
Nutrition Labeling and Education Act (NLEA), 325, 326,
    329–33
    see also Food labeling
Nuts:
    recommended consumption of, 32, 33, 35
    serving size for, 34

Oatmeal, 328–29
Oils, 23, 36–38
    cooking, reducing amount of, 30
    recommended consumption of, 33
    trans fatty acids in, 36–37
Olive oil, 37, 38
    mail-order sources for, 27
Olives, mail-order source for, 27
Oranges, 336
Organically raised food, 21, 334, 335–36
    mail-order sources for, 26, 27
Ornish, Dean, 40
Osteoporosis, 331
Oven temperature equivalents, 11

Packaged products, 22–23
Palm oil, 36
Pans, 28, 29, 30
Pantry items, 23–25
Parasites:
    in ocean fish, 342–43, 344
    in pork, 344, 345
Pasta, 19, 25, 40
    recommended consumption of, 32, 33, 35
    serving size for, 34
PCB's, 343
Peanut oil, 37, 38
Peas, 39, 40

Persimmons, mail-order source for, 26
Pesticides, 321, 322, 334–36
    joint EPA, FDA, and USDA announcement on, 324,
        327–28
    and washing and peeling of fruits and vegetables, 335,
        336
Pitofsky, Robert, 328
Plastic wrap, microwave cooking and, 345
Politics of food, 321–33
    Congress and, 321–22, 326, 328, 329, 337
    cooking and handling instructions and, 341
    EPA and, 321, 324, 327–28, 335
    FDA and, 321, 322, 324, 326–28, 329, 332, 337, 338–39,
        340, 342, 344
    Food Guide Pyramid and, 322–24
    food irradiation and, 340
    food labeling and, 322, 324, 325, 326, 328–33
    FTC and, 321, 328–29
    organic food and, 336
    pesticides and, 321, 322, 324, 327–28, 336
    state governments and, 326, 328–29
    USDA and, 321, 322–26, 329, 332, 341, 344
Polyunsaturated fat, 36, 37–38
Pork, 21
    cooking in microwave, 345
    grilling, 345–46
    trichinosis and, 344, 345
    see also Meat
Potatoes, 35
Pots, 28, 29
Poultry, 21
    bacterial contamination of, 325, 326, 340–41,
        344
    cooking and handling instructions for, 341
    cooking in microwave, 345
    grilling, 345–46
    ground, 21
    inspection of, 322, 325, 326, 342, 344
    labeling of, 332
    mail-order source for, 26
    recommended consumption of, 33, 35
    serving size for, 34
    skin of, 21, 345
    stuffed, 340, 345
    tips for safe handling of, 340
Pregnancy, 32
    lead and, 346, 347–48
    seafood and, 343
Preserves, mail-order source for, 28
Procter & Gamble, 326

Protein, 32, 40
    food labeling and, 332
    hydrolized, 333
Prunes, mail-order source for, 27
Pure Food Campaign, 337

Quaker Oats Company, 328–29
Quick, low-fat cooking:
    equipment for, 28–29
    fat-reducing techniques for, 30
    ingredients for, 16–28
    strategies for, 15–16

Rabbit, mail-order source for, 26
Radiation, *see* Food irradiation
rBGH (bovine growth hormone), 327, 336–37
rBST (recombinant bovine somatotropin), 327, 336–337
Reagan administration, 322, 326, 328, 341
Recipes, planning and, 44–45
"Reduced," labeling regulations and, 331
Relishes, mail-order source for, 28
Republicans, 321–22
Rice, 19
    mail-order sources for, 27
    recommended consumption of, 32, 33, 35
    serving size for, 34
Rifkin, Jeremy, 337
Root vegetables, 336
Roux, substitute for, 30

Safety of food, 334–48
    bacterial contamination and, 322, 325, 326, 334, 340–345
    biotechnology and, 336–39
    food irradiation and, 339–40
    grilling and, 345–46
    lead and, 346–48
    organic farming and, 334, 335–36
    pesticides and, 321, 322, 324, 327–28, 334–36
Safflower oil, 37, 38
Salad dressings, reducing fat in, 30
Salmonella, 325, 340, 341, 344, 345
Salt, 32, 39
    see also Sodium
Saturated fat, 13, 32, 35, 36, 38
    labeling regulations and, 331, 332
    in oils, 37–38
Sauces, reducing fat in, 30
Sausages, mail-order source for, 26

Seafood, *see* Fish and shellfish
Seeds, 35
Serving sizes, 34
    food labeling and, 331
Sesame oil, 37, 38
Shellfish, *see* Fish and shellfish
Shopping, 16, 17
Shortenings, vegetable, 36, 37
Simple carbohydrates, 39
Smoky flavor, 30
Sodium, 38–39
    food labeling and, 331, 332
    recommended consumption of, 32, 38–39
Sodium caseinate, 332
Sour cream, 20, 30
Soybean oil, 36
Soy oil, 37, 38
Spices, 23–24
Spinach, 336
Spoons, 29
Starches, 20, 25
    recommended consumption of, 32, 33, 35
State governments, 326, 328–29
Steamer baskets, 28
Stocks, 22
Stroke, 31
Sugar, 39
    labeling regulations and, 331
Sunflower oil, 37, 38
Supplements, 41–43, 322
Sushi, 343

Tahini, 22
Taylor, Michael, 325, 326
Thiamin, 339
Third-party certificates, 335
Tomatoes:
    canned, 22
    genetically engineered (FlavrSavr), 338–339
    sun-dried, mail-order source for, 27
Tortillas, 20
Trans fatty acids, 36–37
Trichinosis, 344, 345
Tucker, Kathleen, 339
"Tufts University Diet & Nutrition Letter," 349
Turkey, 21
    see also Poultry
Tyson Industries, 325

Union of Concerned Scientists, 338
"University of California at Berkeley Wellness Letter," 349
Utensils, 28, 29

Van Gemert, Marcia, 340
Veal, mail-order source for, 26
Vegetable oils, 36–38
Vegetables, 13, 18, 31, 39, 40, 41, 43
    frozen, 22
    irradiation of, 339–40
    mail-order sources for, 26
    pesticides and, 328, 334–36
    ready-cut, 18
    recommended consumption of, 32, 33, 35
    serving size for, 34
    washing and peeling of, 335, 336
    waxed, 333, 336
Venison, mail-order source for, 26
Vinegars, 23
    mail-order source for, 27
Vitamin A, 41
    food labeling and, 330, 332
Vitamin C, 41, 42, 339
    food labeling and, 330, 332

Vitamin E, 41–42, 339
Vitamins, 40–42
    dietary supplements and, 41–42

Walnut oil, 37, 38
Walnuts, mail-order source for, 27
Water, lead in, 347–48
Waxed fruits and vegetables, 333, 336
"Way We Grow, The" (Garland), 335–36
Webb, Tony, 339
Weight, 32
Weight loss, complex carbohydrates and, 40
Whipped cream, reducing fat in, 30
Willett, Walter, 41
Willow bark, 43
Women's Health Network, 337
Wotecki, Catherine, 41
Wüsthof knives, 28

Yogurt, 20
    "cheese," 30
    nonfat, 30
    recommended consumption of, 33

Now available!

20-Minute Menus

Time-Wise Recipes & Strategic Plans for Freshly Cooked Meals Every Day

If you've enjoyed using *Eating Well Is the Best Revenge,* you'll want a copy of Marian Burros's *20-Minute Menus,* available at your favorite bookstore. The perfect book for everyday cooking, *20-Minute Menus* contains 100 from-scratch menus that have been designed and tested to get the best-tasting meal on the table in the least amount of time.